W9-AIJ-461

ALOHA ALOHA ALOHA ALOHA

ALOHA ALOHA ALOHA ALOHA

THE
BEST OF

ALOHA.

The Magazine of Hawaii and the Pacific

THE BEST OF
ALOHA.

The Magazine of Hawaii and the Pacific

Produced and published by
ISLAND HERITAGE PUBLISHING

Designer and photography editor, Paul Turley.

Front cover: Young hula dancer Celeste Noelani Kalama.
Back cover: Leis adorn an assortment of Hawaiian
instruments. Photography by Joe Carini,
Hawaiian Legends©.

First Edition
First Printing, 1990
Copyright© Island Heritage Publishing
Please address orders and correspondence to:

 ISLAND HERITAGE PUBLISHING
A division of The Madden Corporation
99-880 Iwaena Street
Aiea, Hawaii 96701
(808) 487-7299

ISBN 0-89610-167-3

All rights reserved. No portion of this book
may be modified, reproduced, modified or enhanced
without the prior written consent from
Island Heritage Publishing.

Printed in Hong Kong

TABLE OF CONTENTS

HAWAII
OUR ISLAND HOME

BY RITA ARIYOSHI

Landfall Hawaii—it is night. The ocean is dark. We have been flying for hours in inky blackness, suspended in air by the grace of God and the power of a jet engine. Suddenly, very suddenly, below us there are lights twinkling in the void—hundreds, thousands of lights. There are people here in the middle of the ocean, in the dark of night, and they have prepared a landing place for us, with lights to guide us in. Hawaii glistens like a jewel set in black velvet.

Approaching these remote islands on the face of the Earth by night is always like that—a bit miraculous. Finding land where no land should be, experiencing discovery, receiving the place as a gift is forever the experience of coming to Hawaii.

The Islands were born in fire, far from human eyes. For eons, mighty volcanoes beneath the ocean's surface spewed forth molten lava and rock from the middle of the Earth, forming pillows of land, one mounded on top of the other, until finally, in a fiery burst with towering columns of smoke and great clouds of steam, Hawaii emerged from the waves.

2

Lovely Hawaiian wahine, Diane Ahrens-Obedoza.

Of the eight major islands, Kauai was the first to be formed and Hawaii, the Big Island, is the youngest, but not the last. Scientists are studying the birth of the newest Hawaiian island, Loihi, being formed near the Big Island. Divers have photographed the incredible process of creation, the undersea mount at work, piling up the lava that will one day be a new island that no one now living will ever see. Loihi—even the concept of our planet still in the creation process after all we have done to it is wondrous.

The first people to set eyes upon Hawaiian shores had sailed for weeks, perhaps months, in huge voyaging canoes, sixty to eighty feet long, propelled by sails made of tree bark. They had left their homeland in the Marquesas far to the south. They set their course by the stars, following the winds, the ocean currents and the voices of their gods, who promised them far islands, green and fruitful.

For centuries, these first Polynesian settlers had Hawaii to themselves. They were joined later by Polynesian voyagers from Tahiti. For years, there was commerce between Hawaii and Tahiti, and then, for some reason, the ocean voyages ceased and contact with the outside world was severed. The homeland became a memory and eventually a myth. They sang about it in chants and danced its praises in the hula, keeping the record of Havaiki, the lost home of men and gods.

In isolation, the people of Hawaii developed a highly structured society and enjoyed the greatest flowering of Polynesian culture. They lived in harmony with their limited island environment, taking their sustenance carefully from the land and the sea. They were robust, healthy. Disease was unknown. Even today, the bones of early Hawaiians are easily identified without radiocarbon testing, for they had perfect teeth.

It wasn't Eden, for they had imperious, ambitious rulers and fought among themselves. They were subject to the caprices of nature—earthquakes, tidal waves and storms. What they also had, however, was a climate as nearly perfect as any on Earth, a land of breathtaking natural beauty and a sense of spirituality that gave birth to the philosophy of aloha, of love. Aloha is the recognition that all life is sacred and that even the stranger stands in the presence of God.

How bitter it must have been when those first foreign ships dropped anchor in Waimea Bay, Kauai in 1778, and the welcome turned into death within the year, for with the strangers came new diseases to which the Hawaiians had developed no immunities—measles, plague, syphilis, leprosy. They died by the thousands. Whole valleys succumbed.

It was during the early days of contact with the outside world that Hawaii's greatest leader emerged, a Big Island chief, Kamehameha. Through warfare and intrigue, the wily warrior succeeded in binding all the Hawaiian islands into one kingdom. For the first time in centuries there was peace on every island, and the people were united in their response to the outside world.

Upon the death of Kamehameha I, his son, Liholiho, ascended to the throne and the title, Kamehameha II. He was twenty-two and an easy target for his ambitious stepmother, Kaahumanu, who was anxious to break the power of the priests. She invited the young king to dine with her publicly, an act strictly forbidden by the ancient religion. After several days of anguished deliberation, the king accepted the invitation of the woman he had been raised to respect and obey.

The people were stunned. The sacred kapu had been broken and the gods were seen to be impotent. They burned their temples and be-

Performer from Kealiikaapunihonua Keena Ao Hula Halau at the Merrie Monarch Hula Festival, Hilo, island of Hawaii.

Waikiki at twilight.

Afternoon stroll along the Hilton Hawaiian Village's lagoon, Waikiki.

*Lily Kama demonstrates the art of Hawaiian quilting,
Polynesian Cultural Center, Laie, Oahu.*

A new Hawaii was emerging. The people spoke many languages and observed intriguing rituals. Perhaps it was the sense of geographic isolation that made them all pull together, perhaps a recognition that the Islands were small and everyone had better get along. Most likely, the cooperation, the racial tolerance, the respect was born of the aloha spirit, which some say was born of the land itself. This legacy from the early Hawaiians has been the single most dominant factor in the shaping of modern Hawaii. It is the life of Hawaii.

The second most influential factor is statehood in the United States.

It is natural that tourism became the major industry of a place so blessed with sunshine and gentle trade winds, and endowed with such incredible beauty. What makes tourism so successful, however, is not so much Hawaii's obvious physical charms, for many places have beaches as lovely, abundant sunshine and majestic mountains. It is, again, that spirit of aloha, of welcoming the stranger with love. Hospitality is not a Hawaiian art so much as it is a Hawaiian perspective. There is, in fact, no Hawaiian word for welcome, for welcome is always assumed. It just is, like the air we breathe.

It is important to acknowledge the many contributions of the first settlers of these islands, the art and culture they developed, the system of law, and the way they cared for the land and the sea that they passed to us in almost pristine condition. The most important heritage we received, however, is the most fragile—aloha.

In the tradition of that love, ALOHA Magazine has been making a friend of the stranger, sharing to the best of our ability, the beauty, truth and wondrous sense of the holiness of all life that is our legacy—and our mandate.

Since the following stories appeared in ALOHA's tenth anniversary issue in July/August 1987, Hawaii has experienced changes in the realms of both politics and resort development. Some of the islands have new mayors. With the exception of Molokai, all have new hotels: The Hawaii Prince on Oahu; Embassy Suites and the Four Seasons Resort Wailea on Maui; the Ritz Carlton on the Big Island; the Hyatt Regency Kauai on the Garden Island; and the Lodge at Koele on Lanai. All of the hotels that were under construction when these stories first appeared have opened and are prospering. Tourism in the Islands continues to grow—in 1989, the Hawaii Visitors Bureau tallied more than 6,500,000 visitors statewide. Hawaii's people warmly welcome these friends from all over the world who have succumbed to the bewitching magic that pervades this, our Island home.

came, overnight, a people without a god and without the constraints of their religious law.

While the temples were burning, halfway across the world in New England, a party of Christian missionaries was setting sail for Hawaii.

The deep sense of spirituality that was so much a part of the Hawaiian character prepared them to embrace the new faith. They became enthusiastic students of both The Word and the almost equally powerful written word.

There are times in the history of a place when the historical record seems to be playing at a faster RPM than it should. Time, events, motives—all become blurred and distorted by speed. In a relatively short period, the Kamehameha dynasty died out, the monarchy became constitutional and was eventually overthrown by foreign interests, predominantly American, and Hawaii was annexed by the United States in 1898.

Against this dramatic background, the native population was continuing its decline, the great sugar and pineapple plantations were built, and workers were arriving in waves from China, Japan, Portugal and the Philippines. The Hawaii that Cook found had all but disappeared.

7

OAHU
HITTING A HIGH NOTE
BY MARTY WENTZEL

Sunbathers at Waikiki Beach.

awaii's most populated island sings a song all its
own. Open your heart and
listen well, for it is a complex song; there are many verses to
be sung, many more still to be written.

Oahu's song began four to six
million years ago when volcanoes
erupted at the bottom of the sea,
spewing molten lava that gave the
island its shape. Crashing waves cut
its shoreline, persistent streams chis-
eled its valleys.

No one is quite sure what the
word "Oahu" means. Somehow,
somewhere, during the course of
history, the literal translation of the
word was lost.

Oahu, the island, is as difficult to
define as Oahu, the word. It is today
a place where many different worlds
meet. Bustling Honolulu is the hub
of business and government in the
state. Just an hour's drive away, the
mellow North Shore is dotted with
small country towns, banana and
papaya groves, surfing havens and
breeze-kissed beaches that invite a
languorous lifestyle.

For those who delight in the cultural arts, Oahu offers ballet, opera,
symphony concerts and Broadway
plays. It also offers Island tradition in
the form of such colorful annual
events as Aloha Week, the Japanese
Cherry Blossom Festival and the
Chinese Narcissus Festival.

Waikiki is the quintessential tourist mecca, hosting an average of
65,000 guests each day. Embracing
fine restaurants, theaters, shops, scenic sights and hotels, it is the unri-
valed entertainment capital of the
Pacific. In contrast, Oahu's tranquil,
upland regions provide sanctuaries
for those yearning to escape life in
the fast lane. These hidden forests
and lushly blanketed valleys harbor
secrets of the island's past—of ancient gods and their great powers, of
legends that inspire wonder, of an
industrious people who developed a
rich and enduring culture.

Kodak Hula Show entertainers, Waikiki.

Oahu's earliest inhabitants were
Polynesians who steered their canoes by the stars to reach their new
home. They fished, farmed and led a
simple but productive existence. Life
on Oahu grew in complexity with
each new contingent of visitors:
British explorer Captain James Cook;
French and Russian traders; American whalers and missionaries; Chinese and Japanese plantation workers. Each group brought its own
unique language and customs to what
was becoming a cosmopolitan mix
on Oahu.

In 1850, the alii moved their official headquarters from Lahaina,
Maui, to Honolulu, the new seat of
government. The reign of King David
Kalakaua (1874-1891), who was
nicknamed the "Merrie Monarch"

because of his fondness for music
and dance, was marked by lavish
balls in Iolani Palace. This rather
carefree period preceded a time of
great trial for the Hawaiian people.

In 1893, the Island monarchy
tumbled at the hands of heavily armed
American businessmen and marines.
The reigning queen, Liliuokalani,
was imprisoned in Iolani Palace, and
Hawaii became a republic, then a
territory of the United States. Oahu's
song crescendoed in 1941 when
Japanese fighter planes attacked Pearl
Harbor, plunging the United States
into World War II. Following that
turbulent era, in 1959, the Stars and
Stripes were raised over Honolulu,
capital of America's new fiftieth state.

Although it has seen rapid changes over the years, Oahu's song is far

from finished. Downtown Honolulu is experiencing its own eruption in
the form of concrete and glass. Mul-
timillion-dollar skyscrapers stretch
toward the sky. A parade of condominiums and hotels marches through
Waikiki. A network of freeways supports a steady stream of traffic. Huge
subdivisions extend outward from
Honolulu in all directions.

Honolulu Mayor Frank Fasi explains Oahu's need for development
this way: "As long as our population
keeps growing, we will need housing
for our people. That's number one.
When you stop building, it only
means trouble for everyone. Business falls, rents rise, jobs disappear
and the brains of the community
move away. The people who are op-
posed to growth only make it tough-

Hanauma Bay.

er for our children and grandchildren to stay here."

But look again. Look at the silhouettes of yachts cruising along the Waikiki coastline at sunset. Admire the twin spires of Mount Olomana piercing the sky under a full moon. Study the beauty and precision of outrigger canoe paddlers perfecting their strokes along the Ala Wai Canal. Marvel as refreshing showers bathe Nuuanu Pali's ageless splendor. Look, and you can hear it: Another chord in Oahu's song.

True to its popular nickname,

"The Gathering Place," Oahu houses eighty percent of Hawaii's one million residents, yet there is still room for its primeval beauty to flourish in a contemporary environment. Oahu's upper reaches are kept green and cool by almost daily rains, and its native forests are filled with fragrant stands of ferns, ohia, ginger, eucalyptus and lilikoi. Its most famous figure—Diamond Head— watches over Kapiolani Park to the south, while the Waianae Mountains protect the rural west. Hiking trails tickle the spine of the Koolau

range on Oahu's windward side, where a simpler way of life prevails.

The North Shore is a haven of old Hawaii. Freeways give way to two-lane country roads, and life's frantic complexities surrender themselves to a slower pace. There are towns here whose names slide off the tongue like ancient Hawaiian chants: Kaaawa, Laie, Kahuku, Haleiwa. On the North Shore, you can let yourself go. As you dig your toes in the sands of palm-fringed beaches or wander back into deep-cut valleys dressed in forests of guava and bamboo, some-

Fun in the sun on the windward side.

Trumpet player in the Aloha Week Parade, Waikiki.

Sailboats, Kaneohe Bay.

Feeding pigeons at Honolulu Zoo, Waikiki.

Byodo-In Temple, Kahaluu.

how you feel less hurried. Here—more than anywhere else on the island—the past reaches out to you.

You can see it in centuries old fishponds, some so well-preserved that they are still being used today. You can feel it in the winds which sweep across Waimea Bay through Puu o Mahuka, the largest heiau on the island. And you can hear it in the rush of the ocean, where surfers enjoy a sport which traces its beginnings back to the fifteenth century.

Diversity is Oahu's gift, and you can visualize it through its beaches—210 miles of ivory avenues which have aged gracefully next to cobalt blue seas. Waikiki, with its perpetual sunshine and reef protected waters, has been billed as "Life's Greatest Beach." Ala Moana attracts a parade of families who come for day-long picnics beside its placid waters. Makapuu's mighty waves challenge the strength and prowess of the Islands' best bodysurfers. At Lanikai, regattas of windsurfers worship steady, off-shore breezes and pray that their next ride will be the ride that tops them all. Sunset's gigantic winter curls provide a wonderful playground for surfers who travel around the world in search of the best waves. Waimea Bay is as calm as a lake in the summer, but characterized by dangerous swells in the winter. The magnificent underwater landscape of serene Hanauma Bay, a marine conservation district, is perfect for snorkeling.

Equally varied pleasures define Oahu's culinary scene; it's a global binge. Within a half-mile block along Kapahulu Avenue, for instance, you can find savory Thai *sateh*, steamy Korean *man doo*, sweet Portuguese *malasadas*, smoky kalua pig, hot-and-sour Chinese soup, Japanese *ramen* and the ubiquitous American burger. Oahu also serves the most sophisticated continental cuisine this side of the Pacific, in settings exuding true elegance.

The island's people, too, reflect a blend of East and West, of old ways with new. At Triangle Park in the heart of the posh Kahala neighborhood, *tai chi* students perform graceful movements, creating living tableaus against the low light of dawn. Contemplative Zen archers at Kapiolani Park practice their sport as joggers and soccer buffs engage in theirs. Honolulu's Chinatown is perhaps the clearest example of the state's remarkable ethnic potpourri. Filipino, Thai, Vietnamese, Taiwanese and Chinese entrepreneurs operate neighboring shops—lei-makers peddling brightly colored floral creations, herbalists selling bizarre remedies, butchers slicing juicy chunks of *char siu*, grocers offering salted cracked seed and exotic herbal teas. Stroll through Ala Moana Shopping Center on any day and you'll notice a United Nations melange of faces.

Said Mayor Fasi, "On Oahu, we tend to judge our people by what they have to offer, not by the color of their skin or the shape of their eyes. Our racial problems are miniscule compared to what I see in other parts of the world. If every country lived the way we do here, we'd never have another war."

The University of Hawaii boasts an enrollment of 21,000 students from America's fifty states and sixty foreign countries at its picturesque Manoa campus. Since 1907, the university has achieved nationwide respect for its work in such fields as tropical agriculture, astronomy, geophysics and biology. Its pioneering program in Travel Industry Management has been applauded worldwide, and hotels throughout the state support the school by hiring its interns and graduates. Also housed on campus is the federally funded East-West Center, which brings together scholars from throughout Asia, the Pacific Basin and the United States to participate in an unparalleled program of cultural exchange.

Wedged into this hodgepodge, adding their own cadence to Oahu's song, is the military, an undeniable presence occupying one-fourth of the island's land and numbering one-eighth of its resident population. Most of them are housed at such self-contained settlements as Fort Shafter, Schofield Barracks, Hickam Air Force Base and Kaneohe Marine Corps Air Station. They emerge from time to time to play visible roles in Oahu's civilian community—for example, jogging in formation, hundreds strong, in the annual Great Aloha Run for charity held in February.

Oahu and its military forces share a crucial interdependence. Due to its strategic Pacific location, Pearl Harbor has served as a key base of activities for the U.S. Navy since 1902. On a hillside above it looms Camp Smith and the U.S. Pacific Command (CINCPAC), which di-

Diamond Head Lighthouse.

13

Picnic on the Kaneohe Sandbar.

rects the operations of all American military forces in the Pacific and Indian Ocean areas. The military also serves as the largest employer in the state, annually pumping nearly $2.5 billion into Hawaii's economy. If it were to shut down its Island operations, nearly 30,000 civilians in the state would lose their jobs.

A gleaming white memorial stands respectfully above the battleship *Arizona*, which sank with 1,102 men on board when the Japanese bombed Pearl Harbor on December 7, 1941. Interestingly, the state's most popular visitor attraction is another war memorial—the National Cemetery of the Pacific in Punchbowl crater, where more than 26,000 of America's servicemen and women have been laid to rest. Also buried here is Island-born astronaut Ellison Onizuka, who died in the *Challenger* space shuttle tragedy in January 1986. More than four million people come to Punchbowl each year to honor these fallen heroes and to tour the cemetery's impeccably maintained grounds.

Oahu's other popular attractions celebrate Hawaii's specialness. Sea Life Park, poised on the ridge above Makapuu Beach, loosens the boundaries between land and sea with marine exhibits and shows starring dolphins, whales and other fascinating creatures of the Pacific deep. Opened in 1904, the Waikiki Aquarium displays 250 different species of South Pacific fish, a shark exhibit and an outdoor pool populated by rare Hawaiian monk seals. The aquarium was the first institution in the United States to exhibit the intricately structured chambered nautilus and to breed it in captivity.

Paradise Park is an oasis of performing birds, babbling brooks, waterfalls and tropical flowers in the cool of Manoa Valley. At Waimea Falls Park, the archaeological remains of an ancient Island community are tucked away in a valley rich with rare plants and animals.

The Polynesian Cultural Center authentically recreates the cultures of seven South Pacific destinations. Visitors are invited not only to observe, but to participate in games, crafts, dances and other activities unique to each Polynesian group. Moanalua Gardens, once a royal estate and center of Hawaiian arts, pays tribute to the spirit of Hawaiian dance during its Prince Lot Hula Festival, held every year in July.

The Honolulu Academy of Arts showcases a notable collection of treasures from all over the world in thirty galleries surrounded by six spacious courtyards. Built in 1927, the academy's gracious Spanish-style architecture has garnered it a coveted spot in both the state and national registers of historic places.

The Bernice Pauahi Bishop Museum was founded in 1889 by prominent Honolulu businessman Charles Reed Bishop as a memorial to his wife, Princess Bernice Pauahi Bishop, great-granddaughter and last surviving direct descendant of Kamehameha I, unifier of the Hawaiian Islands. It was Bishop's intent that Bishop Museum "rank with the museums of the world," and throughout its ninety-eight-year history, the museum has pursued a course of scientific research and acquisitions that has realized that intent. Today, Bishop Museum is recognized as the principal museum of the Pacific and one of the world's leading scientific and historical institutions.

From 1882 to 1893, Iolani Palace was the official residence of King Kalakaua and Queen Liliuokalani, the last reigning monarchs of Hawaii. Its cornerstone was laid on December 31, 1879; construction, which called for the services of three different architects, was completed in 1882 at a cost of just under $360,000. After the demise of the monarchy, Iolani Palace served as the capital for the republic, territory and, finally, state of Hawaii from 1893 until 1968.

A float carries the Aloha Week court, which represents Hawaiian alii.

Granny Kealoha Lake brings Queen Liliuokalani to life.

The state legislature appropriated over $6 million for the renovation project currently underway, and a major effort is being made to locate many of the palace's original furnishings.

Queen Emma Summer Palace in Nuuanu and the Mission Houses Museum in downtown Honolulu also are preserving the Hawaii of yesteryear through intriguing displays of Island artifacts.

History, in fact, is an ongoing presence on Oahu. Sunday services are still held in Hawaiian at Kawaiahao Church, which was built of sturdy coral blocks by Protestant missionaries in 1842. Favorite Island tunes fill the air at the Iolani Palace bandstand each week, courtesy of the Royal Hawaiian Band, which was founded in 1836 by King Kamehameha III. Punahou School, established by Congregational missionaries in 1841 as an educational center for their children, is the oldest college preparatory school west of the Rocky Mountains. Its physical plant reflects its long and distinguished history; stone buildings from the turn of the century stand on its lovely, seventy-six-acre campus in Manoa along with such sleek, contemporary structures as the Bishop Learning Center.

For many people, Hawaii begins and ends on Oahu. With its glitter and simplicity, its wilderness and Waikiki, its wealth of people and resources, Oahu shares a glorious song, indeed.

MAUI
BRINGING OUT ITS BEST
BY *KAUI GORING*

Sisters Julie, Jill and Joy Pascua, Wailea.

16

L ong ago, so legend goes, the sky hung so close to the earth, the people of Maui were forced to walk with their heads bowed to the ground. Maui, the demigod for whom this island is named, supposedly used his mighty powers to lift the clouds one day, enabling everyone to stand tall and, for the first time, take a good look around them. What they saw was an island of flawless white sand beaches, fern-framed waterfalls, majestic sea cliffs and valleys cut deep into the bosom of nature.

Maui's nickname, the Valley Island, merely hints at its incredible beauty. Mauians prefer to say of their home: "Maui no ka oi"—Maui is the best.

Two million visitors come to Maui each year, most of them headed for luxurious resorts on the island's western and southern shores. In March, Hawaiian Air opened the Kapalua-West Maui Airport after several years of public debate over its impact on the quality of life on the west end. Serviced by smaller prop planes, the new airport should ease some of the traffic at Maui's main Kahului terminal.

Along with Hawaii's statehood in 1959 came a blueprint for the island's first planned resort development on 1,200 acres along three picturesque miles of

Molokini Island, off the west coast of Maui.

beach at Kaanapali, on the far west coast. Until just prior to World War II, the landing at Kaanapali was used to ship tons of sugar processed at nearby Pioneer Mill.

In 1963, the Sheraton Maui became the first hotel to open at the Kaanapali Beach Resort. Perched on Black Rock, a lava promontory from which early Hawaiians believed the spirits of the dead jumped into the afterlife, the Sheraton anchors one end of the self-contained resort, 600 acres of which have been developed to date. At the other end, developer

Chris Hemmeter's $80 million Hyatt Regency Maui sparkles with a $2-million collection of art treasures gathered from around the world. In between are more than a dozen other hotels and condominiums, an open-air shopping complex and two championship golf courses.

Hemmeter's attention is now focused on a $155 million renovation project at the former Maui Surf. The hotel, scheduled to reopen in August as the Westin Maui, will have an elegant new look, including a sun-filled atrium surrounded by fresh

flowers, waterfalls and miniature lakes.

Five miles away, the Kapalua resort, constructed in the mid-1970s on fields once planted in pineapple, stretches over 750 beautifully landscaped acres. The Kapalua Bay Hotel, overlooking a picture-perfect cove, hosts a prestigious music festival and wine symposium each summer.

Kapalua's two championship golf courses were designed by Arnold Palmer. The Bay Course is the site of the $600,000 Isuzu Kapalua International Golf Tournament each November, a nationally televised event which draws top-name players from all over the world.

About eight miles away, the town of Lahaina blends history with Carmel cuteness. Tee-shirt boutiques and curio shops on Front Street are nestled among such gracious reminders of the past as Pioneer Inn which, built in 1901, was Maui's first hotel; the Carthaginian II, a replica of a nineteenth-century whaling ship that now serves as a museum; and the venerable Wo Hing Society Building, which is still used for community meetings. In 1962, Lahaina was designated as a National Historic Landmark. Two years later, ordinances to protect the town's unique architectural features were

Kaanapali Beach.

passed by the Maui Historic Commission.

From 1810 to the mid-1800s, Lahaina was the capital of King Kamehameha I's newly united kingdom. This was the height of the whaling era, and ships, often hundreds at a time, would anchor at the port of Lahaina to reprovision, turning their sea-weary men loose in town for a few days of rest and recreation before setting sail again. Many drunken, rowdy sailors were confined in Hale Paahao, the "House of Irons," to sober up. Today, the courtyard of the restored, 137-year-

Windsurfer Robbie Naish, Hookipa Beach.

Young Hawaiian girl, Hana.

old prison, constructed of massive coral blocks, is often the site of wine-tasting parties and wedding receptions.

New England missionaries arrived in Lahaina in 1823, hoping to offset the influence of the bawdy whalers by introducing Christian values to the Hawaiian people. One of the most prominent missionaries in Maui's history was Doctor Dwight Baldwin, whose home, built in 1834, is now a museum displaying many fascinating artifacts. Each week, the ladies of Lahaina gather on the steps of the Baldwin house to string leis to be sold to visitors. All proceeds benefit a local charity.

In the hills overlooking Lahaina, Lahainaluna School, the oldest school west of the Rocky Mountains, was founded in 1831. Housed here is Hale Pai, the printing house, which turned out volumes of books printed in both the Hawaiian and English languages.

Certainly among Maui's "best" attractions are the humpback whales which make the 3,000-mile journey from Alaska to Hawaii from November through May to bear their young in warmer Pacific waters. Internationally recognized marine biologists set up their headquarters on Maui during that period so they can conduct close-up studies of the elusive mammal, which is an endangered species.

People pull their cars off to the side of the highway all along the western coastline, hoping to catch a glimpse of the mammoth yet graceful creatures frolicking in the waves offshore. "Whale-watching" cruises leave from Lahaina on a regular basis during the peak season. In fact, interest in Maui's humpbacks has soared over the past six years, spawning a brand new industry which has brought in a total estimated revenue thus far of more than $100 million.

Until two decades ago, the area stretching from Kihei to Makena seemed to be desirable only for pig farming and weekend fishing. The only signs of civilization used to be beach houses belonging to Maui's kamaaina families, which were tucked down sandy driveways amidst rows of dry kiawe trees. Today, Kihei is a maze of condominiums, shopping centers, fast-food outlets, and booths promoting snorkeling and sailing tours.

A few years ago, the new Piilani State Highway opened, bypassing the old Kihei Road which hugs the ocean. The highway has provided a straight path to the blossoming Wailea and Makena resort areas.

Spread over 1,500 acres, Wailea encompasses luxury hotels, condominiums and homes, golf and tennis facilities, a charming shopping village and five lovely white sand beaches. Just offshore, the crescent-shaped islet of Molokini is a popular playground for snorkelers.

Beyond Wailea, the Seibu corporation of Japan has planned a 1,000-acre resort adjoining the Makena golf course designed by Robert Trent Jones, Jr. The newly opened Maui Prince Hotel is a vision of elegance overlooking the vast blue Pacific.

In contrast, the serenity and simplicity of rural life can be found in Maui's fertile up-country region. Cabbages, tomatoes, turnips, carrots and another of Maui's "bests"—an onion so sweet it is often mistaken for raw sugarcane—are among the bountiful crops Kula farmers are harvesting. Fields of brightly colored protea also flourish in Kula's cool, crisp climate. These exotic blooms are being shipped to destinations as far away as New York, Japan, France and Italy.

Tedeschi Winery has also put up-country Maui on the map with its sweet pineapple wine called Maui Blanc. It also produces a fine quality champagne, Maui Brut Blanc de Noirs, which was served at President Ronald Reagan's second inaugural dinner in January 1985. The winery is a joint partnership of Ulupalakua Ranch owner Pardee Erdman and Emil Tedeschi, who grew up working in the vineyards of Napa Valley.

Each Fourth of July weekend, the rustic cowtown of Makawao comes alive as it hosts the biggest—and best—rodeo in the state. Crowds of spectators arrive at the Oskie Rice Arena to watch more than 100 of the best paniolo in Hawaii compete for valuable prizes. From April through August, the field adjacent to the arena is the setting for fast-paced Sunday polo matches.

Haleakala, whose name translates as "House of the Sun," is one of Maui's most spectacular lures. Maui, the demigod, is said to have lassoed La, the sun, here long ago, slowing its pace so the people of Maui would have more daylight hours to accomplish their tasks. Today, scores of early birds brave thirty-degree temperatures to greet perfect sunrises at the dormant volcano's 10,023-foot summit. Hiking, hunting, camping and horseback riding are among Haleakala's recreational options. Many visitors also come to view the rare silversword plant, which, interestingly, blooms only on Haleakala and the mountainous regions of the Big Island.

Maui's two major towns, Wailuku and Kahului, have gradually merged together along Kaahumanu Avenue in the central part of the island. Wailuku is the county seat, although most of Maui's population resides in Kahului. Battles are currently raging over development plans in Wailuku. On one hand, people cite the need for more office space; on the other are those who would like to preserve the charm of the town's older structures.

Lahaina Harbor.

Sunset, Kapalua shoreline.

21

Haleakala Crater.

Just outside of Wailuku is peaceful Iao Valley, which, though it's now difficult to believe, was the site of a battle between King Kamehameha I and the chiefs of Maui in 1790—a battle so fierce, history records that the Wailuku River ran red with blood. One of Iao Valley's scenic highlights is an intriguing natural rock formation called Iao Needle. A short distance away is lovely Kepaniwai Heritage Gardens, in which stands a memorial to Sun Yat Sen, the "Father of the Chinese Republic," who spent his years of exile on Maui in the early 1900s.

East of Kahului Airport is the old plantation town of Paia, built in the 1870s. Paia was deserted in the late 1950s when sugar workers moved to their "dream city," Kahului, but in recent years, it has been given new life and a new identity. Windsurfing has transformed the town into an international sports center. Young, well-tanned board sailors from as far away as Japan and France line up daily outside Picnics, Dillon's or the Paia General Store for plate lunches before hitting the waves at Hookipa a mile up the coast, one of the best windsurfing spots in the state.

Superstars like Robby Naish, Alan Cadiz and Debbie Brown compete each year in such events as the Marui-O'Neill Invitational and the Citizen Aloha Classic for the chance to win purses as large as $30,000. Geoff Bourne and Barry Spanier found the sport so lucrative, they switched from manufacturing yacht sails to making windsurf sails. It is estimated that windsurfing generates $10 million in annual revenues.

If you're game enough to take on the 617 curves and fifty-six bridges leading to sleepy Hana, be sure to fill up your gas tank in Paia; there are no other gas stations along the way. Most people find Hana to be worth the grueling but scenic ride, which winds through lush forests of bamboo, kukui and wild ginger. Depending on the number of stops you make for picture-taking, the trip can take as long as three hours, even though the actual distance from Kahului to Hana is only fifty-five miles.

Hana, too, was once a bustling sugar town. Its plantation closed in 1944, and today, most of its activities center around the Hana Ranch and the Hotel Hana Maui.

Hana has always been unpretentious, despite the fact that it attracts such celebrities as George Harrison, Jim Nabors, Kris Kristofferson and Richard Pryor, who savor its slower pace. Famed aviator Charles Lindbergh spent much time during the last years of his life in Hana, and prior to his death in 1974, he requested that his final resting place be at tranquil Kipahulu, a few miles away.

Maui is a place of many pleasures. It is fast becoming world-renowned as a haven for the fine arts. The Maui Philharmonic Society has sponsored such celebrated international talent as Japan's Kodo drummers, in addition to offering its own full season of classical music performances. Na Mele o Maui, in its fifteenth year, is a three-day festival of Hawaii's musical heritage held at Kaanapali each November.

Maui is the largest seller of marine art in the world. The fourth annual Maui Marine Art Expo, held in February and March at the Maui Inter-Continental Wailea Hotel, gained national attention when it brought Jean-Michel Cousteau, son of famous marine scientist Jacques Cousteau, to the Valley Island. Expo producer Gary Koeppel contributed $20,000 to the Cousteau Society, an

amount raised from poster sales and a gala luau attended by 300 people.

Art Maui, the annual exhibition of Valley Island artists' creations, becomes more prestigious each year. In 1986, one of the show's judges, a British artist of international repute, said, "I think many of the pieces shown here could easily stand up in a world market."

The Maui Community Arts and Cultural Center, now in its planning stages, "will inspire innovative and creative thinking, rooted in the wisdom of our rich cultural traditions," according to Executive Director David Harder. The state has pledged $7 million in matching funds for the center, groundbreaking for which Harder hopes will take place by the end of the year on a fifteen-acre site in Wailuku donated by Maui County.

Commenting on the island's vigorous population and economic growth and the need to expand its infrastructure, Mayor Hannibal Tavares recently said, "Our concern is more than just meeting our present needs, but in carefully preparing for the future so that we may maintain for our children and future generations Maui's 'no ka oi' standing."

Sunset, Black Rock, Kaanapali.

23

HAWAII, THE BIG ISLAND

BIG SURPRISES, BIG CHANGES

BY BETTY FULLARD-LEO

H awaii, the Big Island, has always been described in superlatives. The largest and youngest of all the Hawaiian Islands, it stirs the senses and triggers profound musings, for more so than any other island in the Hawaiian chain, it is volatile—a vast arena of constant change.

Steeped in legend, the Big Island is a giant that is still growing. Pele, the volcano goddess in Hawaiian lore, is said to have used her magic digging tool, Paoa, to make a firepit at Kilauea. Even today, the crater periodically springs to life, indicating to many believers that Pele still makes her home there. At the end of 1986, slender fingers of glowing lava snaked down the slopes of Kilauea toward the sea, adding seventeen acres of new oceanfront land.

With 266 miles of coastline and five rugged volcanic mountains—Mauna Loa, Mauna Kea, Kilauea, Hualalai and Kohala, the Big Island is so large and so varied that Mayor Dante Carpenter divides it into four sections when he discusses its diversity and the problems of unifying the sectors. "Kona," he says, "is where the jobs are. Hilo and the Puna district are where the people are. For years (when sugarcane was the biggest income-producing crop), the Hilo side basically supported whatever infrastructure there was in Kona. Now Kona is maturing and their tax contributions are perhaps greater than (those from Hilo)."

Kaui Carreira offers a chant to Pele as molten lava from Kilauea Volcano spills into the sea.

For it is the Kona-Kohala coast in the western sector of the island that is taking off economically with the development of tourism. A five-mile string of hotels and condominiums along the water's edge is anchored by the King Kamehameha Hotel at the northern end of Kailua town and the Kona Surf Hotel at the southern end in Keauhou.

Further south along this sun-drowsy coast are precious reminders of the past. Puuhonua o Honaunau was designated as a national histori-cal park by Congress in 1961. As early as the twelfth century, Hawai-ians who had broken a sacred kapu could swim through a bay known as "the den of the shark," then climb over a ten-foot lava rock wall into the sanctuary to do penance for their sins and gain absolution from the kahu-na.

It was at nearby Kealakekua Bay that Captain Cook made landfall in 1778, becoming the first white man on record to discover the Hawaiian Islands. A year later, when Cook again sailed into Kealakekua Bay, he was killed by Hawaiians in a battle over a boat stolen from one of his ships. Today, the bay is a marine conservation district and visitors can snorkel in the sparkling waters near a monument that honors Cook.

Kailua was a sleepy little fishing village for years, coming awake an-nually for the Kona Coffee Festival in November; the Hawaiian Interna-tional Billfish Tournament, the Mil-lion Dollar Golden Marlin Jackpot

and Chuck Machado's Luau Fishing Tournaments in August and Sep-tember; and the grueling Ironman Triathlon in October.

With its bougainvillea-dotted yards, opalescent seas, sparkling air and fine dining in a balmy, seaside setting, Kailua-Kona now draws droves of repeat visitors. Kailua town is as appealing now as it was in 1812 when King Kamehameha I chose to build Kamakahonu, his principal residence from which he ruled Ha-waii in his later years, in a large en-closure flanked on one side by Ahu-ena Heiau. The black lava rock plat-form of the restored heiau stands right next to the pier where Kailua's fishermen weigh their daily catches of marlin.

After his wars to unite the Islands, Kamehameha the Great retired in Kailua, where he died in 1819. The kapu system was eventually abol-ished, opening the way for mission-aries from New England to establish the Christian religion in Hawaii. Standing in Kailua is Mokuaikaua Church, which, built in 1837 of coral and lava rock, holds the dis-tinction of being the first Christian church erected in the Islands. Across the street is Hulihee Palace, con-structed a year later by a cousin of Kamehameha I, Big Island Gover-nor John Adams Kuakini, and occu-pied in subsequent years by mem-bers of the royal family.

According to Mayor Carpenter, "Everyone thinks of Kailua-Kona as one little spot. North Kona and South Kona comprise sixty miles of communities with people tending to migrate above the village of Kai-lua on the slopes of Hualalai. The population is exploding there. They have the equivalent need of a new school every year for the next five years."

Shiny-leaved coffee trees cover acres of land in Kona's up-country area. Until the 1960s, schools de-clared a holiday during the coffee harvest so children could help pick

Kazo and Fujie Tanima at their Holualoa coffee farm.

Paniolo Charlie Kimura astride his horse at Parker Ranch, Waimea.

Cattle graze on Parker Ranch pastureland.

the labor-intensive crop. Farmers in Captain Cook, Kealakekua, Honalo and Holualoa, eked out a living. After years of hard work to establish it as a viable product, Kona coffee is now in demand as a gourmet brew. The largest crop in thirteen years is expected this year. With a value of $8.7 million, it will place coffee into the top ten of the Big Island's diversified crops.

The complexion of Kona's upcountry towns is gradually changing, Holualoa being a prime example. On one hand, Holualoa still retains some of its plantation town flavor with small, family-run businesses like the lau hala shop seventy-nine-year-old Tsuryo Kimura runs with the help of her two daughters. Kimura's father started the business as a general store in the late 1800s. Just down the road is the "new" Holualoa. The old coffee mill has been the Kona Arts Center ever since Bob and Carol Rogers moved from California to teach art classes in Holualoa more than twenty years

A youngster steps gingerly on a lava-covered section of the highway.

Picturesque scene along the Hamakua coast.

Canoe paddlers at sunset, Kona coast.

Paniolo herd cattle into a pen, Parker Ranch.

ago. With four art galleries displaying a wide range of creations, Holualoa is truly becoming an enclave of artists.

The area undergoing the most change on the Big Island is the barren, lava-covered South Kohala Coast. Presently nestled along this twenty-mile stretch between Kailua and the harbor at Kawaihae are the 100 thatch-roofed hales of the Kona Village Resort and three high-rise luxury resorts—the Royal Waikoloan, the Mauna Lani Bay Resort and Bungalows, and the Mauna Kea Beach Hotel, each with its own spectacular golf course.

In the wings are resorts or real estate developments on virtually every available piece of property, from Kona to Kawaihae. Under construction by Hawaii's golden boy of resort development, Chris Hemmeter, is the 1,200-room Hyatt Regency Waikoloa Hotel. Hemmeter has announced plans to expand this master plan to a two-to-three-billion dollar development with anywhere from 6,500 to 13,000 rooms that could create some 15,000 to 30,000 new jobs.

According to Mayor Carpenter, "This plan is a short-range plan—it's like six years. My initial reaction is terrific, but then all the red lights come on, too, because I know damn well that a massive infrastructure (is) required." Carpenter and the mem-bers of the Kohala Coast Resort Development Association are also well aware of the threat to the area's basically rural lifestyle and of the need to preserve multiple historic sites in the area.

The lava flows that found their way to the South Kohala seacoast centuries ago are etched with petroglyphs. Kona Village and the Royal Waikoloan have preserved petroglyph sites on their own grounds, but the most varied and abundant examples are found at Puako, at the end of an easy fifteen-minute walk from the road. From Puako, past Kawaihae Harbor, are vast stretches of empty land, once planted in plantation cane, now open range for cattle. At Lapakahi, the state's only historical state park, are house sites and shrines reflecting the everyday lives of ancient Hawaiians. Further up the road is 500-year-old Mookini Heiau, a national historic landmark, and a sign marking the birthplace of King Kamehameha the Great. At Kapaau is the original Kamehameha statue (its better-known replica stands in front of the judiciary building in Honolulu). The road ends at Pololu with a spectacular misty view of cliffs meeting the sea.

Rolling green ranch land defines the Waimea district of the Big Island. Even cattle ranching in Hawaii is changing. At 22,000-acre Kahua Ranch, owner Monte Richards is turning to science and diversified farming in order to realize a profit. There are 198 windmills on a hill behind the neatly painted, century-old ranchhouse. The 3.5-megawatt windfarm produces electricity for Hawaiian Electric Company and income for Kahua Ranch. In one pasture, sheep graze contentedly. The lambs and a limited amount of wool are marketed on the Big Island. Half an acre of greenhouses are laid out on another hill where long-stemmed carnations are grown for Honolulu nurseries.

Richards runs the ranch from an office equipped with computers and citizen band radios. His twenty paniolo (a few represent the third and fourth generations of their families to work at Kahua) carry walkie-talkies when they ride the range, and often they herd cattle astride motorcycles instead of horses. Ranch employee Judy Hancock explains the reason for the changes at Kahua: "We're struggling to stay alive because we like our lifestyle. If we weren't here, there's not much other than development to come in."

A couple of years ago, Richards and Polo Von Holt of an adjoining ranch, sold 10,000 acres of land to Kohala Ranch for subdivision and resale. According to Hancock, "Monte and Polo made a pledge that would be the last land they would ever sell. The money allowed us to diversify."

Waimea town, on the cool inland slope of the Kohala Mountains, has always been the Saturday shopping hub of the ranching community. It also has become a popular stop for tourists. A shopping center houses the Parker Ranch Visitors' Center and Museum where a slide show portrays the history of the sprawling 225,000-acre Parker Ranch, one of the largest individually owned ranches in America.

The drive from Waimea and Hilo meanders through miles of waving sugarcane and macadamia orchards along the Hamakua coast. If you stop to explore the plantation towns that look like relics from the past with wooden boardwalks and dogs dozing in backyards, it can be a full day's excursion, or you can make the trip in just over an hour.

A side trip via four-wheel drive into Waipio Valley reveals why this "Valley of the Kings" was once a favorite retreat for Hawaiian royalty. Cliffs drop 2,000 feet into the pastoral valley. Only eight families live in Waipio, farming taro and other crops along the river that flows from the twin waterfalls of Hiilawe at the back of the valley. Tom Araki opened the five-room Waipio No Name Hotel when he retired from construction work a few years ago. Guests must bring their own food, but Araki supplies kerosene and lamps because there is no electricity. Still, he says, "I've had visitors from all over the country—from forty-eight states, from Bombay and Australia."

Honokaa is where the first macadamia nut trees were planted in Hawaii in 1881. Macadamias have become big business on the Big Island, supplying ninety percent of the state's yield. Towns with music in their names pass quickly—Laupahoehoe, Papaaloa, Ninole, Honohina, Hakalau, Honomu, Pepeekeo and Papaikou—until finally, around the last deep-cut green gorge, past the last field of cane, you enter Hilo.

Hilo was devastated by a tidal wave in the early morning on May 22, 1960. Old-time residents still remember how the water in Hilo Bay receded and the sand flats sprouted fresh water springs before a series of huge seismic waves swept away businesses and homes near the water's edge, ultimately killing sixty-one people.

Hotels now rim the water's edge along tree-shaded Banyan Drive. Liliuokalani Garden is an adjoining thirty-acre oriental park with arched bridges and waterways filled with opae and tilapia.

Lei-bedecked friends at their high school graduation, Hilo.

The capital of the Big Island, Hilo is a fascinating dichotomy of old and new. Government affairs are handled in modern state and county buildings. By contrast, the Lyman House Memorial Museum, built in 1839, offers a glimpse of the Islands' missionary era.

Kilauea Avenue is lined with specialty shops in renovated one- and two-story wooden buildings which sell clothing, kitchen wares, handcrafted gift items, maps and charts. Mixed in are Japanese *mochi* shops, old-fashioned soda fountains, a taxidermist and Chinese stores selling preserved fruits in big glass jars. In residential areas, little wooden houses with rust-stained tin roofs are surrounded by neat-as-a-pin yards. At the edge of town, the modern, air-conditioned Prince Kuhio Plaza shopping mall was recently completed.

Hilo is known for its abundant rainfall. An average of 121 inches per year keeps three nearby tropical gardens—Nani Mau, Hilo Tropical Gardens and the Hawaii Tropical Botanical Garden—lush and green. The rains also keep picturesque Akaka Falls and Rainbow Falls flowing.

Residents joke that Hilo's streets roll up at dusk. But every morning about eight o'clock, a crowd gathers to watch the bidding at the Suisan Fish Market. Opakapaka, uhu, aweoweo, aku, ahi and marlin are laid out in a colorful display and the fish are auctioned to local retailers.

In mid-April, no hotel rooms are available in Hilo for an entire week. That's when the best halau in the state meet to participate in the state's most prestigious hula competition, the Merrie Monarch Festival.

On the outskirts of Hilo are nurseries with bright red anthuriums peeking through the shady fronds of tree ferns under acres of protective netting. Anthuriums bring more than $7 million a year into the Big Island's economy.

Sprawled across 220,000 acres on the slopes of Kilauea and Mauna Loa, Hawaii Volcanoes National Park was established in 1916. Rift zones on Kilauea's southeast side have been erupting periodically for the past four years; Mauna Loa last erupted in 1984. A portion of the park is a cool, green preserve with giant tree fems towering overhead. In the next moment, you might round a bend in the Chain of Craters Road and the thick vegetation will give way to an

A fountain of lava spurts more than 1,000 feet into the air, Kilauea Iki Crater.

The rich colors of twilight bathe the snow-covered cinder cones of Mauna Kea.

enormous barren caldera, a circular depression black with cinder and ancient lava. An eleven-mile Crater Rim drive circles Kilauea Caldera, with Halemaumau emitting steam and sulfurous fumes at its center.

At the U.S. Geological Survey—Hawaiian Volcano Observatory, perched on the edge of Kilauea Caldera, scientists with seismographs and tilt meters measure carbon dioxide at steaming fumeroles, as well as the actual tonnage of molten lava emitted, to predict each new volcanic episode.

The dining room of the thirty-seven-room Volcano House looks out over Kilauea Crater's vast depression. Ohia logs blaze in the fireplace in a cozy den, and the goddess Pele, captured in a bronze sculpture, smiles from above the flames. A few steps away, a path leads to an earlier Volcano House built in 1871, which has been restored to house the Volcano Arts Center. Next door at park

headquarters is the Thomas A. Jaggar Memorial Museum, where films of recent eruptions are shown in a 340-seat theater and rangers explain the exhibits and dispense information about the park's 150 miles of hiking trails.

The dramatic Chain of Craters Road descends to the coast where Kilauea's latest lava flow crossed the road after destroying seventeen homes in the Kalapana Gardens subdivision last year. Around the next bend in the road, the deep blue of the ocean bursts into white surf along the ebony-covered Kaimu Black Sand Beach. A trail through the Lava Tree State Park at Pahoa winds around eerie tree stumps encased in lava—grim reminders of the destructive forces of a long-ago flow.

From the island's infamous Saddle Road, a poorly maintained sixty-mile stretch that cuts through a desolate expanse, a ribbon of blacktop snakes off to the Ellison Shuji Oni-

zuka Memorial Center, the midway point to the top of Mauna Kea, which, rising 13,196 feet from the sea, is touted as the highest mountain in the world from its base on the ocean floor. Here, five major astronomical observatories search skies that, because of the altitude, are exceptionally clear and dark. In March, Mauna Kea was chosen as the site for the construction of the world's largest telescope by the National Optical Astronomy Observatories.

When snow falls at the base of the huge mushroom-shaped observatories, skiing on an island that is known for its tropical resorts becomes a surprising reality. The area can be reached only by four-wheel drive vehicles and there are no ski lifts, lodges or tow ropes—only snow; cold, clean air; and a panoramic view that extends to sun-sparkling beaches and the blue ocean beyond.

The future promises more change

and development for the Big Island. Ka Lae, the southernmost tip of the United States, is being considered as the site of a space port to launch missiles. Mayor Carpenter has other visionary ideas. At the beginning of the year, he was visited by Japanese businessmen who proposed building tracks for a bullet train from Hilo to the Kohala coast which would reduce commuting time from more than one hour to about thirty minutes. Carpenter feels train service is a viable solution to the Big Island's problem of unifying 4,000 square miles of land area.

Carpenter has also asked a special committee on sports to investigate the possibility of holding winter Olympics atop Mauna Kea "in 1992, or if that's too early, 1996, or if that's too early, the year 2000. We can make snow, using geothermal energy, or wind energy out of the Kohala windmills, or ocean thermal energy conversion out of the Kealakehe

Adze quarry shrine, Mauna Kea.

Window shopping during Christmas, Kainaliu.

area." Carpenter grins, thinking of the reaction of possible critics, then adds, "I like to stir the pot a little."

After all, the Big Island of Hawaii has always been a place to think big.

Volcano update: Thus far, during its seven-year eruptive phase, Kilauea has consumed more than 100 homes, a National Park visitor center, a church, a grocery store, Kaimu Black Sand Beach and the community of Kalapana. Hawaii Volcanoes National Park rangers, however, assure visitors that Kilauea poses no threat; because its eruptions are for the most part passive (non-explosive), spectators can get fairly close to active lava flows without being endangered.

A worker harvests anthuriums, Hilo.

33

Hanalei Valley.

KAUAI
IN PERFECT RHYTHM

BY RITA ARIYOSHI

A restaurant hostess welcomes guests, Hanalei.

Searching for a home in Hawaii, the fire goddess Pele tried each of the northwestern islands, one by one, but found no fire in the earth and moved on. She came to Kauai, traveling along the Na Pali coast, digging in vain in each of the green valleys—Awaawapuhi, Honopu, Kalalau, Hanakapiai—not even an ember.

Darkness fell. Sitting disconsolately on the sand, she heard a pounding that was not the surf on the shore—rhythmic, powerful, compelling. There were words on the wind, chanted to the beat of the drum:

"In the forests, on the ridges
Of the mountains stands Laka;
Dwelling in the source of the mists.
Laka, mistress of the hula,
Has climbed the wooded haunts
of the gods..."

The oli and the pahu echoed from ridge to ridge, coming from the direction of Haena. She followed the sound of the drums and reached the shore. Above her, on the hillside, was an enclosure. Inside, people were gathered around an altar. They were dancing, fifty across, their bodies glowing with exertion, with the light of the flames. There was smoke and the scent of maile, palapalai, ginger, akolea, lauae and pili, each one sacred.

Pele, as a beautiful young woman, entered the compound. Her ehu hair, her stature, her magnificent dark eyes commanded immediate attention. She was brought before the king, Lohiau, an exceptionally handsome man. Pele decided at once that she wanted him for herself. Frantically, she scratched in the earth at Haena. No fire. Almost in a panic, she mined all the way to Koloa and still could not find the volcanic fire necessary to her survival.

Reluctantly, she departed from Kauai, vowing to return for Lohiau. Many times in the course of her journey, and even after she was settled in Halemaumau on the island of Hawaii, her spirit would awaken to the sound of the drums and return to Kauai to be with Lohiau.

The love affair ended tragically for Lohiau, for it was dangerous to be loved by the goddess of fire, but the tale remains one of the favorite legends of the Islands.

The drums that had called to Pele were the hula drums of Kilioe, sister of Lohiau. Kilioe was considered to be the master hula teacher of the day. Dancers, chanters and kumu from all the islands would come to the heiau at Haena, called Ka Ulu a Paoa, with its 100-foot roofed hula pavilion and shrine dedicated to Laka, goddess of the dance.

Today, dancers still come reverently to the remains of the huge heiau for ritual performances. Kumu hula Roselle Bailey has taken it upon herself to keep the site clean. She teaches her young students not only the time-honored choreography, but also respect for their ancestors and for the surrounding forest that provides the vines and flowers sacred to the dance and to Laka.

The first drum ever to echo across the Hawaiian landscape was brought to Kauai from Tahiti by Laamaikahiki, the son of Moikeha, the legendary Tahitian lord who once ruled over Kauai. Made of a hollowed coconut

Anahola Baptist Church.

log, with sharkskin stretched taut across the top, the drum was the model for many drums that would be used in the dance and in the dark rituals of human sacrifice introduced by the Tahitians.

Kauai has always been more closely linked with the other Polynesian islands than its windward neighbors. Prehistoric artifacts unearthed on Kauai can be directly linked to central Polynesia. Captain James Cook, whose first contact with Hawaiians was at Waimea Bay, Kauai,

noted in his journal of January 9, 1778, that the people of Kauai were "of the same nation as the people of Otahiete (Tahiti)..." As late as the 1870s, language expert Abraham Fornander noted the similarities in language between Kauai and Tahiti and the corresponding differences between the speech of Kauai and the other Hawaiian islands.

Kauai was the only island never to be conquered by Kamehameha. The great warrior planned two invasions. In the first, his armada of 1,500 war

canoes ran into a storm in the Kaieie Waho Channel, and many ships and men were lost, forcing him to abandon the action. In anger, he vowed to "drink the water of Wailua, battle in the water of Namolokama, eat the mullet that swim in Kawaimakua at Haena and wreathe ourselves with the moss of Polihale..."

To keep his promise, Kamehameha gathered a second invasion force of 7,000 Hawaiians and fifty Europeans, most of them armed with muskets. He also counted in his

arsenal eight cannons, forty swivel guns and six mortars. In addition to his fleet of war canoes, he had twenty-one armed schooners. The army was poised at Kaaawa, Oahu when disaster again struck, this time in the form of an unnamed disease, probably typhoid. More men were lost to the sickness than would have perished in battle. Even Kamehameha was struck, but he was one of the fortunate few to survive.

Images of unconquered Kauai continued to taunt the warrior mon-

Wailua Falls.

arch, while Kaumualii, king of Kauai, regarded Kamehameha with increasing fear as reports of the Big Island chief's military and strategic successes continued to reach Kauai.

Eventually, Kaumualii was persuaded to meet with Kamehameha. When he sailed into Honolulu Harbor, dressed in his magnificent feather robes and flanked by his war chiefs and priests, Kamehameha came out to greet him. According to accounts of the day, Kaumualii shook Kamehameha's hand and said, "Here I am. Is it face up or face down?"

Kamehameha reportedly ignored the greeting and got right down to business. The two kings worked out an arrangement whereby Kaumualii agreed to acknowledge Kamehameha as sovereign while Kamehameha agreed to let Kaumualii continue to govern Kauai exactly as he chose without threats or interference. The arrangement worked until Kamehameha's death.

In an audacious power play, Kamehameha's widow, Kaahumanu, had Kaumualii kidnapped and brought to Oahu where she married both him and his son. Kaumualii never returned to Kauai. Upon his death, there was a brief but bloody rebellion on Kauai against Kamehameha II and the central Hawaiian government. In reprisal, most of Kauai's chiefs were sent in exile to other islands and their lands seized by relatives and allies of Kamehameha II.

Kauai has always been slightly, and proudly, out of step with the rest of the Hawaiian islands. Kauaians march, as people say, to the beat of a different drum.

Tourism, which has been the major economic force of the other islands for decades, has come more slowly, more gently to Kauai, the oldest of Hawaii's major islands. While other islands have permitted high-rise hotels and condominiums to proliferate along their shores, Kauai has imposed a treetop limit. No building may be taller than a coconut palm, a height that has been

Taro fields, Hanalei.

designated as four stories. The island welcomed a million visitors in 1986, while the statewide total topped five million that year. Kauai's count reflected a twenty-two percent growth over the previous year.

According to the island's mayor, Tony Kunimura, Hurricane Iwa, which struck in November 1982, was one of the best things to happen to Kauai. "We were fortunate to be devastated. We reconstructed and went into restoration. We made it better. People were in a mood to cooperate. Because of the disaster, the lion and the little rabbit huddled together in the brook. That's when you've got to take command."

Kunimura talks tough: "We dictate who can come, when they can come and the quality of what they do. Honky-tonk—no welcome." He lolls back in his chair. "I can practice government with a bayonet—or practice a philosophy of voluntary compliance." It is obvious that he prefers the voluntary compliance, and equally obvious that the symbolic bayonet of power could be wielded against those who do not voluntarily cooperate.

Kunimura backs up what he says, reminding people he is also a sheriff—and one to be reckoned with. By night, he drives around his island in a jeep. If he sees anything suspicious, anyone out of line, he radios the police. If he stops in a restaurant, he insists on being served last. He'll wait for a table, let visitors go first. "If you're going to be the head of the house, you better set a good example. This business is so fragile, like delicate crystal. I tell people Kauai is a special place. We don't have tourism. We have a visitor industry. There are no tourists, only visitors, guests." Depending on personal perspective, people credit or damn Kunimura for the growth of Kauai's tourism.

Kauai's first hotel was the Fairview in Lihue, which opened in 1890 with William Rice, Junior as manager. Later renamed the Lihue Hotel,

it had a beachside annex for water sports. Prior to the Fairview, everyone on Kauai—from Queen Deborah Kapule on down—was in the hospitality business, offering lodging to visitors to the island.

Today, Kauai has 6,000 visitor units (hotel rooms and condominium units) and four thriving resort areas: Lihue, Poipu, Wailua-Waipouli and Princeville-Hanalei. When the Westin Kauai opens in late 1987, the inventory will increase by 800. It will also mean 1,000 to 1,600 new jobs.

Tourism currently employs 6,000 people out of a total population of 44,600. It is the island's number one industry.

Number two is sugar. For the first time in many years, 1986 saw Lihue Plantation in the black by about $100,000. Kunimura says, "We're doing everything to help sugar stay alive." The first sugar mill in Hawaii was built in Koloa in 1836. Fields of waving sugarcane carpet most of Kauai's lowlands and creep up the hillsides in emerald aprons. The plantations have endowed the face of Kauai with a distinctly rural character. Most of the people live in plantation towns with populations under 4,000. Some of these towns, like Hanapepe, hugging the banks of the Hanapepe River, are unadorned country hamlets. Others, like Koloa, have been refurbished, recycled and reborn as cute resort shopping centers. Hanalei and Kapaa are straddling the times with new boutiques and restaurants standing side by side with dusty, charming old general stores.

For a country place, Kauai probably has more for visitors to do than many more sophisticated resorts. It has been called nature's Disneyland.

Book a rubber raft. Traverse an inaccessible coastline. Look for whales leaping out of the water. See spinning dolphins. Watch flying fish streak across the bow. God and Captain Zodiac will arrange it all.

Step back in time to a more gracious era of great mansions and smiling servants, of lavish furniture and sweeping lawns. Ride in a horse-drawn coach past workers' quaint cottages and lovely gardens. Dine on the lanai. Browse among the lovely shops in the parlor, in the bedrooms, even in the bathrooms. Don't miss Kilohana Estate.

Admire beautiful koa furnishings in a spacious, turn-of-the-century house. Nibble on delicious cookies baked in a wood-burning stove. Experience life on a sugar plantation at Grove Farm.

Wander in fantastic gardens where the plants look like atomic mutants of your common house plants. See philodendron running amok, riots of bright heliconia, huge torch ginger, a hundred varieties of hibiscus, the world's largest collection of palms, whole mountainsides of bougainvillea, a pond of lilies with pads big enough to hold a sixty-pound person. Find these wonders at the Pacific Tropical Botanical Garden—or Olu Pua, Menehune Gardens or Smith's Tropical Garden. Kauai has definitely earned its nickname of "Garden Island."

See how the ancient Hawaiians lived. Watch them pound poi, weave lau hala baskets, make fishnets—all this at Kamokila Hawaiian Village for an admission charge of only $5.

Swim at Lumahai Beach, site of the film "South Pacific." Tread in the footsteps of Harrison Ford and King Kong. Kauai has been the location for a host of films because Hollywood has always had an eye for beauty.

Cruise up a tropical river past Amazon-like jungles. Enter a beautiful, mysterious fern-choked grotto. Be serenaded. Repeat your wedding vows—or get married.

Walk along an ancient roadway into the Valley of the Lost Tribe. Bathe beneath a waterfall. Pick ripe guava from the trees. This one's tricky, however. There are no aerial trams. The Kalalau Trail is rugged

and not for the faint of heart, but it is exceedingly splendid, perhaps the experience of a lifetime. A tip: Most of the best scenery is in the first mile of the hike. Another tip: There are about a thousand helicopter flight-seeing tours a month. The price is a bit high, and you don't get to eat the guavas, but unlike the hikers, you'll dance that night.

Do your dancing at a high-tech disco with lights, camera and video—a surprise at the sedate, upscale Sheraton Princeville.

Go to a luau. Go to two. Kauai has a couple of the Islands' best luaus—down-home and as close to authentic as they get these days—one at the Sheraton Coconut Beach at Coconut Plantation, the other at the carefully casual Tahiti Nui.

More activities? Play golf on one of Kauai's breathtaking courses, enjoy a match or two on acres of tennis courts, ride the range. Paddle up a river. Book a tour that puts you on a picnic, shows you a waterfall and seats you in a canoe.

Kauai has a Sleeping Giant and Menehune Fish Ponds. The giant is a natural formation in the mountains near Kapaa. The ponds are archaeological treasures constructed by unknown pre-Hawaiian people. Legends say they were a race of pygmies who worked prodigiously and completed their tasks all in one evening. The story says that they left Hawaii after the arrival of the Polynesians, departing on a floating island. In a census taken on Kauai in the early 1800s, sixty-five people in Wainiha Valley stated their nationality as Menehune.

Waimea Canyon, the "Grand Canyon of the Pacific," slices through the heart of Kauai, exposing layers of geological history and displaying it in shades of russet, amber, rose and gold. It is a wild place, a vastness of wind and silence.

The rugged Na Pali Coast is a natural fortress, defying the might of the ocean. The green ramparts

Waimea Canyon.

have been standing solidly for centuries. Eons from now they will finally fall and the ocean will claim Kauai again.

To see both the canyon and the coast, you hardly have to leave your car. Along Route Fifty-five are three lookout points—one for the canyon, one for the valley and the third for the "forbidden island" of Niihau. Seventeen miles away, this small island, a part of Kauai County, is privately owned and closed to outsiders. Niihau residents are almost all pure Hawaiians whose primary language is still Hawaiian. The lookout is as close a view of Niihau as most people will ever have, unless the Robinson family, owners of Niihau, succeed in obtaining a permit to helicopter

tourists to a remote site on the island, far from the residents, just so people can say they've been there.

At the canyon lookout, Waimea spreads to the horizon, with shadows dancing among the clefts and crags. From the upper lookout, the Na Pali Coast and broad Kalalau Valley are revealed in tantalizing fragments, majestic and aloof.

Then, of course, there are the beaches, ranging from the sunny stretches of Poipu—where you can pick your beach for your purpose (there's one for bodysurfing, one for swimming and one for surfing)—to the secluded coves of Hanalei.

Even with a million visitors a year, Kauai has not lost any of its rural charm. At the Shell Station on

crowded Kuhio Highway that runs through Lihue, they sell, in addition to fuel for the car, boiled peanuts, chips and preserved seeds, patele, manapua and laulau. At the other end of the food chain, there is Nobles Restaurant at the Sheraton Princeville, where the chef creates gourmet delicacies from local specialties—like boats of filo pastry with taro leaves and lobster tails. In between are the kinds of dining discoveries people really want to hear about, like Kauai Chop Suey, Atami Japanese restaurant, Fez's Pizza and Hamura Saimin Stand.

Most Kauaians welcome the surge in the economy generated by tourism. Talented people have outlets; young people don't have to leave home to find work. The most outspoken opponents of tourism are the "instant locals," the Mainlanders who have found nirvana on Kauai, like it just the way it is, and want to pull up the bridges before anyone else gets there and "spoils it."

Officially, Kauai is beating the drums for tourism, while encouraging sugar, ranching and diversified agriculture. A brand new air terminal at Lihue welcomes daily flights direct from the Mainland.

So far, Kauai is one island that is managing to hold on to a rural Hawaiian lifestyle while opening itself to visitors. Kauaians remind everyone, however, that the sky's not the limit. The treetops are.

41

Spouting Horn showing off.

MOLOKAI
ONE OF THE LAST HAWAIIAN OUTPOSTS

BY CHERYL CHEE TSUTSUMI

Waterfall, Halawa Valley.

M olokai lies just twenty-six miles from Oahu across the Kaiwi Channel, but the two islands are worlds apart in terms of mood, style and pace. While Honolulu wrestles with traffic, pollution and all the other problems that come with urbanization, Molokai is relishing its peaceful, rural existence. It has no freeways, stoplights, movie theaters, bowling alleys, elevators, nightclubs, shopping centers, supermarket chains or fast-food outlets. None of its buildings stands more than three stories high. Newcomers may regard Molokai as being unsophisticated, perhaps even backward, but those who know it best recognize the magic in its simplicity.

Geographically, the island is characterized by two dormant volcanic mountains connected by a plain. Kamakou, to the east, reigns over miles of lush, mist-shrouded valleys; pristine forests filled with the fresh scent of rain and tropical fruit; and rugged lava cliffs that dramatically plunge to frothing surf 3,000 feet below. On the west end, Maunaloa looks out over acres of flat, arid land targeted for major development.

Molokai measures a mere thirty-eight miles long and ten miles wide. Its total land area is 261 square miles—making it smaller than New York City—but what it lacks in size,

it more than makes up for in spirit. In many ways, Molokai is the most "Hawaiian" of the major Hawaiian islands. Close to fifty percent of its population of 6,000 claim they are of Hawaiian ancestry. With the exception of privately owned Niihau, that figure represents the highest island percentage in the state.

"E komo mai" is more than a saying on Molokai; it is a daily practice. Most residents never lock their cars or their homes. There is no need, they say, for crime on the island is virtually non-existent.

Molokaians speak with great pride of their rich heritage. Kaana, located on the slopes of Maunaloa, is believed to be the birthplace of the hula. It is said that long ago, Laka, the goddess of the hula, set forth from Kaana to teach the dance to people throughout the Islands. One of renowned kumu hula John Kaimikaua's favorite ancient chants, an incredible 928 lines long, tells of the travels of Laka and her experiences in establishing the hula as an integral part of the Hawaiian culture.

Kaimikaua's family hails from Molokai. Although he was born and raised on Oahu, he spent many summers at his grandfather's forty-acre homestead in Hoolehua. Each visit brought him more in tune with the special spirit of the island.

42

Sunset at the beach fronting the Kaluakoi Resort.

43

Said Kaimikaua, "I like to go to Molokai to rejuvenate myself. It is a very powerful place, and yet at the same time, very subdued. The first thing you must do before you can really experience Molokai is quiet your soul. Just sit on the land, on a grassy field, close your eyes and let your soul absorb everything around you. The land speaks to you through your feelings. If you go to Molokai to see the beauty with only your physical eyes, you won't fully enjoy it. But if you see Molokai with your spiritual eyes, with your feelings,

you will come to truly understand it and you will love it forever."

Once a year, Kaimikaua takes his students to the sites on Molokai mentioned in many of the songs they perform. "I take them right to the place where a particular chant came from, and I make them dance that number right there, so that they can get a feel of that place," he said. "When we go to these places, we always pray and ask if it is God's will, that He will let us feel the spirits of those of the past as we dance and that we will be able to understand the

things they felt when these chants were being written. For some of my students, it is such an overwhelming experience, they become tearful."

Molokai's strong link with the past is evident in its wealth of archaeological treasures. The largest and best preserved concentration of ancient fish ponds in the state is found along the scenic thirty-mile coastline stretching from the main town of Kaunakakai to Halawa Valley, on the verdant east end of the island. Two of the ponds, Keawanui and Ualapue, have been placed in the

National Register of Historic Places.

Also awarded that distinction is Iliiliopae, which, measuring a massive 320 feet long and 120 feet wide, is one of the largest heiau still standing in Hawaii. Legend says the heiau, which dates back to the thirteenth century, was constructed by the Menehune out of smooth stones which were transported over the Kamakou Mountains from the shores of Wailau Valley to the north. All the work was supposedly done in one night and as a reward, each Menehune received one shrimp; hence,

Country living on the east side of the island.

44

the temple's name "Iliiliopae," The Heiau of the Shrimp.

Throughout Island history, Molokai has been regarded as a place of great religious significance. Its nickname, "Friendly Isle," is a modern-day one. Anciently, it was known as "Molokai Pule Oo," Molokai of the Potent Prayers. Its kahuna were feared throughout the Islands for their mystical powers. It is for this reason that outsiders avoided Molokai, and it was spared much of the bloodshed and turmoil that plagued the other islands during the eighteenth and early nineteenth centuries as chiefs waged war against each other in the hopes of gaining more land and power. Kamehameha I emerged as the ultimate victor in 1810.

A decade later, the first contingent of Christian missionaries arrived in Hawaii, bringing with them a new religion and a new way of life. Molokai did not remain untouched by their presence. The Reverend Harvey Hitchcock and his wife, Rebecca, arrived in 1832 and established Molokai's first Protestant school and church at Kaluaaha, on the southeastern coast. This marked the beginning of rapid social change on the island.

Rudolph Wilhelm Meyer, an engineer and surveyor who came to the Islands from Germany in 1850, remains a formidable figure in Molokai's history. Meyer settled on the island in 1851 after marrying Dorcas Kalama Waha, a Hawaiian chiefess. They raised eleven children in the cool, upland region of Kalae.

Among a score of duties, Meyer served as the overseer for the vast ranch lands of the Kamehamehas. Until the 1870s, the majority of Molokai's land had been devoted to cattle raising, but, recognizing the need to diversify to ensure economic stability, Meyer encouraged the introduction of a number of experimental commercial crops, including coffee, corn, wheat, white potatoes,

Church framed by palm trees.

Visitors befriend a giraffe on the Molokai Wildlife Safari.

cotton, bananas, beans and sugarcane.

From 1878 to 1889, he operated a sugar plantation and mill at Kalae. A $1.5 million project to restore the historic mill is currently underway. Long-range plans call for the erection of a museum on the one-acre site, which would serve as a research center and repository for valuable artifacts collected by the Meyer family over the years.

Preserving what "was" on Molokai is in many instances preserving what "is," for life—at least in the two towns of any consequence—has changed very little in the past fifty years.

Days pass gently in Kaunakakai. Its parade of old wooden storefronts presents a humble facade, yet there are truly lovely finds tucked away on store shelves—solid brass knick-

Kalaupapa coastline.

knacks, gleaming milo bracelets, and necklaces woven out of Job's tears, wiliwili, royal poinciana and seashells.

Molokai Fish and Dive boasts the best collection of souvenir tee-shirts in town—all custom-designed by owner Jim Drocker and his staff. It's also the place to get acquainted with Big Bull, Rosebud, Pee Wee, Sun Dancer or any one of a dozen other macaws, cockatoos, cockatiels, parrots and parakeets that Drocker brings to work with him every day.

Nearly all of the businesses in Kaunakakai are family-run. Kanemitsu Bakery is known statewide for its delicious breads, and Mid-Nite Inn for its fresh fish entrees. Customers can still buy groceries on credit at Friendly Market, Misaki's and Kaunakakai Groceteria. Outside C. Pascua Store, old-timers enjoy leisure hours sipping beers and "talking story."

Blink and you could miss drowsy Maunaloa town, which has a charm

all its own. You can find beautiful deerhorn jewelry, handmade coconut fiber dolls and hihiwai shell necklaces at The Plantation Gallery; pick up "Molokai Red Dirt Shirts" at a shop with the same name; and stop at JoJo's Cafe for a refreshing lilikoi sundae and a look at a magnificent mahogany bar that was shipped around the Cape of Good Hope in the 1800s.

At Jonathan Socher's store, something fun is always in the wind. Crammed into his cozy Big Wind Kite Factory are kites of all colors, sizes and designs, among them hula girls, pandas, whales, unicorns, penguins and rainbows.

"Quietness" lured Socher and his wife, Daphne, to Molokai from the urban sprawl of Los Angeles eleven years ago. "The business was very slow to start with," Socher admitted. "We would end up playing chess in the back room. The last two years have been insane. We now get an enormous amount of tourist traffic."

Some see tourism as Molokai's savior since the shutdown of Dole's pineapple operations in 1975, and the devastating announcement in May that Del Monte will close its plantation in late 1988. Life on Molokai had revolved around pineapple for fifty years, and kamaaina are still reeling from the sudden shift in economic focus. The island's average unemployment rate is fifteen percent—the highest in the state.

The Destination Molokai Association was founded in 1983 to give tourism—and the economy—on the island a shot in the arm. Gena Sasada is the association's current executive director and also the general manager of Rare Adventures, Ltd., which operates the island's top attraction, the Molokai Mule Ride. In Sasada's opinion, "What Molokai offers is peace, tranquility and a chance for people to get away from it all. There's enough to do on Molokai to keep you very busy for a week. On the

other hand, you don't have to do a blessed thing if you don't want to. Molokai has many things for you to do—and nothing for you to do. It's your choice."

Sasada's mule ride winds its way more than three miles down the face of a 1,600-foot cliff, graced with silvery ribbons of waterfalls, to the remote seaside community of Kalaupapa, where people stricken with Hansen's Disease were once banished. Belgian priest Father Damien de Veuster arrived at Kalaupapa in 1873 and devoted the rest of his life to serving a congregation of outcasts.

About 100 patients have chosen to remain at Kalaupapa even though, thanks to modern medicine, Hansen's Disease is no longer a public threat and they have been free to leave since 1969. The area was designated as a national historical park in 1980, under the joint administration of the State Department of Health and the National Park Service.

Kalaupapa's poignant story is an unforgettable chapter in the island's history, but there is so much more to Molokai. On a tour of the Molokai Ranch Wildlife Park, picture-taking becomes a real adventure. Eland, ibex, Barbary sheep, greater kudu and axis deer are among the hundreds of animals who roam across 2,000 acres that resemble the African veld.

Enjoy guided four-wheel-drive and hiking tours of the Nature Conservancy's 2,700-acre Kamakou Preserve, a tropical rain forest harboring several endangered bird species and 219 varieties of plants which can now be found only in Hawaii.

Troll for marlin, mahimahi and ono aboard a vessel specially equipped for deep-sea sport fishing. Soar in a helicopter above the world's highest sea cliffs, Hawaii's longest waterfall and largest white sand beach. Paddle a kayak along the spectacular wilderness that defines Molokai's northeast coast. Snorkel, surf and swim in secluded coves.

Seven months ago, Howard and Sarah Selnick's Hawaiian Horsemanship Unlimited became the local representative for Fits Equestrian, an international riding tour organization based in Solvang, California. The Selnicks welcome horsemen from all over the globe to Molokai, which has, as Sarah says, "the most beautiful riding country in the world. There are areas that look like the Black Forest of Germany because pine trees are spread like a canopy over your head. There are fern grottoes there, and waterfalls, and fruit growing wild—plums, Bartlett pears, guavas, lilikois, papayas and avocados. Other areas look like the Cliffs of Dover in Ireland. You can gallop across a plateau of soft grass right next to sheer cliffs. Some spots on Molokai look like Africa and others remind me of Australia—and, of course, there are so

many beautiful beaches. It's incredible! Molokai is horse heaven."

Glenn and Mahealani Davis and their three children have found their own bit of heaven in the serenity of Halawa Valley, where the first Polynesians on Molokai are believed to have settled around 650 A.D. The family lives just steps from the sea in a modest home that has no electricity, telephone or television. Glenn makes a living by selling fish that he catches in coastal waters teeming with weke, kumu, enenue and other delicacies. When the ocean is calm, his twenty-five-foot, twin-engine *Mahealani* doubles as a tour boat, taking visitors on a half-day cruise to some of the most isolated—and beautiful—spots in Hawaii.

At their haven in Halawa, the Davises have been blessed with ample spiritual and physical nourishment. In addition to fresh fish, their

table is always laden with deer, pig or goat that Glenn has brought back from hunting expeditions in the valley. Mahealani raises won bok, eggplant, taro, beans, carrots, spinach and a fragrant variety of spices in a garden fronting the house. They are deservedly proud of their self-sufficiency.

Said Mahealani, "This is a good place to raise the children. They've got a different set of values than if they were growing up in a city. Our son can go out and catch a fish, and he knows how to clean it and cook it. He's durable; he can survive off the land. Along with that comes a lot of self-confidence. Our children don't feel inhibited or threatened. They are polite and respectful. We teach them to share and to care about each other. We're talking family values. Hawaiian values. People don't get a chance to be 'Hawaiian' too often

nowadays. We have a chance here to be Hawaiian.

"We have access to a TV; we can watch it if we choose to. But not having it here where the children can constantly turn it on keeps that distraction out of the home. There are other things that educate them. They read more. They learn from the earth."

Added Glenn, "Halawa Valley is the home we had been looking for all our lives. It's beautiful! The ocean is right in front of our house; the mountains are in the back. We can go hunting, fishing, kayaking, swimming, surfing, horseback riding. Whenever I get depressed, I go to the beach, look around and see what I've got. This is paradise."

On the west end of the island, the Kaluakoi Corporation, a wholly-owned subsidiary of The Louisiana Land and Exploration Company, is

Enjoying early morning solitude near the Hotel Molokai.

developing its own concept of paradise. Its master plan calls for 1,100 hotel units, 1,200 condominium units, 1,000 single family dwellings and a shopping village to be constructed on 6,700 well-manicured acres over the next fifteen to twenty years. The Kaluakoi Resort presently encompasses two condominiums, a championship golf course, a ten-acre beach park, and the Kaluakoi Hotel and Golf Club.

Near Kaunakakai, two smaller hotels exude the down-home flavor of Molokai. At the Pau Hana Inn, clean, no-frills rooms go for $25 a night. Hotel Molokai takes the island's "get away from it all" promise very seriously; its comfortable bungalows have no televisions or telephones.

Many believe tourism, supported by this kind of low-rise, low-density development, is the hope for Molokai's future. Others feel the answer lies in agriculture. In 1921, Congress passed the Hawaiian Homes Act, which set aside approximately 33,200 acres in the central portion of Molokai for native Hawaiians' "return to the land." There are presently 421 homesteads on the island in active cultivation, ranging in size from two to forty acres.

Molokai is the state's largest producer of watermelons, sweet potatoes and green beans. Other major crops include bell peppers, onions, herbs, and such "specialty produce" as miniature corn and carrots.

Doctor Noa Emmett Aluli speaks eloquently of the need for Molokai to retain the vitality of its land. "The alternative (to tourism development) is diversified agriculture, strong and clear. Molokai has always been known for its subsistence kind of living. The community has been strong because of the ingenuity people have had in growing things. The good thing about agriculture here is that it's a family enterprise where sons, daughters, nieces, nephews, aunts, cousins and grandparents work in the fields, take care of the books. That keeps the Hawaiian tradition of family togetherness alive. Everybody works together and everybody benefits. What we want to see is this community grow in a Hawaiian fashion."

John Kaimikaua concurs. "I believe Molokai is meant to be the breadbasket of Hawaii, and it can be, with Hawaiians farming and managing their own land. Molokai is a very special place, a very Hawaiian place, and it should be preserved as such. Molokai is a place for the future of the Hawaiian people."

49

The thrilling Molokai Mule Ride.

Ronnette and Jennifer-Hope Arevalo.

LANAI

ISLAND OF SPIRITS AND DREAMERS

BY ALLAN SEIDEN

The fast-moving storm quickly devoured a landscape that had been bathed in sunlight only minutes before. It didn't take long for us to realize we were lost. Driving through pineapple fields that seemed to reach to the horizon, we'd followed a dirt road into the hills, eventually brought to a halt by a cul-de-sac of ironwood pines that bordered rock-strewn, erosion-gouged terrain. The trees fought hard to survive here, assaulted and shaped by the trade winds, drawing moisture from the dry, hard-packed soil that prompted the Hawaiians to call this land "red Lanai."

With skies still clear, I left my friend and wandered off in search of a lookout that might reveal the lay of the land. I was heading back to the jeep, following a Hansel and Gretel trail of visual clues, when the weather suddenly changed. Rainclouds and a soft gray mist accompanied a fast-blowing wind, hiding the landscape, obscuring the trees, rocks and broken branches that were meant to guide me.

At first it felt as though I was only playing at being lost. As earth-hugging clouds raced toward the southeast, I was momentarily amused at the thought of being thrust into some exhilarating adventure patterned after a Hollywood script. The thought of being in possible danger didn't seem real. After all, this was Lanai—a mere 140 square miles of island only nine cross-channel miles from neighboring Maui and Molokai—not a sprawling continental wilderness.

As windblown rain drenched me with pinpoint insistency and dense gray absorbed all sense of space and time, I recalled Hawaiian legends that peopled Lanai with malevolent ghosts and remembered whispered stories of spirits still to be found here—stories told with an over-the-shoulder glance and a look of urgency that quickly implied they should be taken seriously.

For many centuries after the Polynesians settled Hawaii, they had avoided Lanai. While some legends referred to it as the landfall of Hina and Wakea, progenitors of the Hawaiian people and their pantheon of gods, in the popular imagination it was haunted by ka polo, evil ghosts who feasted on those humans foolish enough to try to spend a night on the island.

It was Kaululaau, the son of a Maui chief, who was the first to challenge Lanai's isolation. Exiled to Lanai for repeatedly disobeying his father's edicts, he was forced to confront the ka polo aided only by his aumakua, the godly ancestors who helped him avoid the ghosts in their nightly search for unwary humans. Night after night the ka polo were outwitted, drowned and bumped by Kaululaau's trickery. Soon, only the two wiliest ka polo remained, and

Kaululaau prepared a final trap to free Lanai of its ghostly inhabitants.

In the night, with a full moon overhead, he sat beside a large pool, with his reflection clearly visible. When the two kapolo saw him, they climbed a hala tree. The first spirit leaped at the image and drowned in the pool. The second declared his defeat and rushed off to join others of his kind on neighboring Kahoolawe.

Each night thereafter, Kaululaau went to the beach at Naha, on the coast directly across from Lahaina on the island of Maui. There he lit fires to attract the attention of his kinsmen. Curiosity outweighing fear, they set out to discover the cause of these blazing nightly fires. Finding Kaululaau alive and repentant, they brought him back to Lahaina, a hero. But the lure of Lanai did not fade from Kaululaau's memory. Accompanied by others, he returned to settle the no-longer-forbidden isle.

The sea provided for these first Hawaiian settlers. Slowly they moved inland, planting taro in the narrow valleys of the windward coast and yams in the fertile soil of the Palawai basin, the great erosion-flattened crater that centuries later would embrace the world's largest pineapple plantation.

Brought back to the present, with an unrelenting head wind as a companion, I was given very real meaning to that otherwise out-of-context bit of information, trekking through fields that seemed to repeat themselves as if Lanai were a single bit of reality endlessly recycled.

I'd left the jeep at noon. An hour had passed in my search for it and my friend. In a hollering wind, even my loudest efforts to communicate turned fragile. It was three-thirty when the clouds thinned enough for me to catch a glimpse of the rolled-tin roofs of Lanai City's older plantation homes.

Without a horizon line or the sun to provide a sense of direction, it was

Garden of the Gods.

Lehua Pate and her daughter, Kauwela.

the wind that provided the clue I needed to head back to town. Earlier that day, from atop Lanaihale Road that curves its way along the island's summit, I'd noted a strong wind blowing from the northwest. Sketching a mental map of the island, I traced a route from my cloud-covered world back to Lanai City.

The path back took me through dense scrub and flash-flood gullies before returning me to the edge of the Palawai's 14,000 acres of pineapple. Two-and-a-half hours later, rain-drenched and caked with pounds of Lanai's red earth, I wandered from the fields onto Lanai City's blessedly paved streets, joyful and touched by the power and immensity of spirit that gives life to this bit of Hawaiian aina.

Wu Tu Tsin was the first foreigner to settle on Lanai. He arrived in 1802, twenty-three years after the island had been sighted by Captain James Cook's ships as they retreated from the confrontation on the Big Island that had cost Cook his life. Wu Tsin came to grow sugar, hoping to make use of the sugarcane he'd seen growing wild while en route to Maui. As he soon found out, Lanai's dry climate was an erratic ally. After

View of Lanai from West Maui.

Dancer at sunrise atop Puu Pehe, "Sweetheart Rock."

54

producing Hawaii's first crop of sugar, he departed for greener pastures.

Other visionaries followed their dreams to Lanai. In 1836, Maui-based missionaries Dwight Baldwin and William Richards came and quickly departed, finding the conservative Lanaians clinging to belief in their ancestral gods. A group of American and Hawaiian Mormons arrived in 1854 with a mandate from their leader, Brigham Young, to establish a community "where the brethren can collect in peace and sustain themselves unmolested."

Iosepa, their City of Joseph, was built on the fertile Palawai plains, on lands owned by Oahu Chief Haalelea, who hoped to lease his acreage for the royal sum of $175 annually. Fields were planted in beans, sweet potato, corn and melon. Cattle and supplies were rowed in from Lahaina, followed by additional settlers from Maui. But two years of drought proved to be devastating to these early Lanai pioneers and by 1857, Iosepa was closed despite Chief Haalelea's offer to sell his 10,000 Palawai acres for $300.

It was the controversial Walter Murray Gibson who would next set his sights on Lanai. In 1860, he set sail from New York in search of an island on which to raise his children and nurture his dreams. Gibson was a free spirit, a self-made millionaire turned practicing idealist, a philosopher turned entrepreneur, an inventor turned linguist, author and diplomat.

"This is the best land of the Sandwich Islands," he wrote. "I could make a glorious little kingdom of this or any such place with such people, so loving and obedient. I would fill this lovely crater (Palawai) with corn and vine and oil and babies and love and health and brotherly rejoicing..."

Gibson's "kingdom" came in the form of a ranch that covered the Palawai lands he had bought for twenty-five cents an acre and had populated with sheep and goats that could appreciate its sparse vegetation. His utopian goal established to his satisfaction, Gibson left his son-in-law on Lanai to manage his properties, and headed to Honolulu where he kept up a high profile as owner/editor of the *Honolulu Advertiser*, legislator, minister of the interior and prime minister under King David Kalakaua.

Ultimately, the Palawai ranch lands would pass from Gibson's control, to be used as collateral for loans made in support of the royal government. In January 1888, far from Lanai, Gibson died of tuberculosis in San Francisco.

Sugarcane crops on Lanai, meanwhile, had been attempted and failed. Some blamed the failure on the destruction of the Kahea Heiau when tracks were being laid for a cane haul railroad. At the time, ranching was the mainstay, with Lanai serving as home to thousands of head of cattle and sheep, but fewer than 200 people.

Ranching had been given a boost by the arrival of Charles Gay in 1904. Landing at Manele on the chartered interisland steamer *S.S. Kauai*, he unloaded livestock, the makings of a household, family and friends. Gay was no wishful adventurer. His utopia seemed already half accomplished; he already owned a good part of Lanai.

Gay came from an illustrious family. His grandmother was Eliza Sinclair, the New Zealand matriarch who had moved to Hawaii in 1874, lock, stock and gold bars, buying Niihau from King David Kalakaua and expansive tracts on Kauai from its chiefs. Now it was Gay's turn, and Lanai was the object of his attention.

Two years earlier, at age forty, Gay had bought the Palawai holdings of the bankrupt Gibson estate for

$108,000. He quickly added to this acreage, purchasing the ahupuaa of Kaa and Kaohai from the Spreckles family, who had bought it from Princess Ruth Keelikolani. A year later, Gay bought the coastal acreage of the failed Maunalei Sugar Company from Gibson's son-in-law.

By 1908, the whole island was his. But three years of drought followed, leaving Gay deeply in debt and unable to secure new loans. Lanai, minus the 600 acres Gay was able to retain, was sold by his creditors for $375,000.

Fourteen years later, Jim Dole paid $1.1 million for an island he told Gay was worth at least $20 million. He then set out to prove his point, combining the idealism of Lanai's nineteenth-century dreamers and the pragmatism of a successful entrepreneur to transform red Lanai into the Pineapple Island.

Gay had already planted pineapple, agreeing in 1921 to grow pineapple for Maui's Haiku Pineapple Company. But Dole had a full-scale plantation in mind, and proceeded to lay out Lanai City on flatlands where the Palawai crater met the foothills of Lanaihale, the mountain that climbs 3,370 feet to the summit of the island. Next he planted 3,000 Palawai acres in pineapple, and directed the construction of a harbor from which to ship Lanai's first harvest.

Dole's plantation proved to be a model effort, with well-paid workers living in well-maintained homes on large plots that faced Lanai City's grid of streets. By 1926, when the first harvest of fruit was shipped to Honolulu, Lanai City boasted tennis courts, a gymnasium, theater, post office, hospital, churches and a school. With more than 16,000 acres eventually planted, Lanai and the Dole Plantation came to mean the same thing. Red Lanai was now the

This pineapple picker is well-protected from the merciless sun.

Workers harvest a crop of pineapple.

largest pineapple plantation in the world.

As much as the rest of Hawaii has changed in the past ten years, Lanai has remained the same. Lanai City is still a small town; the island itself can be described as a great plantation surrounded by an often eerie wilderness. On the jeep track called the Munro Trail that winds its way along the summit spine of Lanaihale, winds provoke an air of mystery. Sentinels of the storm, they oversee a dense tangle of fern and dwarf lehua and the vertical wilderness of Lanai's southern slopes. At the Garden of the Gods, boulders lie scattered on the hard-packed earth, and deep gullies scar hillsides, a cosmic landscape in natural disarray.

Today, close to 14,000 acres on Lanai are still committed to pineapple. Drip irrigation has been installed, the money spent taken as evidence that "pine" still has a future here. Irrigation has made pineapple growing more efficient, speeding up the eighteen months it normally takes for the exotic bromeliad to mature in the hot dry weather of up-country Palawai. Per acre yields have also increased, more than compensating for the recent loss of some 3,000 plantation acres.

Change is coming to Lanai, with what was once inevitable now imminent. No one is sure of the impact that hotels, condominiums and a new non-plantation population will have. Castle & Cooke, which, via its Dole subsidiary, is landlord to more than ninety-five percent of Lanai's population, is about to embark on an island-wide master plan that includes construction of a 102-room lodge on the outskirts of Lanai City. Managed by Rockresorts, it will be elegant and upscale—a dramatic contrast to the rustic, ten-room Hotel Lanai which now provides lodgings for hunters, state and county employees, businessmen and an off-the-beaten-path type of visitor.

The plan also calls for the construction of a 250-room, luxury hotel on a promontory overlooking Hulopoe Beach, which will be relandscaped and expanded as a public park. The Manele Bay Hotel, also to be managed by Rockresorts, is slated for a spring 1991 opening, with later additions possible thanks to zoning for 400 rooms. A small condominium and 275 home lots are also part of the plan for Hulopoe.

Few on Lanai express outright opposition. There's a passive acceptance tinged with excitement over the prospect of being drawn a bit more into the mainstream. More money, more options, expanded horizons are all part of the bargain.

Simplicity, ohana and aloha are still Lanai's rewards. Just how much development will impact that sense of things remains to be seen. For those with a fear of the momentum of change, there's no doubt that some of Lanai's intimacy will be lost, dissipated by the intrusion of the outside world. There are many who love Lanai just as it is.

It is 5:00 A.M. on a Friday morning and a siren is wailing a pre-dawn message that there will be work today. By 7:00 A.M., when the workday begins for many on the plantation, a thick mist starts rising from the ground, drifting its way through the branches of the Norfolk pines that fill Lanai City with an up-country fragrance. Youngsters on bikes head to school, their mothers making a morning stop at one of the several grocery stores or shops facing the town common.

People stop to talk, lingering in front of the post office to check out the latest information on the glass-cased bulletin boards. Hunting schedules (axis deer and Barbary sheep range Lanai's backcountry), travel opportunities, family news, and notices advertising self-improvement programs and jeeps for sale are all tacked up.

Lanai City's grid of streets are lined with colorfully painted plantation homes, most with well-tended gardens. Many of the streets are unpaved. Along some, tall trees provide welcome shade. Others are more open, giving an often powerful sun free reign. Many of Lanai City's residents are recent immigrants from the Philippines, establishing Filipinos as Lanai's ethnic majority. There are also Hawaiians, Japanese, Mainland haoles and their diverse racial blends.

Later, on this typical Lanai day, rainbows crown the landscape. In the fields, millions of pineapple plants absorb life from the sun. The scene is radiant with color, life and well-being. Looking around, my eyes focus on the distant hills that provide a west rim for the Palawai crater, and an image replays in my mind: The rush of wind, the swirl of gray clouds, the mist and cold of a past adventure.

The sound of laughter draws me once again into the present. The brilliance of a sunny day returns. Hopefully, echoes of this light and laughter and the freedom of spirit they represent will guide Lanai, island of spirits and dreamers, into the future.

Castle & Cooke recently announced its plans to phase out pineapple production on the Pineapple Island within the next two years and turn its attention instead to tourism. It will maintain only about 100 acres of pineapple, which will be used by Lanai's new hotels.

Gorgeous Lanai sunset.

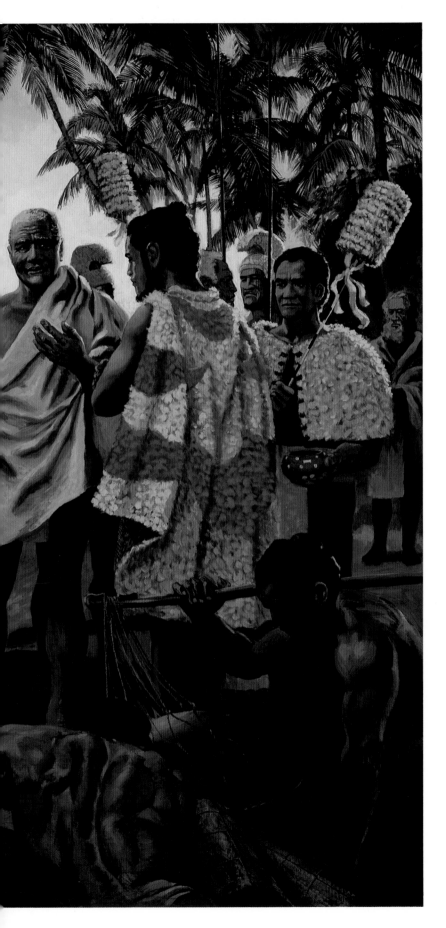

KAMEHAMEHA
HAWAII'S GREAT WARRIOR KING

BY ALLAN SEIDEN
ILLUSTRATIONS BY HERB KAWAINUI KANE

Kamehameha, the lonely one, he had been named. With several wives, dozens of children and an Island kingdom of his own making, his loneliness was more associated with greatness than with isolation. His destiny was to transform a society—to unite seemingly irreconcilable forces and use them to build a powerful dynasty that would rule the Islands for nearly a century.

It is difficult to separate the man from the many legends that surround his life. Kamehameha was born in Kokoiki in the Kohala district, near the northernmost tip of the Big Island. The exact date of his birth is unknown, although authoritative sources estimate it was sometime in 1753. It is said that when he was born, a comet blazed across the night sky—an omen of his ultimate rise to power. He was removed from the birth chamber by a Big Island chief and taken to nearby Mookini Heiau for his birth rites.

Much of Kamehameha's life is a mixture of myth and fact. He is believed to have spent his early childhood years in the peaceful, lush wilderness of Waipio Valley. At the age of five, he was accepted into the court of his great-uncle, Big Island high chief Alapai. Here he received the usual training accorded a boy of high rank. He was taught the ways of the ocean, and from a very young age, demonstrated his prowess in swimming and surfing. Kamehameha was also schooled in religion, the arts and sciences, court etiquette and the proper carriage of an alii. He excelled in every area.

59

Kamehameha at Kamakahonu.

In his early teens, Kamehameha supposedly moved the immense Naha Stone in Hilo, fulfilling a prophecy that the man who could do so would unify the Hawaiian Islands into one kingdom. By his late teens, his strength and skill as a warrior had been proven in wars fought by high chief Alapai and Alapai's nephew and successor, Kalaniopuu, who was also Kamehameha's uncle.

Only a few pictures of Kamehameha exist, painted or sketched in a stylized manner by European artists employed on round-the-world voyages of exploration. He is said to have been a massive man, six feet six inches in height with what Lieutenant James King, third in command to Captain James Cook, described as "as savage looking a face as I ever saw."

Timing played a critical role in Kamehameha's rise to power. By 1778, when Cook made his first Hawaiian landfall, the population of the Islands had grown to an estimated 400,000, providing the critical mass to fuel kingly ambitions. At one time, battles had been fought between neighboring districts for control of a single island. As Kamehameha reached manhood, the stakes began to change. A multi-island Hawaiian kingdom was now the ultimate goal, and Kamehameha's royal relatives already were engaging in warfare with that objective in mind when Cook made his appearance.

In his mid-twenties when Cook arrived, Kamehameha was very impressed with what he saw of Western technology. Inquisitive, intelligent and ambitious, he was granted permission to spend the night aboard the *Resolution* after his first meeting with Cook. It was weaponry that captured Kamehameha's attention. In future years, he would make good use of cannons and muskets in his successful effort to establish the kingdom of Hawaii.

60

Arrival of Keoua at Puukohola.

As a member of Kalaniopuu's royal court, Kamehameha met Cook several times and was likely present when the British captain was killed at Kealakekua Bay in 1779. Injured in the cannonade, Kamehameha supposedly was given Cook's scalp as his share of the captain's mana.

Although his high alii status is not in question, his genealogy—all-important in establishing legitimacy and rank in Hawaii—remains uncertain. Big Island chiefess Kekuiapoiwa held the undisputed claim of mothering the future king. Officially, the Big Island chief Keoua, nephew of Alapai, was accepted as Kamehameha's father. As Alapai's grandnephew, Kamehameha was not in direct line for the Big Island chieftancy, although rumor had it that Alapai had killed his brother, Kamehameha's grandfather, and usurped authority that by right of descent was Kamehameha's. Further complicating the matter are claims that Kamehameha was actually the son of Kekuiapoiwa and Maui's King Kahekili.

As a youth, Kamehameha was sensitive to rumors of his uncertain parentage. His belief in his mana, enhanced by the favor shown to him by the war god Kukailimoku, proved to be a motivating force in his drive for power.

Before his death in 1781, Big Island high chief Kalaniopuu named his son, Kiwalao, as his successor and empowered his nephew Kamehameha as guardian of Kukailimoku. Already renowned as a warrior from his participation in Kalaniopuu's attacks on neighboring Maui, Kamehameha defied his uncle's wishes that Kiwalao, not he, take over the Big Island chieftancy. Mustering support in Kona, his home district of Kohala and the northern half of Hamakua down to Laupahoehoe,

Outrigger canoes like this one provided transportation for Kamehameha and his warriors in ancient times.

Kamehameha established himself as one of three contenders vying for control of the entire Big Island.

Of the three, Kamehameha was by far the most sophisticated and inventive. Having seen Cook's arsenal and the terrifying damage it could inflict, he had been quick to understand its potential. As the wars on the Big Island drifted into a stalemate and trade ships began to make Hawaii a reprovisioning port of call, Kamehameha focused his attention on securing European vessels and weapons for the battles yet to come.

The first opportunity to obtain such goods did not come until 1788, when Kamehameha was able to acquire a small field cannon and some Brown Betties, the standard musket of the British navy. Two years later, the capture of the ship *Fair American* and an encounter with its sister ship, the *Eleanora*, provided a more significant haul, adding not only cannons and muskets, but the first two of a number of haole advisors who would help Kamehameha in battle and governance.

In the eight years following Kalaniopuu's death, Maui chief Kahekili (the man whom some believe was Kamehameha's father) had taken advantage of civil war on the Big Island to pursue his own territorial ambitions elsewhere in the archipelago. By 1790, Kahekili was in control of Molokai, Lanai and Oahu in addition to Maui. In alliance with his half-brother, Kaeo, he also dominated Kauai.

When revolts on Oahu drew Kahekili from Maui, Kamehameha seized the opportunity and prepared for an invasion of Kahekili's home island. A great fleet of war canoes was readied. What followed were fierce battles in Hana and Wailuku, and combat in Iao Valley that, for the first time, proved the impact of cannons and muskets. This bloody encounter was called Ke Pani Wai, or Battle of the Damming Waters, so named because the bodies of fallen

63

This statue of Kamehameha stands in front of the Judiciary Building in Honolulu.

warriors were said to have blocked the flow of Iao Stream.

Still in Waikiki, Kahekili decided to pay Kamehameha back in kind by supporting his Big Island rival, Kalaniopuu's son, Keoua, who was chief of the Puna and Kau districts. Taking advantage of Kamehameha's absence, Keoua moved through Hilo to capture the northern coast, from Laupahoehoe to Waipio Valley.

Shifting his focus from Maui, Kamehameha returned to the Big Island, pursuing Keoua as he pulled back to the village of Koapapa, near Honokaa. Routed by the onslaught of Kamehameha's warriors and the bombardment of cannons and muskets, Keoua escaped with only a remnant of his army.

Kamehameha traveled back to Kawaihae, in the northern sector of the island, where, on the advice of the kahuna Kapoukahi, he began construction of Puukohola Heiau, which was to be dedicated to Kukailimoku, the war god who was his lifelong patron. Before the heiau was completed, Kahekili engaged Kamehameha in a sea battle off the Waipio Valley coast. This time, both sides made use of cannons and muskets, and the results were indecisive.

After the confrontation off Waipio, the venerable Kahekili withdrew, first to Maui and then to Waikiki, where he died in 1794. Some say it was on his deathbed that he revealed that he was indeed Kamehameha's real father.

Keoua's fate was tragic. As he and his troops were en route to their home base in Kau, in retreat from an indecisive skirmish with Kamehameha's forces, Kilauea Volcano erupted. Fire, steam and poisonous gases assailed them, killing many of the men.

Within a year, the demoralized Keoua accepted an invitation to talk peace with Kamehameha. Disembarking at Kawaihae, within sight of Puukohola Heiau, Keoua was stabbed to death by Keeaumoku, one of Kamehameha's trusted lieutenants. Many others in Keoua's party were then killed before Kamehameha put a stop to the violence. The body of his dead cousin was carried to Puukohola, where it was sacrificed to the war god Kukailimoku and Kamehameha's goal of a unified kingdom.

With the Big Island under control and Kahekili dead, Kamehameha, in 1795, trained his sights on Oahu, preparing a war fleet designed to assure victory over Kahekili's heir, Kalanikupule. Gaining control of Maui and Molokai en route to Oahu, Kamehameha's armada included hundreds of war canoes, Western-style ships equipped with cannons and muskets, and thousands of troops outfitted with traditional Hawaiian weapons of combat.

Kamehameha anchored his fleet along a five-mile stretch of coast that ran from Waialae to Waikiki, then headed inland, prepared to meet Kalanikupule's army at their encampment in Nuuanu Valley. Historian Abraham Fornander describes what followed: "At Puiwa the hostile forces met, and for a while, the victory was hotly contested; but the superiority of Kamehameha's artillery, the number of his guns, and the better practice of his soldiers, soon turned the day in his favor, and the defeat of the Oahu forces became an accelerated route and a promiscuous slaughter. Of those who were not killed...a large number were driven over the pali at Nuuanu, a precipice several hundred feet in height, and perished miserably. Kalanikupule was hotly pursued... finally he was captured...killed, brought to Kamehameha and sacrificed to the war god Kukailimoku."

Having secured control of Oahu, the Big Island, Maui, Molokai and Lanai, Kamehameha, in his early forties, now felt the need to establish a dynasty. He married the sacred alii Keopuolani in 1795; with her royal bloodlines, he could now father children of the highest alii rank—the sacred niau pio caste. Only three of their eleven children, however, lived to adulthood—Princes Liholiho (Kamehameha II) and Kauikeaouli (Kamehameha III) and Princess Nahienaena.

Kamehameha had met and married Kaahumanu, the great love of his life, a decade earlier in 1785, while he was in the midst of establishing his claim to Kalaniopuu's Big Island kingdom. At the time, he was in his thirties and she was seventeen. Renowned for her beauty, Kaahumanu, a regal six feet tall, was every bit the match for Kamehameha in style, lineage and temperament. Although she never bore him children, it was Kaahumanu, not Keopuolani, who proved to be the power behind the throne, ultimately ruling as regent for several of Kamehameha's high-born heirs.

The year 1795 marked a full decade since Kamehameha began his great conquests, and with the exception of Kauai, he was now ruler of an Island kingdom. With Kauai's surrender in mind, he expanded his fleet to include more than 600 war canoes, and in 1796 set out from Oahu on the first of two ill-fated attempts to invade this westernmost and most isolated of Hawaii's main islands. Halfway across the Kauai Channel, his ships were hit by a terrible storm. Boats capsized and a sizeable number of warriors drowned.

Six years passed before Kamehameha again tried to invade Kauai, which was under the rule of high chief Kaumualii. This time, his fleet included 800 canoes and twenty Western-style vessels, each weighing twenty to forty tons. Anxious for victory, Kamehameha commanded an army of 16,000 men. Prince Liholiho was now already five, and Kamehameha, who was approaching fifty, was determined to finalize the borders of the kingdom his niao pio heir would inherit.

But the gods seemed equally determined to thwart Kamehameha's will. As the fleet prepared to depart Oahu, his ally Keeaumoku died. Some accounts report it was on Keeaumoku's deathbed that Kamehameha was told of his descent from Kahekili. A greater shock to his plans followed in the form of a devastating plague that wiped out half his forces.

Kamehameha mellowed in the decade that followed the plague. Pursuing elusive Kauai with diplomacy, he succeeded where his martial plans had failed. In 1810, Kaumualii made a voyage of obeisance to Kamehameha. It is said Kamehameha refused to accept Kaumualii's homage, deferring the final unification of the Islands to the reign of his son, Liholiho. That was really a matter of detail, for Kaumualii's offer proved a fait accompli; the Island kingdom was now completely unified under Kamehameha's rule.

In 1812, Kamehameha moved his court from Waikiki to Kailua-Kona on the Big Island. Nearing the age of sixty, survivor of many battles and a lifetime of change, he was now ready to retire quietly to the land of his roots. From his royal compound on the shores of Kailua Bay, Kamehameha could scan the ocean and the mountains. Life was still tied to tradition here, the old ways not yet supplanted by the foreign influences that were turning Honolulu into an international port.

Kamehameha was most likely very content during his last years in Kailua-Kona. The kingdom he had fought for was now at peace. His mana had been confirmed by acts of heroism that had made him legendary. His children were of the highest caste. Trade, in the form of provisions and sandalwood for the China clippers, was bringing prosperity to the Islands. And the outside world still represented more of a challenge than a threat.

More than a chief, Kamehameha was the embodiment of a way of life. Even after he died in May of 1819, attended by Kaahumanu and the royal offspring he'd fathered with Keopuolani, it was his mana that gave legitimacy to the monarchy that followed. And today, nearly 200 years after his passing, it is his mana that still inspires Hawaiians with a sense of greatness and pride.

"Kamehameha, Hawaii's Great Warrior King" was first published in January/February 1988.

65

Lithograph of Kamehameha done after a drawing by Louis Choris, c. 1822.

THE TREE
FOR A KING'S CANOE

BY BARBARA B. ROBINSON
ILLUSTRATIONS BY HERB KAWAINUI KANE

A thousand years before Columbus embarked on his adventures, Polynesian navigators had already explored the Pacific. The *Santa Maria's* crossing of the narrow Atlantic has been applauded, and rightly so. But how many appreciate the achievement of the great double-hulled canoes that traveled over the Pacific, an ocean spanning a third of our water-skinned planet? These Polynesian voyaging canoes were masterpieces of utility and grace. Swifter, more maneuverable than the *Santa Maria*, many were longer than the ships of explorers Cook and Vancouver, and longer than the *Thaddeus*, which another four centuries after Columbus, brought missionaries to Hawaii.

And yet—consider: The Polynesian builders created their ships in island cultures that had no metals and no writing systems. Their tools were of wood and sennit, bone and stone. How then was it possible for these stone-age artisans to create such splendid ocean-going craft? Certainly the task seems impossible. But the key to Polynesian canoe-building was the tree.

To the Polynesians, a sailing canoe was not a mere thing. It was a living creation, metamorphosed from sacred trees with the aid of the great gods Kanaloa, Kane and Ku. It was crafted with offerings and poetry and rev-

Canoe of Atiu, *collection of the State Foundation on Culture and the Arts.*

A wooden canoe from Fiji.

erence. And, when finished, the vessel was an honored being—a voyager with spirit, power and a carefully chosen name.

Only a high-ranking chief with extraordinary planning ability could achieve such a canoe. Since his entire district might be involved in its construction for more than two years, his workers had to plant extra crops to feed the canoe's craftsmen who were taken from their regular jobs.

In preparation for the canoe's construction, tools had to be made, materials gathered, and a huge hangar-like canoe shed erected near the beach to keep the unfinished hull from cracking in the hot sun while the months of scraping and polish-

ing were going on and its braces, booms, masts and rigging were being fitted.

Handsome gifts of feather capes, bowls, mats, tapa cloth and weapons had to be prepared as gifts for other chiefs, to persuade them to offer special materials that might be lacking in the canoe builder's own lands.

In some Pacific islands where trees were sparse, canoe hulls were stitched together from small planks. But the mountainous rain forests of Hawaii yielded trees so huge a canoe hull was carved from a single tree trunk.

For a waa kaulua, a twin-hulled canoe like Hawaii's *Hokulea*, two tall, straight, unblemished trees of reasonably similar size were required.

The koa, a native mahogany, was highly favored for its strength, resilience and its beautiful grain. Such trees were not easily obtained.

A chief's woodlands, therefore, were carefully guarded by his forest kahuna. The kahuna were the professionals—the special priests, the experts and technicians in the affairs of life, of weather, medicine, planting, building, and all matters between men and gods.

Over the generations, the kahuna, the priests of the forests, ranged over their chief's lands. They planted bushy close-crowding shrubs around the young koa trees to make them grow tall and straight. They trimmed lower branches and suckers to pre-

vent knotholes, and kept a mental inventory of growth, storm damage and locality.

The kahuna ka lai waa was the high priest of canoe making. He directed all ceremonies and construction, surveyed the canoe-hauling roads and interpreted messages from the goddess Lea, wife of Ku and patron of the forest.

Upon receiving the chief's demand for a canoe, the kahuna ka lai waa led an expedition up into the mountains to seek out the special tree. When a prospective tree was discovered, Lea manifested herself in the form of an elepaio bird, a native woodpecker, which walked over the tree's upper trunk and large branches. If the bird paused and pecked at the bark, it was surmised that the tree was blemished and the search was resumed. But if the bird inspected the tree and departed without pecking, the tree was assumed to be free of termites, other wood borers and rot, and preliminary tree-felling activities were put in motion.

Before actual work on the tree could begin, however, the canoe's craftsmen had to make new sets of special adzes and chisels. For this tool-making project, the craftsmen traveled to some secret mountain quarry, usually located on a volcanic summit where a particularly hard basalt or obsidian was found. Here they lived in cold windy loneliness. Here they cut and split the black stone into tapering fragments and immersed them in water so escaping air bubbles would reveal inner pockets and hairline cracks. Flawed pieces were discarded. Perfectly solid stone was then soaked in a mixture of saps and juices of green kukui candlenut and palai fern. These and other secret ingredients were used to make the stone easier to chip and to imbue the new cutting blade with its mana, the spirit-power needed to help change a great forest being into a new ocean being.

The solid basalt wedge was beveled with diagonal blows of a chipping stone. After the chipped-out blade-blank was ground to a smooth sharp edge on a sand-sprinkled grinding rock, the finished adze blade was lashed to its new wood handle with fine sennit cord braided from coconut husk fiber.

When all was finished, the workmen returned from the mountains carrying their new adzes and chisels. They were met by the kahuna ka lai waa, who conducted them, with their tools, to the heiau, the temple where the workmen and tools were consecrated with chants and ceremony to the coming task. That night, tools and workmen slept in the heiau.

Next morning, before sunrise, the workmen waded into the sea and dipped their sleeping adzes into the water chanting: "Awake to work for Kane great god of the artisans…"

The chief and his craftsmen then followed the kahuna up into the forest to the selected tree. To this chosen tree the chief brought offerings of red fish, coconuts, awa drink and a black pig to appease the great god Kane for taking one of his forest children and to invoke his continued protection over his tree-child in its new form.

To fell and shape a tree of this enormous size took months of work up in the cold rain forest so shelters for eating and sleeping were built on the site.

Cutting began according to established protocol. After the rituals of cooking the fish and pig and the ceremonial feasting, the kahuna ka lai waa addressed Kane with a chant asking Kane for guidance. He then chipped two horizontal scarfs, or grooves, about a yard apart, around the base of the tree. Adze-men then stepped to the tree. Layer by layer they chipped out the bark and wood between the two scarf lines, deeper and deeper until at last the tree toppled and fell, its crash summoning the elepaio bird, who paraded up and down the fallen trunk, her thorough unhesitating inspection and rapid departure signifying Lea's final approval.

Rough shaping of the hull was done on the spot.

In Hawaii, canoes were not charred out with fire, and cutting with stone adzes was long tedious labor. Even so, though steel blades can chop bigger bites, stone adzes had the advantage of never going too deep, never ripping up a split along the grain. And, moreover, Polynesian craftsmen worked rapidly. Indeed, their cutting strokes were so rapid that their adzes became hot and brittle and had to be cooled frequently by slashing them into the juicy-soft stumps of green banana plants. In the meantime, another adze in the workman's set was put to work.

Since stone blades needed frequent sharpening, grinding specialists worked in a kind of assembly line near the adze-men. These crews of sharpeners received the dull adzes, unbound them from their handles and whetted them on wet sand-powdered slabs of smooth stone. Binding specialists, using thin braided sennit twine, then lashed the blades again onto their handles. Thus the work went surprisingly fast.

After the great tree had been trimmed of its branches, the huge limbs were taken away for carving into booms, gunwales, partitions, bracings and other fittings. Then the enormous trunk itself was hewn to its outer dimensions. This might be a hull-blank forty to eighty feet long. (Canoes even longer have been reported by Vancouver and Cook.) After this, the hull-blank was turned over and the inside chipped out. Sections of wood were left outstanding within the hull where bracings and fitting would later be carved into its final contours.

Green, newly cut koa wood, if brought suddenly to a hot dry area, was likely to split in great long cracks. So the new rough hull, therefore, was left where it was for many months, to cure slowly in the cool forest. In those times, however, even in Hawaii, this was reasonably safe because many of the destructive termites and wood-boring insects had not yet arrived.

Over the centuries, some of the best routes down the mountain were developed into wide canoe-hauling roads. Even so, in preparation for moving the hull, the entire route was newly surveyed and cleared of hazardous rocks and shrubs. Great bundles of grass were laid down to cushion the keel and to help slide the hull more easily over the ground.

At last, when all was ready, the villagers were summoned to help move the enormous hollowed log from the mountain to the sea. The kahuna conducted prayers and ceremonies asking Kane to protect it from damage during its dangerous journey down the mountainside, the villagers attached long guide ropes to the hull and the hazardous haul began.

The long dead weight was steered and braked by heaving on the guide ropes as the villagers wrestled it across ravines and down muddy slopes, while a pilot, sometimes riding in the bow, signaled directions. Particular care was taken when lowering it down steep cliffs. Accompanied by hauling chants, the villagers moved the long hull onward.

Throughout its progress, the kahuna ka lai waa followed at some distance. No one was allowed behind him because this space was reserved for the ship building gods who were present in spirit. One of them, for example, was Kuhooholo-pali, or Ku-the-guider-over-the-cliffs. The hauling chants voiced along the way added to the general excitement, and, eventually, in triumphant procession, Kane's great forest child arrived at its lofty newly-built house by the sea, there to be matched with a twin hull; there to receive masts, booms, a long deck, sails, rigging, bailers, paddles, shaping and final polishing; there to complete its metamorphosis—transformed by stone and sennit, by wise men and gods from rooted tree to rider-of-winds, ready to enter the ocean domain of Tangaroa, great Ocean Father; a tree now transformed into a sailing canoe for a high chief and voyager of the Pacific.

"The Tree for a King's Canoe" was first published in September/October 1980.

RESURRECTING
FATHER DAMIEN'S
CHURCH

BY RITA ARIYOSHI

"A terrible storm visited us last Saturday, and on Sunday morning we found the steeple of our church on the ground."

The words are those of Father Damien de Veuster to his friend, the American naval doctor G.W. Woods. The letter was written in 1888 and concerned Saint Philomena Church at Kalawao, Molokai. Damien had rebuilt the church once before in 1876, but was a little more concerned this time. He continued in his letter, "Being not so strong now, I fear not to be able to do so, myself, a similar difficult work. My disease is progressing, and my hands and feet are undergoing a transformation."

Only months before he died of Hansen's Disease, or leprosy, on April 15, 1889, Damien received a gift of a new tabernacle, along with the materials he needed to not only repair the church, but to substantially reconstruct it in stone, complete with a bell tower over and around the original wooden chapel.

Seeking Damien, a visiting priest, Father Corneille Limburg, found him on the top of the church, nailing on the roof. He reported on Damien's obvious disease: "...the face puffy, the ears, one of which already has broken skin, swollen and elongated, the eyes red and the voice hoarse..." Father Limburg then continued, "You should have seen the wild activity he was directing, giving his orders now to the masons, now to the carpenters, now to the laborers, all lepers. You would have said he was a man in his element and perfectly healthy. This tells you that Father Damien seems not to want to stop until he falls."

Damien didn't. He was dead by Easter.

It has been almost 100 years since Molokai's holy man passed away,

Aerial view of Saint Philomena.

and his church, Saint Philomena, is again in desperate need of repairs. The roof blew off in a storm about a year ago. Volunteers patched together a makeshift roof and put it atop the structure, but it's not attached. It wouldn't take much of a wind to blow it off and completely expose the interior. Termites and time have both taken their toll on the historic church.

In 1872, Brother Bertrant Victorin of the Congregation of the Sacred Hearts missionary order of the Roman Catholic Church, arrived in Kalawao, Molokai's place of exile for victims of leprosy. He set up a tiny chapel that was prefabricated in Honolulu, dedicated it as Saint Philomena and left. No one stayed at Kalawao in those days, unless they were banished there because of the leprosy that was running rampant in the Hawaiian Islands.

Because they had lived for so many centuries with no contact with the outside world, the Hawaiian people had acquired no natural immunities to European and Asiatic diseases, and had no more resistance to the ravages of leprosy than they did to the common cold. In 100 years since Western contact in 1778, the Hawaiian population plunged from approximately 300,000 to 50,000 people. The first authenticated case of leprosy appeared in Hawaii in 1840. By 1868, it had cut such a swath through the population that the Hawaiian government, under King Kamehameha V, decreed a policy of isolation for the infected, and established Kalawao, Molokai as the place of confinement. The disease was epidemic, and there was no cure.

This was the worst plague yet to descend upon the Hawaiians—not just for the obvious horror of the ancient scourge, but because it struck right at the heart of their philosophy, separating them from their loved ones, tearing apart families and wresting parents from children. The

Father Damien de Veuster, c. 1873.

Hawaiians called leprosy "mai hoo-kaawale," the separating sickness. In many cases, families would hide a diseased member, attending to the person themselves, as best they could. When they were found out, the entire family, rather than be separated, would accompany the victim into exile. They would all leave on the boat for Molokai, never to return, for that was the law. The Board of Health became known as the Board of Hell.

In a book titled *Mai Hookaawale: The Separating Sickness,* published by the Social Science Research Institute of the University of Hawaii with a loan from the Maryknoll Fathers, one patient, a Hawaiian man, recalled, "After they caught me, they didn't stop with me. No. They nosed around my family. The Board of Health in those days was not confidential...The social worker came in an official marked car, driven by a chauffeur, dressed in a white gown.

Terrible!...The family felt shame."

Another man, who spent sixty-five years in exile on Molokai, said, "The disease caught me when I was seventeen in 1914. The tall Hawaiian health officer, the one they called the bounty hunter, came to get me at school...That all happened a long time ago. When I think about it though, I still hate the trouble I had with this disease. Yes, I am bitter about my life."

Before Damien, there were no docking facilities at Makanalua Peninsula, now commonly referred to as Kalaupapa. In addition, ship captains were afraid of getting too close to shore, so the sick passengers would be tossed overboard, often into pounding surf, and left to swim ashore with whatever belongings they could carry. Many drowned.

The Hawaiian government did not believe it was acting with cruelty. They had to protect the population at large and this was the only measure available to them. They chose Kalaupapa carefully. The magnificently beautiful place was a natural prison, surrounded on three sides by a rugged lava coastline and surging seas, and on the fourth by towering 2,000- and 3,000-foot cliffs. In ancient times, it had been a fertile farm area, yielding bountiful crops of sweet potatoes and taro. Government officials imagined that the exiles would farm and provide for themselves.

Instead, Kalaupapa became a wild and hostile social environment. The people were bitter, deprived, weakened and desperate. They had nothing to lose, for what sentence could be passed on an offender that could be worse than what he already had? The only governor was Death. The Hawaiians said of it, "Aole kanawai ma keia wahi—in this place there is no law."

Kalaupapa's four square miles were described by American writer and Notre Dame University professor Charles Warren Stoddard as

"sunburnt, dust colored, blackened at the edges." It was hot during the day and cold at night. In winter, the sun went down behind the pali at two in the afternoon, leaving the place in chilled shadow.

There were no shelters and no materials with which to build any. The people lived in caves, under rocks and trees, and a fortunate few in rude huts made of rubble. They fought desperately over the meager rations sent from Honolulu. The people were forsaken, driven from among the living to this terrible limbo. Unclean is the word taken from the Bible's book of Leviticus, which says of the leper, "He shall dwell apart, making his home outside the camp. He shall cry out, 'Unclean, unclean.'"

Still, even in their remoteness, they prickled the consciences of some men. The Roman Catholic vicar of Hawaii, Bishop Louis Maigret, used the occasion of dedicating a church in Wailuku, Maui to express his concern for the sufferers at Kalawao. No one, he reminded the congregation, needed a pastor more than those dying outcasts. The bishop, however, was reluctant to order any priest to such a post, such a fate. Four young priests in the church that day heard the call and settled upon serving Molokai on a rotation basis, taking three-month turns each year. Among the four was Father Joseph Damien de Veuster, a priest from Belgium who had been serving the district of Kohala on the Big Island of Hawaii. He volunteered to go first since he was already away from home.

Seated in the historic church, visitors learn about Kalaupapa's poignant past.

74

Stained glass rendering of Father Damien, Star of the Sea Church, Kalapana, island of Hawaii.

This memorial to Damien stands on the grounds of Saint Philomena Church.

With some cattle, the bishop and fifty new exiles, Damien boarded the inter-island steamer *Kilauea* and set sail for Kalaupapa, arriving Saturday, May 10, 1873 at eleven in the morning. He was thirty-three years old, the same age as Jesus when he was crucified.

The scene is described in the book, *The Heart of Father Damien* by Vital Jourdan: "Leaning on the ship's rail, the Bishop and Father Damien caught sight of the gray cliffs of the pali, with its green patches of straight up-and-down undergrowth. Soon they could see the Kalaupapa beach and behind it some huts and the wooden landing pier. When the patients learned they had arrived, those who were able ran to meet them …during the few hours the Bishop was there, 200 Catholics presented a signed petition asking the prelate for a resident priest. Their joy was boundless when 'Louis our Bishop' presented the priest who had offered to stay among them…Many of them threw themselves at the Bishop's feet, weeping. He was sick at heart. Father Damien had come for a few months only."

Damien, however, knew immediately that this was the place to which God had called him. Two days later, he wrote a letter to the Provincial of his order, Father Modeste, asking him to find a priest to watch over his parish on the Big Island "for I am willing to devote my life to the leprosy victims. It is absolutely necessary for a priest to remain here. The harvest is ripe. The sick are arriving by the boatloads. They die in droves." Eight days after his arrival, Damien was hard at work, making permanent plans.

Because he had left home unprepared for a life's mission, he had taken with him only his breviary. His immediate request was for "some wine, hosts, religious books and some for study, rosaries, shirts, pants, shoes, a sack of flour, a bell and a razor."

From letters and other testimony, it is obvious that Damien had felt his calling even before coming to Kalaupapa. He once confided to Brother Joseph Dutton, a lay member of his congregation who later came to join him in his work, that when he served leprosy patients in Kohala and administered the sacraments to them, he felt his skin prickle and burn.

Four years before going to Molokai he had written in a letter from Kohala, "Leprosy is beginning to be widespread here. A great number of the natives are infected. It doesn't kill them, but cures are rare. This disease is very contagious."

Damien watched the police take away some of his parishioners. It is said he helped some victims hide from the authorities, and was greatly sympathetic to their plight. He later wrote to the Father General of his order, "By order of the Board of Health all the leprosy victims they could collect have been sent to the Settlement of Molokai as to a government prison. Many of our Christians here at Kohala also had to go. I can only attribute to God an undeniable feeling that soon I shall join them. However, eight years of service among Christians you love and who love you have tied us by powerful bonds. Even just joking about my going to Molokai upsets them.

"When I boarded ship for Wailuku, the same voice told me that I would not return to Kohala and that I would never again see our dear children or the four beautiful chapels I built. It was with tears in my eyes that I left my dear Christians."

In his new area of service, as soon as lumber arrived, the first thing Damien did was repair and add on to Saint Philomena Church. He moved the sickest patients into the church until he could build homes and a hospital for them. He himself slept outdoors under a hala tree until every person at Kalawao had a roof overhead.

He wrote to Honolulu, "There's something to keep me busy from morning to night. On my list I have two hundred and ten Catholics and eighty catechumens. Yesterday, high Mass, superb singing, many Communions, and since I arrived, crowds of confessions." He considered the whole population to be his flock and tended to all, regardless of religion.

Damien not only took care of their spiritual needs, he saw to the temporal as well. One of his most persistent tasks was begging. He badgered everyone—the Board of Health, the crown, the church— asking for building supplies, medicine, clothing, food. With the help of patients, Damien tapped the abundant streams in neighboring Waikolu Valley and laid pipes for a water system that still is in use today. An excellent carpenter, he built cottages, a hospital, another church at Kalaupapa and an orphanage. He started farms, visited the sick, dressed wounds and always, almost daily, buried the dead—6,000 of them during his time.

Throughout Damien's ministry, the center of his life and the life of the community was Saint Philomena Church. It was a place of joyous celebration in the midst of the horror and misery. There were processions, songs, pomp and glory. He had the place strewn with leis and fragrant with flowers. Singing in the choir was an honor, though leprosy attacks the vocal chords and the music was often unorthodox. At times it took two pianists to play the hymns, so that together, there would be ten fingers to make the music.

Damien put holes in the floor so his flock could expectorate freely, another manifestation of the disease. He had to expand his church to accommodate those attracted to it. Richard Marks, who is presently a patient at Kalaupapa said, "Everyone became Catholic. It didn't matter what religion Father Damien was, everyone would have joined." When

he died at age forty nine, Damien was buried in a place he had reserved for himself in the cemetery, his "Garden of the Dead," facing the altar of the church and located beneath the hala tree where he had begun his work.

Damien was not an extraordinary man in the beginning. He was repulsed by the disease. He took precautions to protect himself. Of his first days, he wrote to his superiors, "In fulfilling my priestly duties at the lepers' homes, I have been obliged, not only to close my nostrils, but to remain outside to breathe fresh air. To counteract the bad smell, I got myself accustomed to the use of tobacco. The smell of the pipe preserved me somewhat from carrying in my clothes the obnoxious odor of our lepers."

We can only imagine what Damien must have thought as he lay down beneath the hala tree those first nights, staring up at the stars, alone among the most sick and abandoned people on earth, fully realizing that he would most likely become one of them if he stayed, as he knew he would.

Saint Philomena is the only physical legacy of Damien's work. Even his body was unearthed in 1936 and returned to Belgium. Now that modern medicine can control leprosy, almost all of the patients have moved away. A hundred remain at Kalaupapa by choice, because they have lived there all their lives and some bear the scars of the disease, acquired before the sulfone drugs went into use in 1946. Their average

age is sixty-five and they have been promised that they may stay at Kalaupapa until they die. The forty new cases diagnosed in Hawaii each year are treated and the patients continue to live normal lives without danger of communicability.

The peninsula is now the Kalaupapa National Historical Park. The National Park Service has spent more than $3 million on the site, although it has no clear title to the lands. Fittingly, they say they are operating on faith. They have faith that arrangements can be made with the Hawaii Department of Health, the Department of Hawaiian Home Lands, the Department of Transportation, the Department of Land and Natural Resources, and the United States Coast Guard, all of whom have control of parts of the peninsula.

With such a cast of bureaucracies, the red tape could strangle the park. It has definitely ensnared Saint Philomena Church, which is considered by the National Park Service to be the most significant building on the peninsula. The plight of the historic church is further complicated by the laws of separation between church and state. Saint Philomena continued to crumble while the government paperwork mounted.

In November 1986, Henry Law, the federal supervisor at the national park, stated that the best and fastest way to get anything done would be to form an independent organization to save the church.

Law took the initiative, called the first meeting and got the Friends of Father Damien off to a good start. Honorary co-chairpersons of the committee are Hawaii's Governor John Waihee, who has pledged $50,000 from the state legislature, and the Roman Catholic Bishop Jo-

seph Ferrario, who has committed $25,000 from the Catholic diocese. The goal is $500,000.

At the grass roots level, the Hawaii Jazz Society raised more than $25,600 in two concerts sponsored by Hawaiian Air and Hawaiian Electric Company. Dean Hollingshead Knight, of the Episcopal Church in Hawaii, organized Father Damien Sunday, marked by a collection for Saint Philomena in Christian churches throughout the Islands. Politician Patsy Mink is serving as co-chairperson, along with John Howett, while prominent Honolulu businessman Maurice Sullivan is supervising the fund-raising efforts.

Irene Letoto, secretary of the Friends and director of the Damien Museum and Archives in Waikiki, said, "It's been a very good experience—good feelings. It's an ecumenical thing. The cooperation has been tremendous."

A core group of twelve people meets every other week. Letoto said, "It's a 'go' situation. The wheels are in motion. We're going to restore the church. This is an urgent situation. If we don't act, the church may not be there much longer. We've contracted with architects who are examining old photographs very carefully. We don't know exactly how it used to look. At one time, we understand the paint was very garish. It was all donated paint, and it was all different colors. The church would be repainted whenever someone had the strength and the supplies were available. There was a cross that's not there now. The outside entrance is changed."

The restoration work is complicated by the fact that only two barges a year go to Kalaupapa, one in July and the other in September. Retaining a special barge costs $32,000. Letoto said, "We're reluctant to spend our limited funds on that."

Architect Spencer Leineweber, of Spencer Mason Architects, Ltd., has set the point of reference for the

restoration at Christmas Eve, 1932, the date the last regular mass was celebrated in the chapel. Since then, special occasion masses have been celebrated at Saint Philomena once in a while. On April 15, 1987, an anniversary mass was celebrated for Father Damien and attended by an overflow crowd of 200 people, most of whom had flown over from Honolulu for the day. Officiating were Bishop Ferrario and the Reverend Ernest Claes, a grandnephew of Father Damien. Kenso Seki, a Kalaupapa patient since 1928, carried the cross. Other patients made leis for everyone in attendance. The collection basket was filled beyond capacity, the money designated for the restoration fund.

The Friends of Father Damien hope to have the extensive work completed by 1989, the 100th anniversary of the death of Father Damien. All members express excitement at the prospect of the canonization of the Belgian priest.

Father Arsene H. Daenen, of the Congregation of the Sacred Hearts and pastor of Saint Augustine Church in Waikiki, site of the Damien Museum and Archives, said, "We're hoping and praying for canonization. It looks very promising. We don't have anything formal, but the pope has indicated he would love to canonize Damien. Mother Theresa has spoken to him in favor of it. The wheels are churning, but there is all that documentation required. In 1989, we are hoping for a statewide"—he corrected himself with a shy, triumphant smile—"an international celebration."

"Resurrecting Father Damien's Church" was first published in March/April 1988. The restoration of the church has been completed, thanks to the help of hundreds. It remains one of the highlights of a tour to the settlement of Kalaupapa.

Father Damien and Hansen's Disease patients, Kalawao, c. 1880s.

ROYAL HAWAIIAN BAND

KEEPING IN TUNE WITH THE TIMES

BY MARTY WENTZEL

"Listen, the band is coming!" Strains of Sousa and the sweet trills of piccolos punctuate the air. Soon, forty nattily dressed musicians swing snappily into sight, thrilling the crowd lining King Street with the pomp and ceremony of an old-time royal procession. For a few glorious moments in downtown Honolulu, it's difficult to tell whether the year is 1888 or 1988.

As the only musical organization in the country to be founded by royalty, the Royal Hawaiian Band is one of the last remaining links to Hawaii's alii. The words on the side of its blue-and-white truck read: "Royal Hawaiian Band, City and County of Honolulu, established by Kamehameha III in 1836."

Despite its royal ties, the group's beginnings were rather humble; calling itself the "King's Band," it performed in disorganized fashion under the direction of a man known only as Oliver. In 1845, the baton was passed to George Washington Hyatt, a slave from Virginia, who was succeeded three years later by William Merseburg, a German prone to heavy drink.

In 1870, the Austrian ship *Donau* stopped in Honolulu to have repairs done, and during its five-month stay, its band presented many community concerts which were the talk of the town. Sensing the enthusiasm of his

people, King Kamehameha V appointed New Zealander William Northcott as the new conductor of the Island band and directed him to transform a group of wayward youths from the Reform School into an ensemble of which Hawaii could at last be proud. To give the band more widespread appeal, its name was changed from the King's Band to the Royal Hawaiian Band.

Northcott lasted at the podium less than a year. His successor, Frank Medina, a native of Portugal, incurred heavy debts and within a few months, left Hawaii in disguise aboard the vessel *Nebraska*. Finally, Kamehameha V took matters into his own hands and, as a lover of German music, asked the Prussian government to send him an accomplished bandmaster. In 1872, his request was granted. Maestro Heinrich Wilhelm Berger stepped off the ship *Mohongo* onto Hawaiian soil and dramatically changed the future of the Royal Hawaiian Band.

As the band's most celebrated conductor, Berger did much to establish the stellar reputation the group enjoys today. On June 11, 1872, he raised his baton in front of ten Reform School recruits and conducted his first program in Hawaii. Featured was a song which is still part of the band's repertoire, "The Hymn of Kamehameha I." King

David Kalakaua later wrote lyrics to this piece, which became better known as "Hawaii Ponoi." In 1876, the song was chosen as Hawaii's official anthem, which it has remained until today.

Under Berger's expert musicianship, the Royal Hawaiian Band rapidly became an integral part of life in Honolulu. From parades to royal parties, the band brightened every Island occasion with its wonderful blend of Western and Hawaiian songs.

An 1891 entry in the *Hawaiian Annual* outlined its activities: "The services of the band are almost constantly engaged in the following various duties, viz.: at Royal breakfasts, receptions or other requirements of the Palace; concerts at the public squares and at the Hawaiian Hotel; serenade or other services to Diplomats or Cabinet Ministers; concerts at our eleemosynary institutions; at departure of our regular monthly and through steamers—for the benefit of the traveling public—and at receptions on board...By this it will be seen how much our band is interwoven with the social and every-day life of Honolulu. The reader will thus understand why it has such a hold upon us and visiting friends."

With just a few short months of rigorous rehearsals and personal instruction, Berger developed his

"Brown bag" concerts by the Royal Hawaiian Band draw crowds to Iolani Palace every Friday at noon.

Bandmaster Henry Berger (front center) and smartly attired band members on the steps of Iolani Palace, c. 1910.

80

young, inexperienced band members into disciplined, versatile musicians who were capable of performing a varied repertoire. Berger added string instruments to the band, which doubled as an orchestra for the gala balls held during King Kalakaua's extravagant reign. He incorporated European classics and operatic selections into the programs, and featured female vocalists, a tradition that continues today. The first featured singer was Nani Alapai, who performed with the group for forty years and who is noted for being the first to sing Queen Liliuokalani's haunting ballad, "Aloha Oe," in

public. Berger also presented the community with such lovely original compositions as "Beautiful Ilima" and "Sweet Lei Lehua."

A Berger brainstorm was Boat Day, a colorful celebration held at the pier for arriving and departing ships. The festivities always included performances by the Royal Hawaiian Band. An Island tradition which lasted well into the twentieth century, Boat Day helped the band establish worldwide renown. The band's following grew even larger in 1883, when it went to San Francisco and won first place in the Knights' Templar Conclave band competi-

tion. The ensemble also accompanied King Kalakaua and Queen Kapiolani on trips to the Neighbor Islands. Requests for appearances by the band soared.

As of November 8, 1890, Berger's list of local concerts numbered as follows:

Service at the Palace	*785 times*
At Emma Square	*1,108 times*
At the Hawaiian Hotel	*375 times*
At Departure of Steamers	*263 times*
At Thomas Square	*82 times*
At Queen's Hospital	*86 times*
At Insane Asylum	*32 times*

When Hawaii's political structure stood on shaky ground, so did the

band. With Queen Liliuokalani's abdication of the throne in 1893, every member of the band chose to quit rather than take the oath of allegiance to the provisional government. Berger was forced to assemble a new band composed of musicians from Honolulu's Portuguese Band, but eventually, many of the old band members rejoined the group.

As the monarchy gave way to the territorial senate, the band lost favor in the political and cultural circles of the day. During these troubled times, its identity was in jeopardy; within five years, from 1893 to 1898, the group changed its name three

Bandmaster Aaron Mahi studies his music sheets before a performance.

times—from the Provisional Government Band to the Hawaiian Band to the Territorial Band. Its existence was threatened altogether when the House of Representatives withdrew its support of the group. Fortunately, Prince Jonah Kuhio Kalanianaole was in the midst of efforts to form a county government, and when he succeeded in 1905, the band was placed under the jurisdiction of the City and County of Honolulu. It again adopted the name Royal Hawaiian Band.

Although Berger was originally hired as bandmaster for just four years, he ended up devoting forty-three years to the group, conducting it in more than 32,000 concerts. He served under five forms of government and four monarchs: Kamehameha V, Lunalilo, Kalakaua and Liliuokalani, who referred to him fondly as the "Father of Hawaiian Music." He became a naturalized Hawaiian subject in 1879, changed his first name from Heinrich to Henry and lived out the rest of his years in the Islands (he died on October 14, 1929).

Berger continued conducting the band until old age forced him to step down in 1915. The band then went through a long series of conductors who were hired and replaced by various governors appointed by the president of the United States. Since statehood in 1959, the ensemble, which holds the distinction of being the oldest municipal band in the country, has continued to function under the elected heads of state, including William P. Quinn, John A. Burns, George Ariyoshi and today, John Waihee.

After Berger retired, Peter Kalani led the Royal Hawaiian Band for a year. He was followed by Robert M. Baker, who served from 1917 to 1920. One of Berger's top students, Mekia Kealakai, conducted from 1920 to 1926. John Amasiu held the post from 1927 to 1929, and Kealakai again picked up the baton from

1930 to 1932.

Subsequent conductors were Charles E. King (1932-1934 and 1939-1940), Frank J. Vierra (1934-1939), Domenico Moro (1940-1955), William L. Baptiste (1956-1957), Earle Christoph (1958-1963), Lloyd Krause (1964-1968) and Kenneth Kawashima (1969-1980).

Today, the Royal Hawaiian Band is under the able direction of Aaron David Mahi, a large Hawaiian with a gentle disposition and a strong understanding of the band and its role in the community. A boyhood interest in music led Mahi to arrange pieces for the annual song contests at Kamehameha Schools, where he was a student. In 1975, he received his bachelor of arts degree in music education at the Hartt School of Music in West Hartford, Connecticut, then returned to Hawaii to teach music and Hawaiian language in local public schools. He took graduate classes in conducting at the La Sierra Campus of Loma Linda University in California, and played the double bass as a member of the Honolulu Symphony.

"All of my training was leading me toward another form of conducting—orchestral conducting," said Mahi. "So when I was approached by the Friends of the Royal Hawaiian Band and asked to be the conductor, I turned them down, not once, but twice. It just wasn't in my plans."

The third time he was asked, Mahi had a change of heart. "I began to talk with friends about the possibilities. I remember one person saying, 'Isn't it about time the Royal Hawaiian Band had a Hawaiian conductor again?' That kind of encouragement from my associates made me realize that this was a way I could help the Hawaiian people." In January 1981, Mahi took charge of the Royal Hawaiian Band.

"Charles E. King was the last bandmaster who was of Hawaiian ancestry," said Mahi. "He conduct-

ed up until 1940—that's over forty years ago! Since then, there have been an array of good bandmasters, but none who have been closely linked to the (Hawaiian) heritage. I can bring that extra dimension to the band, and that adds special meaning to me."

Mahi takes the role of bandmaster very seriously. "One of my purposes is to help keep Hawaii's traditional music fresh in people's minds. Take, for instance, composers like Kalakaua and Liliuokalani. Berger would notate, organize and orchestrate their melodies, and that's how their old songs survived. It was their relationship with Berger which, in many ways, decided the long tradition; the band became an extension of their musical abilities...The responsibility lies with us to keep those compositions alive."

A modern-day program by the Royal Hawaiian Band is as delightfully diverse as one from Berger's era. Overtures by Rossini, polkas and waltzes by Strauss, traditional Hawaiian works, contemporary show tunes and a song or two by Berger himself—the band offers an entertaining dichotomy of music spanning miles as well as years.

It is this dichotomy which makes the band so well received on its tours away from Hawaii. In 1901, the group went to New York; in 1905, it performed in the Oregon Exposition; in 1906, it went on a tour across the Mainland United States; in 1907, it participated in the Saint Louis International Exposition; in 1974 and 1978, it toured Canada and several Mainland cities; and in 1983, it made a whirlwind swing through Europe, which included performances in the Netherlands, Liechtenstein, Switzerland, France, London, Austria and Berger's homeland of Germany. The European tour included two live Munich-based television appearances reaching 24 million viewers. If funding comes through, the band will tour Asia

sometime in the next few years. In this way, the Royal Hawaiian Band has functioned as a sort of goodwill ambassador, encouraging tourism to the Hawaiian Islands and opening the ears of the world to the universal joys of music.

Mahi is working on building up the band's repertoire to include songs which haven't been played for a long time, including works by previous bandmasters Kalani, Kealakai, Amasiu, King and Moro. He said, "We also need to pay more attention to the music of Hawaii's modern composers like Jay Larrin, Ray Kinney and Robert Cazimero. By playing their music, the band can carry on its original purpose: To preserve the music of the day."

Of his seven-year tenure as bandmaster, Mahi said, "A lot of times, the job can be mundane because we're not only a concert band, we're a service band. It's easy to get in a rut when you perform all the time. But since the day I started conducting the band, I have seen a large change in attitude of the members. I've noticed a heightening of musical standards...The musicians take a more intellectual approach to their musical expression, and the overall impression is a product of very high standards."

Playing in the Royal Hawaiian Band is a full-time job. When seventy-one-year-old Sol Kalima joined the group in 1949, it was the fulfillment of a dream he had had ever since he was in intermediate school. "I started as a trumpeter, then switched to another brass instrument in 1956 under Mr. Baptiste. Then, in 1983, I switched a third time to the bass drum. But no matter what instrument (I've played), I've enjoyed every day I've played with the band."

For Ron Baltazar, becoming a member of the band in 1964 was a destiny he never questioned. "My initials are RHB," he said with a smile. "My father was in the band for

thirty-five years, and as a boy I would watch him play at Aloha Tower. I remember seeing people cry as the band played 'Aloha Oe' for departing ships. That was very moving for me."

Baltazar is most impressed with the achievements of bandmaster Domenico Moro. "He was faced with teaching uneducated musicians to tackle challenging pieces by Verdi, Weber and the like. Today, many of the members have been schooled at Eastman, Julliard and so on, so it's no wonder we sound so good."

One of Mahi's goals is to bring the band into Hawaii's public eye as much as possible. He has arranged concerts in large shopping centers such as Ala Moana, as well as locations in the heart of Honolulu like Tamarind Park and Fort Street Mall. The revival of Boat Day by the Hawaii Maritime Association has also expanded the band's exposure; it plays at the pier for the arrival and departure of large trans-Pacific liners ten or twelve times a year. It has also performed at such special events as the inauguration of Governor John Waihee and the visits of such dignitaries as the Archbishop of Canterbury.

The band is a standard attraction in major parades during Aloha Week in September and on Kamehameha Day in June, and also plays its regular schedule of more than 400 free concerts annually, including one every Sunday afternoon at Kapiolani Park Bandstand in Waikiki.

The Royal Hawaiian Band is, however, most at home playing in the gazebo on the lovely, tranquil grounds of Iolani Palace. Here, each Friday at noon, it turns back the pages of time and transforms them into living, breathing musical history for all of Hawaii to enjoy.

"The Royal Hawaiian Band: Keeping in Tune with the Times" was first published in May/June 1988.

83

Sparkling brass, sparkling music.

THE

Nineteenth-century scrimshaw.

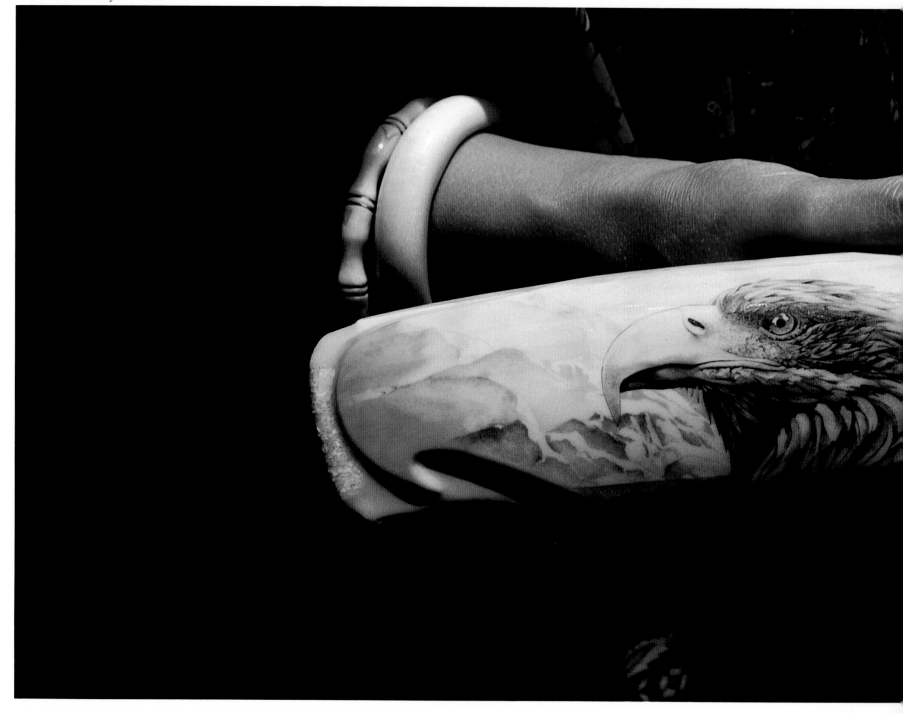

END OF THE WHALE'S TALE

SCRIMSHAW

BY RITA ARIYOSHI

From among the Hebrews, David went out to topple Goliath. One of old Russia's favorite sons, Saint George, took on the terrible dragon. Ancient Greece sent Odysseus to battle the Cyclops.

Monsters of great magnitude have fired the minds of men since the dawn of time, as if something in us has always been cognizant that we inherited our world from the dinosaurs we never saw. Where no monsters existed, we created them. So, it is no wonder that when New England sent her sailors to sea in search of leviathan, the adventure inspired songs, stories and epic works with the breadth of Melville's *Moby Dick*.

It would be nice to think that the mystique of whaling gave birth to what some people claim is the only non-aboriginal, indigenous American folk art—scrimshaw. But it wasn't the thrill of the hunt, the specter of a man in a small boat facing a sixty-five-foot, multi-ton whale, that led men to carve their stories into the teeth and bones of the enemy. It was sheer, utter boredom that drove them to whittling, sculpting and etching the only material they had—the remnants of the whale.

An entry from a whaler's journal of the nineteenth century reads: "But man tires of nothing so quickly as a state of inactivity, and so we were not a week upon the whaling ground, ere every one complained of the weary monotony of such a life...By the time we had gotten a month's experience of the cruising ground, I no longer wondered at the wandering, lackluster look, the shuffling

Excellent examples of scrimshaw on whale's teeth.

walk and awkward appearance, generally, of your regular old whaleman. His mind has been gradually killed by lack of use."

Exactly when sailors began "scrimshoning" (one of the original forms of the word) is not known. The earliest extant piece of shipboard scrimshaw dates back to about 1631, a relic from Holland of the Dutch whaling ventures into the Arctic. Probably the craft never really caught on because the sailor's fingers would have been too cold. A century later, in the warm waters of the Pacific, Yankee whalemen raised scrimshaw to an art form.

There is quite a bit of discussion as to what is really scrimshaw and what is not. E. Norman Flayderman, in his authoritative book *Scrimshaw and Scrimshanders,* defines it as "folk art which was produced by American sailors. The art consisted of useful or decorative objects carved from and on whale's teeth."

Flayderman, however, is the first to point out that the definition is not entirely accurate since whale bone and baleen were also used. The whalemen were specifically American, yet English and French sailors were scrimshanders as well. What also has to be taken into account is that at the height of the whaling era, 1820 to 1865, most of the crew on American ships were Indians, Hawaiians, Eskimos and natives of other countries. Some people assert that the art was learned from these other crew members, many of whom had a cultural tradition of carving whale ivory.

Early Hawaiians artifacts include many examples of whale bone and teeth fashioned for both useful and decorative purposes. The prized lei palaoa worn by the alii, was carved from whale bone.

Shipboard scrimshaw often used material other than whale products. Depending on their ports of call, the sailors might have garnered some fossilized walrus bone or elephant ivory. The themes they chose were as diverse as their material and their own backgrounds. Nautical themes and women predominated. There were ships, rigging, whales, sailors, captains and maps. Women appeared as lassies in tartans, hula dancers, Greek goddesses, Nubians, queens, madonnas, mermaids and trollops. Religious and patriotic themes were popular, depicting mostly crucifixions and eagles.

Sometimes the scrimshaw served practical purposes. The men carved nautical gear, combs, brushes and belt buckles. For their ladies back home, they made corset stays, hairpins and, probably with visions of apple pie dancing in their heads, a wide assortment of artistic pie crimpers. A poem of the day went:
"In many a gale,
Has been the whale,
In which this bone did rest.
His time is past,
His bone at last
Must now support thy breast."

There is great debate today over whether the whaling era scrimshaw is the only real scrimshaw or whether the art as practiced in modern times can be called by the same name. William Gilkerson, himself a scrimshander, suggests in his book, *The Ivory Worker and His Art of Scrimshaw Historical and Contemporary* that the art be divided into two historical periods—old scrimshaw and new scrimshaw, with 1924 being the dividing line. (In that year, the last of the square-rigged Yankee whalers was destroyed by a hurricane which blew her onto the rocks off Buzzards Bay, Massachusetts.)

To appreciate scrimshaw, it is essential to have some understanding of whaling. Melville asserts that Perseus was the first whaleman, having slain a whale which was about to eat the Ethiopian princess, Andromeda. Some South Sea Islanders of old used whale teeth for currency. It is claimed that the Phoenicians launched whaling forays. In the New World, Eskimo whaling villages date back to 100 or 200 A.D. Early European efforts at whaling were primarily salvaging operations, relying on a supply of dead whales washing ashore or live whales becoming stranded by outgoing tides. Whales were so plentiful in those days, with huge pods visible off the European coastlines, that it became obvious that man did not have to rely on chance to send him this valuable creature whose oil lit the lamps of Europe. In the twelfth century, the Basques organized the first whaling "industry," and by the sixteenth century had become so successful that it was necessary for them to establish fisheries in Greenland, Iceland and Spitzenbergen due to a scarcity of the whales in their own offshore waters.

To some settlers, the New World was primarily a new fishery. In 1614, Captain John Smith sailed with a crown permit to take whales. The charter of the Massachusetts Bay Colony established the settlers' rights in whaling. One *Mayflower* voyager's journal read: "Large whales of the best kind for oil and bone came daily alongside and played about the ship."

In 1791, the first American whalers from Nantucket and New Bedford rounded Cape Horn and the great Pacific whale hunt was on. With harpoons and longboats, they plowed the ocean in search of their prey. In the course of things, they discovered and chartered more than 2,000 islands, shoals and reefs, making a record that was used by their descendants who fought in World War II. Ironically, the logs are being used again, this time to help determine the distribution, quantities, and feeding and breeding habits of certain endangered cetacea.

Hawaii, then called the Sandwich Islands, became the whaling capital of the Pacific, serving ships fishing Japan waters and the Baja coast of America north to the Arctic. In 1846,

Pacific Whaling Museum, Sea Life Park.

*Contemporary scrimshaw depicting
Aloha Tower, Honolulu.*

596 whaling vessels visited the Islands, bringing commerce, foreign goods, disease, the mosquito and evangelism. The sailors swarmed ashore in search of rest, recreation, liquor and women. Everyone in the Islands was touched by whaling. Twenty percent of the business in Honolulu at that time was done by grog shops.

Many ship captains, who were Quakers from the northeast United States, preferred Lahaina on the island of Maui as a harbor. It was smaller and the men were more easily contained. The anchorage was free and there were strict laws against liquor and prostitution. The men had to be back on board at sunset and there were high fines for both fornication and spitting in the streets. At one point, the town was fired upon by whalemen from the ship *John Palmer* who had taken some Island women on board in spite of the law forbidding it. When Maui's Governor Hoapili requested the return of the women, the *John Palmer* fired its cannons on the town, hitting, among other things, the home of Protestant missionary Reverend William Richards, the man they blamed for their deprivations.

In one day in November of 1852, there were 3,000 sailors in Honolulu Harbor. One drunken sailor was killed by his jailer when he couldn't be quieted. The result was four days of riots and arson that almost destroyed the city and every ship in port. Providently, there was a gentle Kona wind rather than the usual blustery tradewinds and the fires dissipated.

As for the whales themselves, they cavorted about the ships in the Lahaina roadstead, oblivious to the fact that in the open ocean they would be hunted mercilessly and fearlessly by the same men who could, at that point, hardly stand erect.

Actually, there wasn't much hunting done in Hawaiian waters since the animals, though large, didn't have much fat on them after swimming to Hawaii from their seasonal Arctic habitat. Also, once mortally wounded, they sank fast, and because the ocean is extremely deep around the Islands, it was hard to retrieve the valuable carcasses. Despite this, the Hawaiians had their own whaling fleet launched by King Kamehameha V and by 1858, nineteen whalers were sailing from the Islands under the Hawaiian flag. So many Hawaiians had shipped out as sailors and were dispersed on foreign ships all over the oceans of the world that the king, worried about the decline of his populace, offered a $50 reward for any Hawaiian returned to the Islands, dead or alive. The law didn't achieve the desired effect for many a kanaka came home in a fifty-gallon barrel.

The Hawaiians shared in the loss in 1871 when six of their ships, along with twenty-six American whalers, were caught by an early storm in the Arctic and were crushed by ice. Twelve hundred survivors were returned to Honolulu aboard the remaining Hawaiian and American ships. The Pacific whaling industry had, however, been dealt a fatal blow.

To keep things in perspective, from 1825 through 1860, the height of Pacific whaling, there were fewer whales killed than in 1950 through 1955 when only a few ships were involved in the hunt and slaughter. In the old days, the capture of eight whales was considered a good voyage. The animal, at least, stood a sporting chance and the great sperm whales were known to have rammed and sunk many a ship, destroying their hunters. Today, with sonar and electronically charged and directed harpoons, the beast's fate is sealed.

Surprisingly, in spite of all the whaling activity in Hawaii, later generations found there were very few examples of scrimshaw, the whaler's art, remaining in the Islands though sailors regularly traded the ivory pieces for favors. It is estimated that half of the pieces were pornographic and destroyed by more sensitive souls. The best of what's left, plus an impressive group of pieces from around the world, are now housed in two whaling museums in Hawaii. One is the Pacific Whaling Museum at Sea Life Park on Oahu; the other, fittingly, is near Lahaina, at Kaanapali. In tune with the times, Maui's museum is at the center of a shopping plaza at that prime resort.

Scrimshaw is now traded for money, both hard and plastic. Vern Ignacio has a shop at the Maui Surf Hotel called Kanu Ivory. He said, "I look at scrimshaw as jewelry, only the material is more valuable." Ignacio is a scrimshander himself. "When I bought the store I knew nothing. It was a good buy. I figured I was going to be in the store so I might as well do it. Most scrimshaw I sell goes for $50 to $1,500. I do pointilism, working with dots for depths of colors. Purists claim it's not scrim-

The ships Amelia Wilson *and* Castor
*in the Pacific whaling grounds, painted
in 1825 in London by W.J. Huggins,
marine painter to the king of England.*

Scrimshander at work, Lahaina, Maui.

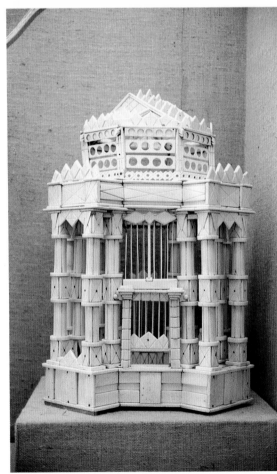

Carved ivory bird cage.

90

shaw unless it's etched in lines by rusty nails—you know.

"Hawaii has a growing number of artists. There are also many on the West Coast and in New England. They seem to gather at seasides. Art students get into it. They already understand form."

Allan Walker, the original owner of the Pier 49 scrimshaw shop in the Whalers Village shopping complex at Kaanapali, was one of the pioneers in reviving the art on the island of Maui. "We took busboys and waitresses with artistic talent and we trained them. They were more motivated by a desire to learn than to make extra money. They were interested in art. Many are now doing some beautiful work in both line and stipple technique. Two to three hundred hours go into a piece." There are now approximately forty professional scrimshanders on Maui with perhaps a dozen able to devote themselves full-time to the art.

Tom Peden who, with partner Howard Konrad, purchased Pier 49, said, "When they (the newer artists) start to see scrimshaw going for $8,000 to $9,000 for one piece, their work starts to really shape up. They really start to develop as artists."

In 1978, Jim Marcum, Walker's Pier 49 manager, went to Seattle to line up additional artists, many of whom had worked for the Alaska Silver and Ivory Company which went bankrupt. Said Walker, "They were looking for work and the timing was right." These Pacific Northwest artists create wildlife and Indian themes, a departure from traditional scrimshaw designs, but popular even in the Islands.

Alyce Valenta has been with Pier 49 since it opened and through the ownership change. She has toured the whaling museums of Massachusetts, read every book she could find on the art and is anxious to share her knowledge with anyone who has the time to listen. In discussing the various kinds of ivory and both the old and new scrimshaw she said, "I try to teach them (potential customers) to see the differences with their own eyes. They will be able to tell the difference between whale ivory and walrus ivory and know which whale teeth are old and which are new. By the time they leave here they are going to appreciate scrimshaw."

Hawaii is reputed to be the largest scrimshaw marketplace in the world, with the trade being plied year-round, an advantage over the closest rivals, Cape Cod and Alaska, which have a two- to four-month season, at best. There have been allegations that illegal ivory is being sold in Lahaina. Commenting on that, Peden said, "Today, you have to show papers. You'd be a fool to sell illegal ivory."

What some people admit is happening is that the Eskimos, who are permitted to sell worked ivory as native handicrafts, are doing minimal etching on the whale and walrus ivory, sometimes amounting to little more than the artisan's initials. As native handicrafts, the ivory can then be authenticated, awarded papers and sold. The piece is then worked by another artist and sold to the public. There is nothing illegal about this practice, but it certainly does circumvent the intent of the law which is the protection of the endangered species.

A more serious threat to a prospective buyer is the imitation scrimshaw being marketed in the United States as "simshaw," which is blatently plastic. However, reports are coming in of unwary buyers who have purchased simshaw abroad thinking that it was ivory. One Islander paid thousands of dollars for a piece of plastic at an antique shop in England and another man suffered the same fate at a swap meet in California.

A man who understands scrimshaw better than most is "Sealskin Charley," Charley McAlpine, who travels from Hawaii to the Pacific Northwest carving a career out of scrimshaw. A burly, red-bearded man, he epitomizes the Alaskan roughneck. "I was looking for adventure and romance in the frozen North. I got all of that I could handle. Yes, indeed. I had floods, fires, plane crashes, hepatitis. One time a guy I was with shot a bear and found he had no more bullets so he grabbed the wounded bear by the back leg and went waltzing all around, kept screaming until help came. I slept through it all.

"I used to hunt whales with the Point Hope Eskimos. There's a lot of religion involved. Eskimos don't need whales for subsistence living (as they and the government assert). They don't need the whale. They love it."

When asked how he got his start in scrimshaw, McAlpine laughed uproariously. "I showed up in Anchorage in moosehide clothes I had bought from some Indians I had met along the way. I even bought a pistol. My leather pants were too big so I held them up with a cartridge belt. When I went to the post office that first day to check general delivery to see if I had any mail, I stopped traffic. I mean pet wolves had even eaten the fringes off the pants. I got rid of that outfit. I soon realized transportation was the key to Alaska. Still is. So I bought a plane and learned to fly. I actually lived out of my plane.

"I got to dealing with the Eskimos in a kind of unique way. I helped them by spotting game in my plane. On the coast I was following the routes of the whaling fleets of old. Made me a pretty valuable guy in their eyes. They like to hunt the small Beluga white whales and caribou. I helped the reindeer herders. Unlike the Laplanders, the Eskimos let the reindeer run free and I helped to find them again at roundup time.

"I started bringing out carvings. I was known as 'the guy' as far as Eskimo crafts went. The scrimshanders knew I was the guy to get material from. So I traded. I wanted their work. I've got a broad range of work of the best of American artists. Incredible work.

"There are a lot of scrimshanders on Maui. Mostly they come from the Mainland. Vern (Ignacio) had been living on the Mainland and wanted to come back. Another local artist is Hamlin Gilmore. He's Hawaiian chop suey, a graduate artist. He does a lot. He's a scrimshaw machine."

Since the passage of the endangered species act of 1973, which protects the giant sea mammal, scrimshanders have turned to material other than whale's teeth and whale products for their craft. The most popular material is fossilized bone and ivory from Alaska. According to McAlpine, fossilized walrus is no problem. "There's not much wooly mammoth tusk left, but there's more than people might think. The wooly mammoth has been dead for 20,000 years so it's hard to classify him as endangered. People kept bringing mammoth bones to the University of Alaska thinking them to be of museum value. They had to put a stop to it. They buried seven tons of fossil ivory."

McAlpine confirmed what everyone can figure out for themselves: "Scrimshaw is going up in value. There are few deposits left and everyone's digging like beavers."

With the passage of the endangered species act, everyone owning ivory had to register it and imports were banned. According to Lewis Eisenberg, a Honolulu scrimshaw collector and dealer, "That act made the price of whale teeth go crazy. Everyone wanted a tooth. It has also allowed better engravers to work on the material because the intrinsic value is now there. We're seeing much finer work. But we're seeing a transition now that teeth are running out. Scrimshanders first turned to elephant ivory. But that presents an ethical problem, too. Fossil ivory is the thing now. The Alaska pipeline unearthed phenomenal deposits.

"It's getting hard to acquire good pieces. People are buying it (scrimshaw) as a hedge against inflation. People are buying for investment rather than a feeling for the pieces. A scrimshaw tooth that was worth $1,000 ten years ago is now worth $25,000 to $30,000."

Eisenberg's own collection plus what he has borrowed from collector friends is now exhibited at the Pacific Whaling Museum. Established as a natural addition to Sea Life Park, the innovative marine park at Oahu's Makapuu Point, it is one of the finest whaling museums in the world and the most extensive west of Connecticut. The museums of Massachusetts may have more exhibits, but Eisenberg's are representative of the finest old scrimshaw art. The Pacific Whaling Museum also houses old photographs of Hawaii's whaling days, whaling paraphernalia and the skeleton of a whale beached at Barber's Point, Oahu.

Capitalizing on the romantic aura of Hawaii's whaling past and returning it once again to the commercial arena, shops throughout the Islands sell scrimshaw. Along Lahaina's Front Street, it's possible to buy a $10,000 piece of scrimshaw carved on whale ivory, authentic Eskimo ivory sled runners or $5 key chains with a ship etched on bone.

A visit to the wholesale showrooms of the Edward Sultan Company in Honolulu revealed a wide range of quality in the scrimshaw that would find its way into Island retail shops. There were cheap souvenir pieces, quality rings, incredible carved Eskimo pieces, truly fine modern examples of the art in objects and jewelry, and some gallery-quality pieces that were breathtaking.

A summation of the experts' advice for prospective scrimshaw buyers is to buy what you like and buy for today. It is obviously an investment, but you still have to buy what you like and have a feeling for the piece. It all depends on whether a buyer wants a souvenir or a piece of fine enduring art.

Scrimshaw, with or without the permission of the purists, is not only surviving as an art form, but prospering. It has, in fact, outlived the whaling industry which sired it. Hopefully, it will not preside over the demise of the creatures which gave it form and life.

"Scrimshaw: The End of the Whale's Tale" was first published in September/October 1981. Pier 49 has since closed. Replacing it in Whalers Village is Lahaina Scrimshaw, which is stocked with scrimshaw of all kinds, from keychains and cuff links to pendants and pillboxes. The shopping complex also boasts a 2,400-square-foot whaling museum, whose exhibits include a priceless collection of antique scrimshaw. Lewis Eisenberg spearheaded the construction of the Whalers Village Museum and is presently serving as its director.

A nineteenth-century whaling scene.

SOICHI SAKAMOTO
MAKING IT FROM MAUI TO THE OLYMPICS

BY CHERYL CHEE TSUTSUMI

Coach Sakamoto is surrounded by memorabilia in his Moiliili, Oahu home.

In a dynamic coaching career spanning forty-five years, Soichi Sakamoto took swimming as a competitive Island sport from an irrigation ditch at Puunene, Maui, to the pools of the World Olympics. Hundreds of youthful swimmers excelled in his training program based on caring and common sense, including six American championship teams, seventeen stars of national repute and four Olympic medalists. But whether or not they were holders of records and ribbons, each athlete left Sakamoto's tutelage with valuable lessons in self-respect and sportsmanship.

At age seventy-seven, Sakamoto is a trim, spry image of the visionary man whose accomplishments earned him a coveted place in the Interna-

tional Swimming Hall of Fame and many other athletic and community distinctions. Although he retired more than a year ago, memories of the challenging, rewarding years he enjoyed as Hawaii's foremost swimming coach rush to his mind in warm, happy waves.

"That irrigation ditch at Puunene has become quite famous," Sakamoto said, surrounded by koa calabashes, photographs, newspaper clippings and certificates that have transformed his living room into an exhibit of memorabilia from his coaching days. "It ran right in front of Puunene Grammar School, and every afternoon, dozens of youngsters would take a dip in it to cool off. This was actually illegal. The sugar plantation people didn't want

to take responsibility for any accidents that might happen. I was a teacher and scoutmaster at Puunene School when I started coaching in the mid-thirties. I appealed to the plantation managers and finally got official approval to use the ditch for swimming practices."

One hundred and twenty boys and girls from ages nine through fourteen became the charter members of Puunene School's swimming squad. Sakamoto demanded commitment and discipline from each youngster. The rules were strict: No smoking, drinking, swearing or gambling. When a student joined the team, he was expected to actively participate. Mandatory workouts were held every day after school from two-thirty until ten, sometimes midnight, and

several hours of practice were also required on weekends and holidays.

Admitting he dove into coaching with a lot of enthusiasm but little experience, Sakamoto said, "I knew nothing about teaching swimming at first. I had no formal training, no medals. I didn't even know good swimming—I thought of myself as only a fair swimmer. Then I began to apply common sense principles in my coaching. I went to the plantation laborers and got ideas from them. They told me you have to work every day or you'll get lazy. If you don't work every day, you won't get extra pay, the bonus. That gave me the idea of practicing every day to get the benefit of top performance. I asked how they could maintain working every day. They said you must be steady and pace yourself. Progress comes a step at a time. When I watched animals moving, they seemed to be so relaxed. That gave me the idea to relax my swimmers. Common sense says anything strong must begin with a good foundation. So I started by establishing sound basics. First the youngsters learned buoyancy and to be confident in the water. Then they learned how to kick, do the armstrokes and breathe properly. Coordinate all three and you have a swimmer. After that, you polish the rough spots and increase the workload."

While Sakamoto's strenuous exercise plan built muscles and endurance in his swimmers, his deep Christian faith and patriotism built character. "I prayed all the time for Him to give me guidance on how to inspire and teach them the importance of being reverent and humble," he said. "I told them we mustn't ever forget God is greater than us and we've got to be humble no matter how good we become. When we win, we should celebrate quietly within ourselves and be thankful that we did well—not show off. I also told them to love our country. I couldn't overlook the responsibility I felt to instill my appreciation of America in them." Without fail, Sakamoto's practices began with prayer, the recitation of the Pledge of Allegiance and the singing of a patriotic song.

In 1937, Sakamoto organized the Three Year Swimming Club with the goal of preparing his protégés for the 1940 Olympics in Helsinki. "I'm great on building air castles and the youngsters sat in the room listening to me, wide-eyed. When word of our plan spread around the school and the community, everyone laughed. They thought I was talking nonsense. The next year we went to Oahu and outclassed everyone at the big meet in Honolulu. In two years, we won our first national team championship. What had been a laughingstock was becoming a re-

ality. We were heralded as heroes on Maui."

Political strife in Europe preceding World War II prompted the cancellation of the 1940 Olympics and interrupted Sakamoto's dream of seeing his swimmers compete against the world's best. But it proved to be a notable year, nonetheless. Impressed by the achievements of the scrappy group from Puunene, Hawaiian Commercial and Sugar Company built a park and pool just a short distance away from the irrigation ditch that had spawned Sakamoto's first set of swimming standouts.

Fifteen-year-old Bill Smith, Jr. came from Honolulu to live and train with Sakamoto in the fall of 1940. As a child, Smith had been stricken with typhoid fever, but through the devoted efforts of his father, was able to build up his health enough through swimming to become a serious competitor. Under Sakamoto's guidance, Smith raced to his first of seventeen national titles in 1941. Seven years later, he was awarded a gold medal for winning the 400-meter men's freestyle event in record time at the Olympic Games in London. It was a highly emotional occasion for Sakamoto, who sat quietly in the bleachers amidst throngs of cheering spectators and watched his dream of a decade materialize.

As one of the United States' Olympic swim team coaches in 1952 and 1956, he was also able to see Bill Woolsey, Thelma Kalama and Evelyn Kawamoto power their way into sports headlines across the world. Many of his other gifted athletes—including Keo Nakama, George Onekea, Dick Cleveland, Jose Balmores, Halo Hirose, Chic Miyamoto and Fujiko Katsutani—made big splashes in national and international swimming circles as well.

Sakamoto is a firm believer in the power of positive thinking. "When you nurture something, whether it be a plant or a person, it'll get bigger and stronger. I would always tell the

youngsters, 'I see in you greatness. You're going to be the next champ—even greater than so-and-so.' Every day I would pat them on the back and say, 'There, see? You're coming along.' All youngsters have it in them to become outstanding swimmers, given time and encouragement. I found each one to be a diamond in the rough that could be polished. You need to respect each person as an individual and each individual as a person, because someday, somewhere, he will show you that he's far greater than you ever thought he'd be."

After the war, Sakamoto accepted an offer to coach swimming at the University of Hawaii in Honolulu, a position he held for twenty-six years. At the time, there was little interest in aquatics at the college level, and he immediately began a building program. In 1945, he founded the Hawaii Swimming Club with the intent of developing swimmers for the university. Now in its thirty-eighth year, the club has a membership of forty youngsters aged five through sixteen, who come from all over Oahu to train at Palolo pool. Sakamoto headed the coaching staff until 1981.

The first bit of counsel Sakamoto shares with aspiring young coaches is always the same. "You must realize you know nothing. Then you must constantly ask for assistance and help from God and others. When I started I was taking youngsters to meets on the Mainland in the midst of big-name coaches. I was nothing but a country boy myself. I asked them to help and they gave so much information to me, so willingly. Once I had that, I combined it with all the ideas I had and I found it brought success to my program."

Other key factors in effective coaching, Sakamoto said, are motivation, dedication and communication. "In their thinking, attitudes and mannerisms, athletes reflect their coach. I told myself I'd never sit down when I was coaching because

when I sit, that gives the appearance of being lazy and tired and I didn't want my swimmers to feel tired. Then I said I wasn't going to wear a jacket no matter how cold the weather got because I didn't want them to feel cold in the water. And I decided I wasn't going to talk to other people during practice—my first concern would be my swimmers."

Today, Sakamoto's priorities lie with home and family. His achievements, however, have not been forgotten. He received the Jefferson Award for outstanding public service in 1982, and was recently inducted into the newly-formed University of Hawaii Sports Hall of Honor as one of only nine charter members.

Sakamoto's only links with his prominent past are the awards and his "youngsters," dozens of them, who have kept in touch with him over the years through phone calls, letters and visits. "The greatest reward of my coaching years comes when I hear them say, 'Thank you, Coach, for all you've done for me—in swimming and even more so in this idea of being someone worthwhile.' I'm humbled when I realize what I had told them about common sense, appreciation and God had sunk into their hearts."

The man without a medal to his name is perhaps the greatest champion of all.

93

"Soichi Sakamoto: Making It from Maui to the Olympics" was first published in March/April 1983. Now eighty-four, Sakamoto enjoys a quiet life filled with wonderful memories of his coaching career.

THE KIMONO QUEEN

BY NAOMI SODETANI

PHOTOGRAPHY BY FRANCO SALMOIRAGHI/PHOTO RESOURCE

Eiko Yorita finished her work, pursed her lips, nodded twice and shuffled to the far edge of the room. There she sat, arthritis-curled hands pressed into her lap. Her eyes searched for any last detail she might have missed; any flaw not smoothed over. But there was none.

Six feet of molded fabric stood before her—red and gold brocade over layers of silk, stiff gilt cloth and soft white gauze. Jutting toward the ceiling at odd angles were pearlescent and metal bangles; an ivory stick protruded from the middle.

The thing actually moved.

Slowly, it slid across the mat, brocade scratching straw. Stopping a few feet away, before Yorita's full-length mirror, the "sculpture's" mouth dropped open. Reflected within was a perfect vision: a young woman dressed in full bridal *kimono* and headdress, with white skin and red lips, holding a *sensu* fan—splendor itself, revisited from twelfth-century Japan.

The woman with the shocked eyes was me.

In two-and-a-half hours, Eiko Yorita's skillful hands had turned me into an utter stranger to myself.

Eiko Yorita, eighty-six, is Hawaii's queen of *kimono*. She is also among a mere handful of persons who still practice the ancient Japanese art of elaborate dressing. When she offered to dress me as part of my research, she said, "You no understand if other way, just talk…" I was honored. More than that, I was intrigued by what her gift might yield. With what part of my ancestral heritage would I connect? Would there be alienation, rejection?

For over forty-six years, Yorita has readied local brides for traditional weddings. Since 1953, she has dressed Cherry Blossom Festival beauty pageant contestants in full regalia, assisted in recent years by Lynn Mari Yorita, a granddaughter whom she trained. Yorita owns perhaps the largest *kimono* collection outside of Japan— over 300 garments individually valued at $500 to $10,000 or more, each with coordinated *obi* accessories and wigs.

In her Kapahulu home, Yorita has filled a huge cabinet with miniature dolls from around the world. While growing up in Kochi, on the island of Shikoku, Japan, she had handcrafted dozens of these dolls, pretending that they were real.

Yorita came to Hawaii in 1919. In 1937, halfway through raising her family, she decided to become a beauty specialist. She tucked a suitcase under one arm, her youngest child under the other, and returned to Japan. Normally, makeup, formal hairdo and *kimono* dressing requires two years of studies. Not only did Yorita train with Japan's finest—the dresser of the imperial household— she walked off with her diploma in just a few months.

She returned to Hawaii, where her business boomed until World War II shut it down. Instantly, all ties to a Japanese past were denied, buried or burned by *issei* and *nisei* wanting to prove their loyalty as Americans.

95

In my parents' wedding photo taken in 1947, my mother's net-veiled hair falls like Joan Crawford's to her shoulders. I see similar touches in her precise eyebrows and dark lips. A virginal satin gown trails behind her. My proud father, whom I think of as an Asian Alan Ladd, wears a white tuxedo.

Today, it strikes me as ironic that I kneel here in *kimono,* discovering a tradition my own mother had rejected.

Yorita pulls pins out of her mouth "Hard, pin up short hair." Our intimacy feels natural; she could be my grandmother. "Put on *juban* now." She hands over a thin slip. When I return to the mat, she has arranged, in two neat rows, hair ornaments, *obi* and sashes, cords, purses and several ornate *kimono.* Suddenly, she slaps my legs. They had sprawled carelessly. "You no sit good, I scold you," she says. My feet in *tabi* tuck back under, properly, as expected.

Yorita's hands gently lower a huge wig over my hair. Each nerve knows its job without asking what comes next. "How does this feel—alright?" she asks. Only eyes reply; my neck is struggling to hold my head upright. The wig weighs at least ten pounds. I must balance this weight, or my head, it seems, will snap off.

Even after World War II, business slumped. Many dressers quit the *kimono* profession; Yorita persisted. In 1953, the newly-formed Japanese Junior Chamber of Commerce started the Cherry Blossom Festival to promote inter-cultural understanding, and Yorita was asked to join its beauty pageant staff. Charm and beauty lessons she had learned so well in Japan were applied to the young women in her charge. She would deftly fold and tie onto each contestant thirty individual garments (two to three *kimono* layers, three *obi, tabi* etc.).

Yorita became a local celebrity. Her presence was sought at cultural events by politicians, businessmen,

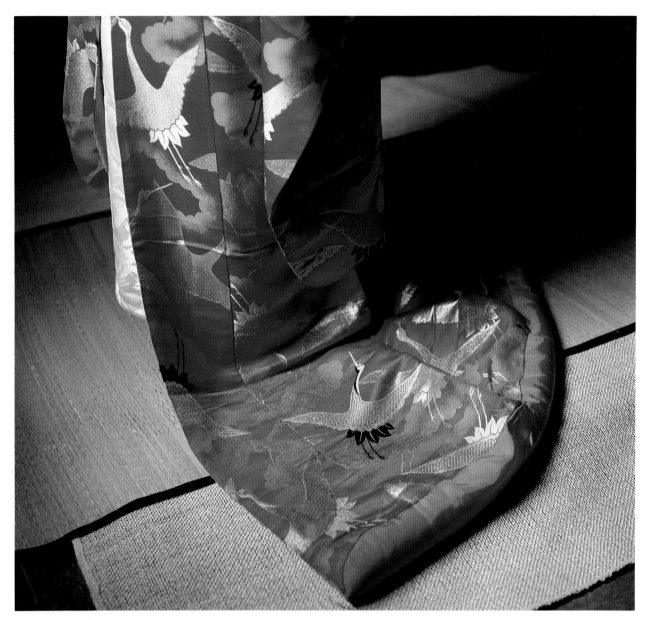

97

and even touring Japanese movie stars such as Toshiro Mifune. A dusty framed photo shows Yorita in her heyday posing with the handsome leading man. The picture says it all: in those post-war years, *kimono* dressing made a comeback— as show business.

The last time I wore a *kimono*, I was eleven years old, readying for the Haleiwa *bon* dance with my cousins. Our mothers would tug off Mickey Mouse T-shirts and pull gangly arms into graceful sleeves that reached our knees. Hair was clasped, or rather winced, into chignons; *obi* became wings; some of us even got rouge on our cheeks. We loved all the fuss and drama that came with the "costume." When we finally flew out the door, giggling, our fathers, uncles and aunts would coo: "*Kirei ne!* How pretty!" Magically, tomboys became girls. And, though none of us ever said it, we also felt curiously Japanese.

Now I'm being groomed as a *yome-san*—bride. Behind me, Yorita constricts a ten-foot long *obi* around my ribs and stops my breathing. All I see are two fists furiously passing it from right to left.

Each time I try to see what she's doing, Yorita tells me to stay still. Finally, she mutters to herself: "*Wakaran.*" Coming around to face me, she drapes a *tsuno-kakushi* over my wig; it is meant to cover the horns of jealously a new bride harbors toward her groom's lovers, past, present or future. She stares intently at the edge of the veil; her fingers coax it into evenness. Then she works on my *kimono* front, where it overlaps.

When I try to straighten up—my neck is sore from bending so long— she says, irritated, "You listen. Don't move around! Don't make head up like this..." She mimics my chin-up, chest-out posture. "Head look only—*massugu*. Look down. Understand?"

like a heap of moultings. *Kimono*, ornaments, wig—each trace of perfection that Yorita labored so long to achieve took seconds to destroy.

Now she grabs my shoulders, smiling. "You *wakarimasu ka*? Understand now?" She starts forming the garments into careful stacks, as I feel a jarring loss. Would she understand if I told her that, while in her *kimono*, I'd felt like a queen who took slow, small steps?

And that for having been shown how sublime a vision could be—even if it lasts but an instant—my hands naturally felt like folding?

"The Kimono Queen" was first published in July/August 1986. Eiko Yorita is now ninety. Because of dimming vision and fingers that are no longer quite as strong or nimble as they used to be, her days of kimono dressing have passed.

Yorita places silver slippers at my feet, then tucks a tiny silver purse halfway into my bodice. Since I had heard that wives used to hide daggers in their clothes with which to commit suicide with their husbands (to avoid disgrace), I ask her if this is true. "No, this one no more knife," she says matter-of-factly.

In 1983, the Hawaii State Legislature read a resolution marking Yorita's official retirement after thirty years with the festival. Today, she still does weddings, and has no intention of ever stopping. "I always like this kind, see? That's why I do."

But demand for wearing the *kimono* has ebbed. Part of the reason is that *kimono* rental is costly, time-consuming and restrictive—you can't dance with guests. Even in Japan, where rental costs for bridal wear are even higher, couples are opting for Western nuptials.

The revival of ethnic pride in the late 1960s to mid-1970s boosted business a bit. "People see 'Roots' on TV, so ring phone," says Yorita. The *sansei* weaned in middle-class American comfort, were eager to reclaim a Japanese heritage as part of their identity.

Yet when I stood before Yorita and peered in her mirror, I saw a "me" I did not recognize at all. I'd been draped in an exquisitely layered shell, but didn't know how to move in it. I held my *sensu* with proper delicacy, but had no modern use for it. Yorita had molded me with Zen-like attention into a living sculpture, but she couldn't curb my feelings of impatience and frustration—or my need to move about uninhibited. Nor could I.

So, the last bit of thick makeup is off; my T-shirt is back on. I marvel at the cast-off layers lying on the mat

Claire Johnson and her family at the Flower Farm.

As a former Mrs. Hawaii, Aloha Week Queen and fashion model, Claire Parker Johnson knows all about glamour, but she has found fulfillment in working the land, "getting very close to what's honest and really clean about living." Aloha aina is her family legacy; her great-great-grandfather was John Palmer Parker, founder of the famed Parker Ranch on 'the Big Island.

Twenty years ago, Johnson began carving her own niche in the business world. Today, she is the president of Flower Farm, Inc., a floral design company and one of the largest bulk retailers of tropical blooms in the state. She has dragged eighteen-foot palm trees through hotel lobbies, cut down coconut fronds at eleven o'clock at night and tramped through muddy fields, scythe in hand, to "get the job done" but she insists, "There is no other work that's more rewarding. I love it, I just love it!"

In 1965, Johnson, her husband Kurt and their children—Ro, Arna and Koa—moved to a beautiful, oceanside home in Kahaluu. Kurt was a jet pilot and colonel in the Hawaii Air National Guard. Said Johnson, "I thought if I could just bring in $200 a month to help out and still be home for the children, I would be so happy."

Johnson saw the potential of growing flowers since their home was surrounded by five acres of fertile soil. The Flower Farm got its start in 1966 with a $200 capital investment and 1,200 red ginger plants that Johnson had obtained from Maunawili Estates in exchange for doing yardwork.

"When I had 1,200 plants in cans, which I got from school cafeterias, I rented a tractor and learned how to plow. I couldn't afford to buy fertilizer so I went to nearby egg farms, hauled out chicken manure and cured it. With the help of my family, I planted a whole field with those 1,200 red ginger plants. I couldn't go anywhere in two years. The weeds grew faster than the plants. I couldn't afford to hire help—my parents would come and help me when they could. Every day, I was out in the fields from early morning, all through the afternoon. Little Koa was scooting all over, getting lost, eating more dirt, earthworms and dog food

CLAIRE PARKER JOHNSON
IN FULL BLOOM
BY CHERYL CHEE TSUTSUMI

that's not romantic. I wanted something that I could look at and admire, something that was beautiful. Flowers celebrate every event in life. They feed your soul."

For Johnson, there were many trials to endure, many lessons to be learned. Two years into the business, she slipped and fell down a hillside with a sickle. One of the fingers on her right hand was cut off. "It took me five years to recuperate emotionally from that accident. But it told me, 'Hey, slow down. Take things slower.' Sometimes I'd put buckets of cut flowers outside and a branch would fall and smash them and I'd have to go out and cut more. Or it would flood after I'd planted a section and I'd see all the flowers—all that hard work—just floating away. I'd have to plant a quarter of an acre all over again. I learned in this business you have to keep your sense of humor."

The Flower Farm is now in full bloom, marketing ti leaves, bird-of-paradise, heliconia, anthuriums, bamboo, fan palms, orchids and other fragrant "exotics." Major clients include airlines, hotels and large conventions. Johnson's first crop of red ginger put $2,000 in the company's bank account; today, the financial records show six-digit figures.

Kurt retired from the Air National Guard two years ago and now serves as Flower Farm's vice-president. "He's so methodical and organized," Johnson said. "He's very good at handling the invoices, accounts receivables and people on the phone. He's learning pricing. There has been no retirement for him. He just jumped into the frenzy of the business."

Ro, Arna and Koa are now pursuing other interests, but when they were young they were mainstays on the farm. From the time they were in the fifth grade, all three paid half of their Punahou tuition with farm earnings. Said Johnson, "I used to work in the fields with them for hours on the weekends when they were growing up. I was lucky I had that opportunity with them. Out there, the children would talk about things they wouldn't talk about at the dining room table. We shared a lot of thoughts. They would just open up. I'd hold my breath and listen because what they were sharing was so precious."

Johnson sees her job as "selling the business." When United Airlines sponsored four months of Hawaii promotions in Europe several years ago, the Flower Farm "provided everything," according to Johnson. "We had to send the leis, flowers, coconut palm leaves, even black sand...The timing was critical because flowers are perishable."

The Flower Farm has also done magnificent floral creations for private parties. One held at the Ilikai Hotel stands out in Johnson's mind. "It was a gourmet dinner done for a very elite group of people. We started planning for it four months in advance. The theme was 'Springtime' and we had a sixty-five-foot stream with carp and ducks swimming in it. We had finches in cages and nymphs sitting on a little island in the middle of a pond. There was a bank of real grass growing around the pond and a burst of spring flowers all around. The hotel provided colored eggs. It was such a challenge to do—but it was just gorgeous. Doing flowers is like doing a painting. It's a creative process. You pour your heart into it."

Last November, Johnson deco-

rated the Hyatt Regency's ballroom with $5,000 worth of donated flowers for a Family Stress Center benefit. "I'd love to do it again. When you start in business, you're very hungry, you can only think of bringing (the money) in. Then there comes a point in your marriage with the business where you want to give it back. That's where I am now."

In addition to directing business operations, Johnson still does all her own cooking and house cleaning. "Sometimes I feel like a juggler. I start the laundry at four o'clock in the morning. I like to start work then because it's quiet and I can get so much done. By the time eight o'clock comes, I've had four hours of work. I sleep only about four hours every night. People sleep too much. A lot of time is wasted sleeping. Late at night, I'm thinking, thinking, thinking about all kinds of ideas.

"I have a lot of energy. I'm fifty-three years old going on fourteen right now. I can still climb a lychee tree, I still run, I still leap over the sidewalk. Life is so much fun and it keeps getting better."

Johnson has been lauded on several occasions as one of the state's outstanding women in business. She is philosophical about her success: "Nature is the most powerful teacher of all. Something happened to me in the process of learning from nature. Patience, endurance, appreciation... the gift has been profound."

"In Full Bloom" was first published in November/December 1986. Claire Johnson and her Flower Farm are still flourishing.

in his baby life than any other kid because he was never in a playpen. He had complete freedom of the place.

"My friends all laughed at me and said, 'Sure, you're going to go from modeling to farming. Yeah, uh huh.' I'd cry at the end of the day because I couldn't even move. Then the next morning, I'd be all fresh and I'd start all over again. Like in any business—it doesn't matter what your dream is—there's always going to be the person who'll say, 'Too bad, you should've planted beans instead. At least you can eat them.' But for me,

The "Mayor of Waikiki."

WAIKIKI'S GOLDEN BOY

BY THELMA CHANG

With a crew of malihini paddlers on board, Steamboat gets set to launch his outrigger.

On this typically sunny Waikiki morning, the silver-blue Pacific is a playground for thousands of swimmers and surfers. One in particular stands out in the waves—a sturdy, husky Hawaiian who rides his surfboard with such ease and grace it looks as though he is one with the ocean.

"Steamboat? You say you're looking for Sammy Steamboat?" says a young woman tending a kiosk promoting canoe rides, surfboard rentals and lessons. "That's him over there—he's walking up now."

His exhilarating ride over, the surfer has paddled to shore and seated himself quietly under the shade of a tree near the kiosk. After watching Steamboat's thrilling performance, it's difficult to believe he's approaching seventy. Crinkles around his eyes and silver hair and eyebrows—a striking contrast to his beautifully bronzed skin—are the only visible hints of his age.

Steamboat is regarded as the unofficial "Mayor of Waikiki" in recognition of his more than fifty years of service as a lifeguard, beachboy and water safety instructor. Of pure Hawaiian blood, he is considered by many to be a cultural treasure.

"Everybody calls me Steamboat," he says. "Not too many people know my real name is Sam Mokuahi. I use the name 'Steamboat' because it's easier for people to say...I remember my dad told this story over and over to us—that my grandmother and grandfather were traveling on a boat from Kau (on the Big Island) to Oahu when my grandmother gave birth to my father...The captain named him 'Steamboat,' then I took over his name."

Steamboat, the eldest of four children, including an adopted brother, was born in Kakaako, today an industrial area near downtown Honolulu. "In the old days, Hawaiian people lived over there—they had a homestead thing going. My family was so poor, I never had time to finish school. In my young days I used to go down to the river, catch fish, sell it. In those days, a few cents was a lot. You could buy a whole aku for twenty-five cents." Steamboat also helped support his family by shining shoes and selling newspapers, among other jobs.

He remembers a job he held as a youth near what is now Ala Moana Shopping Center. "The beachside of Ala Moana was all rubbish dump and I used to dig up that rubbish pile, which sometimes they dumped right next to the road," says Steamboat, whose mother used to send him off to work with his favorite lunch—a peach jelly sandwich. "A single man earned a dollar a day, a married man two dollars."

Some of his memories are dark reminders of the social and political ethos of certain periods in Hawaii's history. He vividly recalls the infamous Massie case of the 1930s, in which a young, haole Navy officer's wife accused five Island men of raping her. In spite of evidence that contradicted Thalia Massie's shaky story and proved the men's innocence, Massie's mother, husband and

103

To Steamboat—
with very best wishes from
Deborah Kerr

Movie star Deborah Kerr enjoys a ride on the Pacific waves with Steamboat.

Navy friends kidnapped Joseph Kahahawai, one of the accused, and shot him to death. The murderers were convicted, but territorial Governor Lawrence Judd commuted their ten-year sentences to just one hour in the custody of the high sheriff. The tragic incident continues to haunt Hawaii even today.

"I came from the same place where all those guys came from—Vineyard," says Steamboat. "See, we moved from Kakaako to the Vineyard Street area (near downtown Honolulu) when I was young. They were nice men and Joseph Kahahawai was an especially good man. What happened was too bad...I don't know how to put it into words."

After fulfilling military obligations during World War II (he worked with the Navy's underwater submarine detection team laying communications cables in the ocean), Steamboat began his service at Waikiki Beach. "Because there was martial law here, this place was all barbed wire, fenced up and down the beach...Back then, the only places beachboys hung around were at the Royal Hawaiian Hotel and the Moana. Waikiki Beach was not like it is today—fewer people and a beach that measured oh, not more than twenty feet (from the edge of the sea to the hotels). The biggest beach was right in front of where the Outrigger Hotel is today. The Royal Hawaiian also had a big part of the beach."

During his many years on the beach in Waikiki, Steamboat has befriended people from all over the world, including such luminaries as Cary Grant, Adlai Stevenson, Gabby Hayes, James Cagney, Deborah Kerr, Judy Garland, Martha Raye and Red Skelton. (He also claims a bit of Hollywood fame himself; he has played supporting roles in several films shot in Hawaii, including *The Old Man and the Sea*.)

"David Niven wanted to go canoe riding with me so much he waited for me every morning," chuckles Steamboat. "He brought me a lot of business because everybody else wanted to come along with us. Niven rode that canoe all day long. I met Alan Ladd long before Niven. He rode the canoe with me once a day when he was in Hawaii. He loved that."

Whether it's canoe paddling, swimming or surfing, Steamboat says children are the easiest to teach. "You tell older people what to do and they think, 'Should I or shouldn't I?' But children just do it. I tell them it's fun to ride the surfboard in but first you've got to work hard to get out there. That's a lesson in life. If I had a whole bunch of kids right now, I'd raise them all on the beach."

For Steamboat, the sea holds meaning that runs as deep as its waters. "I have a lot of friends out there," he says, looking out over the waves. "I took quite a few of them out there, burying their ashes at sea as they wished. My former wife is out there...We take the ashes way out there (in a canoe) and when I stop, all the other canoes surround the boat and make a big circle. Each canoe carries flowers and people who knew the deceased. Some people say a prayer. After we pour the ashes, we put all the flowers into the ocean."

Steamboat belongs to a special breed of beachboys whose lessons often go far beyond the fundamentals of surfing. "In the old days, we took the time to (explain things) to people. And the beach was a different thing, too, because all of the beachboys worked together and if you ever got out of line they would find a way to get you out. Not only one says you've got to go. The whole group agrees. You had to have a good reputation on the beach. That's the way it was."

Memorabilia fills Steamboat's Waikiki apartment, which he shares with his Kansas-born wife, Barbara. (They met while she was on a visit to Hawaii during the late 1970s.) Pic-

Steamboat (back row, center) on the beach with a group of distinguished friends, including comedian Red Skelton (far right). All photos c. 1950s.

tures—including those of his four sons, daughter and many grandchildren—fill scrapbooks and boxes. Three of Steamboat's five children are adopted; one came into his life unexpectedly. "A woman bartender friend says to me one night, 'My daughter has a baby and doesn't want it.' So I said, 'I'll take him.' He's twenty-one now and lives in California. He's my boy."

Two large koa paddles engraved with "Steamboat," a gift from friends, grace one wall. Photos, including one of the late Duke Kahanamoku, decorate another wall. Duke, an Olympic swimming champion, was a close friend of Steamboat's. "A beautiful man," says Steamboat. "I watched him surf. That's why I stand up the way I do (on my board) and relax while surfing. You recognized him by the way he stood."

One morning in 1959, when Steamboat was living in Kailua, on the windward side of Oahu, a powerful tidal wave hit Hilo on the Big Island. Strong reverberations were felt on Oahu. Recalls Steamboat, "I saw this huge wave and I told myself, 'What the hell's going on?' Then I thought, 'Oh my God, I'd like to go surfing.'"

That's probably what you'll find Steamboat doing on any given day in Waikiki. The area's changes are apparent—crowds, traffic, pedicabs, delivery trucks, all vying for their place in the sun. But if you look at the ocean long enough, you're sure to spot Steamboat—a man who stands tall on his surfboard, a man who appears to be one with the ocean, just as he has been for the last fifty-years.

"Waikiki's Golden Boy" was first published in January/February 1988. Although a bad coral cut has slowed his activities in the water somewhat, seventy-three-year-old Sammy Steamboat still enjoys "taking it easy" on the beach in Waikiki.

CHAPTER FOUR: OUR ARTS

LEIS

LOVE THEM AND WEAVE THEM

BY JODI BELKNAP

"Anyone can make a lei, and you can make a lei out of anything!" Malia Solomon joined us beachside at the Halekulani Hotel in Waikiki for a breakfast conversation about Hawaii's lovely garlands made from flowers, ferns, shells, seeds and feathers, and worn by nearly everyone.

An expert on Hawaiian and Polynesian handicrafts, Solomon has been showing eager students and visitors how to create leis for years. She says, "One of our regulars here, a retired schoolteacher who comes down every Tuesday for lunch with her friends, always wears a haku lei on her hat made from whatever happens to be blooming in her yard. She plucks a little bougainvillea, a little of this or that...After all, it's not what's in a lei, but the way it's put together that matters."

Implied, but not spoken, is a principle about the special feeling that goes into creating a lei. A *National Geographic* writer once wrote that a lei was "Hawaii's most tangible expression of aloha." Solomon makes it clear that this is so, with all the attendant meanings expressed by the word aloha. Leis are to enjoy. They are to enhance notable events in life. They are to share. Above all, leis are a gift of love.

Lovely blossom.

107

Best friends Celeste Noelani Kalama and Celina Kanoelani Chow.

There's no exclusivity about who wears leis in Hawaii. Babies, the governor's wife and teen-age boys wear them. Even dust-laden paniolo out rounding up strays on the Big Island wear hats adorned with bands of bright blossoms picked that morning, or, more permanently, of brilliantly colored feathers.

Leis are for special occasions, but it doesn't take much for an occasion to be special enough. A weekly lunch date with friends will do, and, of course, the arrival of a visitor from the Mainland always requires a lei.

Presenting a lei in friendship or wearing one yourself is one of the oldest customs in Polynesia. Ethnologists believe it originated in Asia about 17,000 years ago and traveled to Hawaii with the daring navigators who plied Pacific seas in sturdy canoes. Those early explorers packed their vessels carefully with plants and animals to provide future food supplies: breadfruit, taro, pigs and chickens. In spite of limited space, they included one flowering plant—awapuhi—the blooms of which would be used for leis and headdresses in the new land. This wild ginger, with its heady fragrance, still is one of the favorite flowers for a lei in Hawaii.

At one time, the wearing of leis evolved around ceremonies to appease and honor gods and goddesses, especially those linked with the hula. Leis were made of perishable flowers, ferns and vines gathered in mountain rain forests and placed on the altars of a hula halau before the dance began. Leis were also created from seeds, bone, whale's teeth and feathers. Royalty wore the lei niho

palaoa, fashioned from tightly braided shanks of human hair attached to a hook-like ornament carved from a whale's tooth. Those of ruling rank, the alii, also wore feather leis; yellow and orange were the preferred colors.

Later, the use of leis grew. Mary Kawena Pukui, a respected authority on Hawaiian language and tradition, once said that the word itself means many things: a baby, lovingly remembered by those who reared it, or a sweetheart, or a chanted poem accompanying the gift of a flower garland to someone highly esteemed. Affection is very much a part of lei-making and giving.

Many customs and celebrations involving leis in Hawaii today are twentieth-century introductions. For example, in recent decades when the *Lurline* and other cruise ships sailed away from the Islands, departing passengers waited until the ship was passing Diamond Head before tossing their farewell leis into the sea. If the lei drafted ashore, they were assured of returning to Hawaii someday.

In 1928, Don Blanding, an Island writer and poet, initiated Lei Day, now an annual celebration on May 1 that includes a lei-making competition. Hundreds of gorgeous creations are entered by talented lei-makers on every island. All go on public exhibit at the Waikiki Shell in Kapiolani Park on May Day.

A custom dating from World War II, when there were so many servicemen in Hawaii, is that of presenting a lei with a kiss. Pukui relates that a U.S.O. entertainer was dared by friends to kiss an officer seated at ringside one evening. At first she couldn't think of a good enough excuse. Then suddenly, she removed her lei, placed it on his shoulders, kissed him and declared, "This is a Hawaiian custom." And so has everyone else since.

Another introduced practice, inspired most likely by the Mainland

Maunaloa lei.

tradition of ribbon cutting at the opening of a new road or transportation service, is that of untying a maile lei at the dedication of any new enterprise in Hawaii. It's important, however, that maile be untied, not cut, since a lei also signifies the encompassing love of a family and should not be intentionally harmed.

Hawaii has many holidays when leis are more in evidence than usual. One of the most impressive is celebrated during the second weekend in June to honor King Kamehameha, the Islands' first monarch. The main event is a Saturday parade from Iolani Palace through Waikiki. Each of the major Hawaiian islands spon-

Beautiful leis adorn a Hawaiian entertainer on an Aloha Week Parade float, Waikiki.

Pau rider in front of Iolani Palace.

sors a princess who rides a horse sidesaddle in the parade. She wears a pau, sixteen yards of satin or velvet wrapped around her in girdle fashion and fastened by six kukui nuts tucked in at the waist in a special fold. Completing her costume, which was first worn in the late 1800s, is a haku lei and headdress created from plants and flowers symbolizing the island she represents.

During the Kamehameha Day parade, you'll see the lei of the island of Hawaii, fashioned from feathery red lehua blossoms. These flowers grow on gnarled ohia trees found high on barren volcanic mountainsides.

Maui's lei is made from the pink lokelani, an introduced flower familiar to many as the Castilian rose. In Hawaiian, lokelani means "rose of heaven."

Tiny white blossoms tucked into a thick background of silver-green leaves from the native kukui tree create Molokai's lei. (Fine permanent leis also are made from black, brown and ivory kukui nuts. Leis were not made from the nuts before Europeans arrived in Hawaii but they are popular today, especially for men.)

Hinahina, a beach plant with small white flowers and narrow green leaves, provides material for the rarely seen lei of Kahoolawe, the unin-

A tutu with an armful of leis joins in a May Day celebration, Kapiolani Park, Waikiki.

habited island off Maui which is used by the U.S. Navy as a target for bombing practice.

Dozens of feathery strings of kaunaoa, a leafless parasitic vine, are twisted together to form a stringy, pale orange lei to represent the island of Lanai. Green berries the size of a fingertip and dark, oblong leaves from the native mokihana tree, found only on Kauai, are used for that island's anise-scented lei which lasts as long as the berries take to turn slowly from pale green to brown.

Niihau, the privately-owned island east of Kauai, is symbolized by a shell, not a flower. Strings of pupu Niihau, ivory colored shells shaped like puffed rice and called momi by pure-blooded Hawaiians who live on the island, are strung into highly cherished keepsake leis. Niihau shell leis are rare and costly. A few that are made on the island are on sale at the Bishop Museum. Others occasionally may be purchased at local festivals for prices starting at several hundred dollars for a lei with three or more strands.

Oahu's lei is made from a small, yellow-orange flower, the ilima. It takes 400 to 600 tightly packed blossoms to make one strand of a traditional, waist-length ilima lei. Princess Abigail Kawananakoa, a descendent of King David Kalakaua, who encouraged the revival of the Hawaiian culture in the 1880s, is especially fond of wearing ilima leis. Perhaps because of her admiration for the lei, it has been linked with royalty and is reserved for important people and events.

It's nine o'clock at night and the lights are still on at Mamala Flower Shop, off Kapiolani Boulevard in Honolulu. Inside, manager Barbara Meheula deftly arranges a floral piece for an early morning delivery. At a table beside her, two friends kui or maneuver a long needle through tiny pink rosebuds to make strands for a lei.

Mamala Flower Shop has been open only a year and a half, but everyone works from 6:00 A.M. to 10:00 P.M., seven days a week, to fill the orders pouring in. The rigorous schedule is partly the result of an exciting phenomenon in the Islands. A Hawaiian renaissance is underway; the arts of old Hawaii—the hula, chanting and lei-making among them—are attracting public and private acclaim. Mamala Flower Shop specializes in the lei made as it was in old Hawaii.

From a large refrigerator Meheula retrieves a sturdy tubular sheath cut from a banana tree. About four inches wide, a foot-and-a-half long and cut in half lengthwise, it is a puolo, a container which is used to properly carry a lei to its recipient. Plastic bags are not used in the shop. Instead, finished leis are put in puolo or baskets made from ti, bamboo, palm leaves or coconut leaves.

Meheula removes the top half of the puolo; resting inside is the most beautiful lei I have ever seen. Deep, wine red lehua blossoms nestle in their own small, chartreuse green leaves in a lei for a headdress or hat. The effect is otherworldly. A finishing touch at each end is a bit of palapalai fern. "We use only palapalai in the shop," Meheula says. Together with lehua blossoms, the maile vine and three other plants, it's a fern sacred to Kapo and Laka, goddesses of the hula. The headdress she has created is a lehua laulii lei, as fine a one as any hula dancer might have been proud to wear a thousand years ago.

Poomai Kawananakoa, a descendent of Abigail, owns the shop. "Miss Kawananakoa wanted to offer the forgotten kinds of Hawaiian things," Meheula explains. Materials for these leis are collected in the mountains of Kauai, Maui and the island of Hawaii. Rare or hard-to-obtain items are gleaned from contacts who know where to find them on all the islands.

Five old-style methods are used to make the leis. Hili is a braided lei

Flowers...all kinds...all colors.

made entirely of ferns, vines or other greenery. Haku, another braided lei, includes blossoms backed by greenery. Wili is a lei of both blossoms and greenery wound tightly together. Humuhumu is a sewn lei (large leis for horses are made by sewing). Kui is a strung lei.

"There are forty-five kinds of maile," Meheula says. "We only use one kind, maile laulii. It's strong, with small leaves." About fifteen maile leis made for the shop by a family in the up-country of Kauai are brought in each week for weddings and other notable events. An open lei, maile is worn around the shoulders with long ends hanging in front. Those from the shop are braided together with three strands of the vine so the ends won't unravel.

Ginger leis are another Mamala specialty, made with three intertwining strings instead of one. The result is fragrant and fat, like the soft down of a plump bird's breast. A two-string ginger lei is Meheula's favorite "because they are so dainty to wear."

There are hundreds of legends about flowers and leis. One Meheula relates is about the ieie flowers: Once when gods and men lived in closer proximity to each other, two young lovers longed to marry. For reasons of their own, the gods forbade the union. Despairing, the lovers ran away, far into a mountain rain forest. The gods found them and held a discussion to decide on an appropriate punishment. While they deliberated, the young lovers made a solemn vow that no matter what happened they would seek each other out and unite. Overhearing this, and not being altogether heartless, the gods changed the girl into the exotic pink and green ieie blossom which grows on a vine that is a parasite of the ohia tree. The boy was changed into an apapane bird, so he could seek the ieie in bloom and unite with it.

Visitors to Hawaii frequently are given leis fashioned from tiny, violet vanda orchids. Bred to their small size as a hybrid, vandas are raised in large fields on the island of Hawaii. They're sturdy and long-lasting. Thousands are shipped as leis to the Mainland and Canada annually. A popular style of vanda lei is the maunaloa, in which petals of the flowers are tucked closely together to make an attractive arrangement that lies flat.

More fragile than vanda orchids, but just as popular, is plumeria, or frangipani. Fifty years ago, plumeria trees grew largely in Hawaii's graveyards, and their fragrant yellow, white or pink blooms were not often used for leis. But the plumeria has come a long way since then. On Kamehameha Day every June, dozens of king-size, forty-foot plumeria leis dangle from the statue of Hawaii's first monarch in front of Honolulu's Judiciary Building. They resemble the yellow feather cloaks that royalty once wore in the Islands.

Other popular leis are made from pikake and tuberose. Both are cream-colored and highly fragrant, especially the small, bell-shaped pikake, named in honor of Princess Kaiulani. Pikake is the Hawaiian word for "peacock." The beautiful princess, who lived where the hotel named for her is located today, raised peacocks on her estate near the turn of the century.

Carnations—red, white, pink, multi-colored and sometimes dyed other colors like blue—make lovely, thick leis. Another favorite lei is made from crown flowers—sturdy little white or lavender blossoms resembling miniature crowns. Two leis available seasonally in Hawaii at lei stands are the cigar flower lei and the hala lei. The cigar flower lei, or pua kiki lei, is made from about 2,000 half-inch-long tubular flowers. It will dry out and can then be kept for months. The hala lei, made from a small green-and-gold angular section of the seed from a hala tree, is a favorite lei for New Year's. A traditional Hawaiian lei, it is also long-lasting.

You can try your hand at making a flower lei at home. Kui is the easiest method to use. In Hawaii, twelve-inch needles are available, but a long upholstery needle will do. Thread it with strong, Number Ten white cotton thread. Use a double thickness of thread about a foot longer than you want the finished lei to be.

Pick the flowers you've chosen when they have just bloomed, so they'll last. Any flower with a relatively sturdy center can be used. Run your needle through the bottom of each flower and out the top, through the center. When the needle is full, gentle push the flowers down on the thread, as close together as possible without crushing them. Repeat until the right length is reached. Tie the ends of thread together and trim to finish.

For variety, mix two or more flowers together. Experiment with buds or leaving a little greenery on your blossoms. And, as you work, remember what a lei should be—a little gift of love.

"Leis: Love Them and Weave Them" was first published in April-May-June 1978. Today, "Aunty" Malia Solomon shares her knowledge about leis and other aspects of the Hawaiian culture from her "home base" at the Hyatt Regency Waikiki. Lei-making expert Barbara Meheula has relocated to the Big Island, where she is in charge of creating all the floral arrangements for the Mauna Kea Beach Hotel.

Necklaces made from rare Niihau shells make very lovely accessories.

It takes great skill and patience to create intricate leis like this haku.

Kumu hula Frank Hewett, dressed in the bounty of Oahu's forest.

Detail of a hibiscus blossom.

A traditional tea room in Gojo, Japan depicts different uses of paper in its shoji *windows, painted screens and* fusuma *or paper-covered sliding doors.*

TRACING THE ART OF PAPER

BY JOCELYN FUJII
PHOTOGRAPHY BY FRANCO SALMOIRAGHI/PHOTO RESOURCE

T here are few things in life that bear the simple utility or the fragile magnificence of paper. From the currency that changes hands daily, to the scrolls and scriptures of the ancients, to the Lockean plains of white sheets that move thoughts or freeze a form, paper imbues our lives with reflections of culture and time.

Hawaiian kapa beaters.

As it is with traditions of old, the making of this marvelous substance presents yet another glimpse into worlds, thoughts and values far beyond our own. Eons have elapsed since the techniques of papermaking are said to have traveled from China to Japan in 600 A.D., or since the days when the making of kapa, the cloth-like paper of the Hawaiians, thrived as art, industry and ceremony in pre-Western Hawaii. Yet there are those in Hawaii today who would make the long reach into history to honor and revive those ancient traditions, to celebrate this surface called paper and explore the cultural and aesthetic dimensions of a long overlooked art form.

"It's primarily a going back," reflects Ann Kimura, director of the Temari Center for Asian and Pacific Fibers. "People are going back and trying to discover the sources. Whether you're a painter, writer or watercolor artist, the idea is to go back to the source, to control yet another variable—and that medium is called paper."

Montage of paper designed by Yoichi and Mieko Fujimori.

"The movement in Western and Japanese papermaking started on the Mainland," adds Beatrice Krauss, ethnobotanist at the Lyon Arboretum. "People became interested in books, book-binding and then papermaking. Suddenly in art schools, people wanted to make their own paper."

Honolulu artist Marcia Morse was one of those people. Acknowledged as a primary force in the movement here, Morse uses Western and Asian techniques in making her own paper, then uses that paper in her sculptures, books and tapestries. She says, "I think the reason I make my own paper is that it brings into play so many things—botany, chemistry, history, visual and tactile qualities. I'm an independent sort, and to be able to do it myself is really important. I had to ask myself, what did I need in order to do the work I wanted to do? The more I became involved in making paper, the more I became involved in what the different qualities of paper should say."

In 1980, an international symposium on tapa, Oriental and Western papermaking techniques drew more than 100 participants from four nations to the Honolulu Academy of Arts. They compared techniques and explored the use of tropical fibers, giving root and shape to what was to become an international exchange with a firm niche in Hawaii. In 1983, two Island artists held forth at a tapa-making conference in Kyoto, Japan at which Nepalese, Egyptian, Italian and other papermakers joined in the making of kapa (as Hawaiian tapa is called), demonstrating its place in the world scheme of papermaking.

With interest burgeoning and participants growing in number, last year saw a proliferation of programs, with visiting artists from Japan and, most recently, an international juried exhibit of book arts, right here in the Islands. In January of 1985, leading kapa proponent Pua Van Dorpe unveiled her astounding new work in a series of statewide lectures for the Bishop Museum and the State Foundation on Culture and the Arts.

Artists point to the abundance of native fibers as one reason for the resurgence here. They have only to look to the hills to locate and harvest the fibers that will be cooked, pounded and shaped into handmade sheets of paper. If wauke, or paper mulberry, was difficult to find initially, there has always been breadfruit, hau, banana and many other workable fibers. Papermakers here have ready access to the Orient as well, to the carriers of the Asian traditions that are dominant in Hawaii and which have shaped the worldwide evolution of the craft.

But Hawaii stands alone in the mystery and quality of its own indigenous kapa, revered as the most highly evolved and refined of the many forms of Polynesian paper. While tapa-making still thrives in South Pacific islands, kapa is among the several native art forms that dwindled and eventually vanished from Hawaii with the advent of the West. As a result, authentic Hawaiian kapa is today a rare and elusive entity, reserved for coveted private collections, the Bishop Museum or British museums, where the best examples are said to be stored.

A collection of some sixty-five kapa originals made its way from the hands of a collector into the Lahaina home of Puanani Kanemura Van Dorpe and her husband, Bob. Discovered in Big Island caves, the impeccably preserved kapa pieces date back to the eighteenth and nineteenth centuries. Today, they serve as the standard against which Pua Van Dorpe measures her work.

On this day in Lahaina, Van Dorpe is jubilant. One of her newest successes is a jet black kapa of uncommon perfection, pounded of wauke in traditional Hawaiian fashion and dyed by the natural minerals of a taro field, where it steeped for ten

Pua Van Dorpe examines bast that will be pounded into kapa cloth.

days in the primordial ooze of the earth. It is a triumph, yes, but it's the other piece that excites Van Dorpe.

"I've been beating this piece for three months," she says, displaying an auburn square made from the bark of mamaki, an indigenous Hawaiian plant second only to wauke in the making of kapa. "Although I did fifty previous experiments with mamaki, it was very hard to get it right. This was cooked in an imu with palaa fern to get the right color. This is the first time it's been done in at least 125 years.

"For the past nine years," she continues, "every time I've done an experiment, I take a sample and put it under the microscope to compare against the kapa originals. After nine years of experimenting, I finally got the mamaki to match. My heart stopped beating when I saw it!"

A peek into the microscope reveals that the fiber patterns of her twentieth-century recreation are identical to those of her Big Island kapa original, down to the finest detail of thin and thick areas forming even, parallel, microscopic ridges of fiber. For those of us generally conditioned to judging kapa on its cosmetic merits, this infinitesimal match of fibers presents a new standard of excellence—and a level of integrity impossible to fathom otherwise.

"People look at a piece of kapa and say, 'I want the one with that design,'" says Bob Van Dorpe, project director for Amfac's Hawaiian Sea Village and the Living Arts Center. "But think of the effort involved: It took Pua 500 hours to beat one single sheet of kapa just in the fiber stage and ten hours to do the design. Pua would tell me about the pain involved in doing her work. She beat kapa eight hours a day. She's wanted to quit so many times. Unless you look at the fibers at this level—beyond the cosmetic—it's impossible to understand what the craft was about or what went into it. The kapa maker was making a statement, he was doing something beyond the utilitarian."

The alii of old could be born and could die in kapa. It was used for clothing, peace offerings, and ceremonies marking birth, marriage, death or any other significant occasion. It was used to appease the tax collector or to impress a bride-to-be. And as Bob Van Dorpe points out, it was a feat of measureless commitment to beat, ferment and watermark the bark to achieve the ultimate expression—a perfectly seamless sheet of kapa.

In Japan, where centuries-old techniques are still applied by a dwindling number of papermakers, the reawakening of the West to the values of the craft is making a perceptible difference. "For America, when you see handmade paper, you think it's an art," said Yoichi Fujimori on a visit to the Temari Center this year. Fujimori, a seventh-generation papermaker from Japan, spoke through an interpreter. "That idea is affecting Japan. In Japan, a papermaker is not an artist. He is the one who makes paper for the artist. The papermaker just makes paper from fiber, the kind of paper the artist wants for his own work. Handmade paper is just starting to move into the category of art."

But while attitudes toward the process may differ, the fibers used in kapa and *washi*—Japanese handmade paper—bear striking similarities. The staple of kapa makers was wauke, a close relative of *kozo*, for centuries the most commonly used fiber for *washi*. *Gampi*, similar to the Hawaiians' akia, and *mitsumata* of the Daphne family, are the other two fibers prevalent in Japan, where large tracts of *gampi* are cultivated and entire mountains may be blanketed with wild *kozo*.

In Hawaii, however, the twentieth-century papermakers have had to forage in the wilds for the wauke trees to support their initial endeavors. Pua Van Dorpe recalls her first bonanza, in the plentitude of the Maui wilderness.

"In the beginning, there was no wauke that we knew of," she remembers. "And then one day I went into Iao Valley with a forester, and he found a patch of about 900 wauke plants, overgrown and surrounded by ti leaves and next to it was a patch of mamaki." That patch fueled the papermaking revival, providing slips and cuttings for arboretums and the backyards of those who would nurture them.

There are other suitable fibers as

Sheets of washi *dry on an "iron" heated by burning wood.*

well, and the selection of the plant source depends on the artist's intentions. "For me, it all depends on how I will use the paper," explains Marcia Morse. "For example, some fibers will take printing better than others. If it's a tapestry I'm working on, I'm looking for a paper with body, a paper that will flex and bend. For a collage, it's texture and color I'm looking for." Her favorites among the local fibers, she says, are banana, ginger and heliconia stalks.

Wauke, most popularly used by local craftsmen for both *washi* and kapa, is harvested in even, slender strips, to be soaked and softened until the outer layer can be removed and only the inner bark remains. As they did in old Hawaii, Van Dorpe uses the sharp edge of a shell to

scrape off the outer layer. The clean coils of bast are soaked for varying periods until soft enough to be pounded into the moomoo stage. The moomoo, by this time expanded in width, can be dried and stored until needed.

Water is critical for the soaking, fermenting and preparation of the bark and the dyes, and for this Van Dorpe uses only saltwater from the ocean and fresh water from the streams of Iao Valley. Her jug of stream water is never empty; she may fill her calabash with seawater or she may take the fibers to the sea.

Van Dorpe will wrap the bast in a ti leaf bundle and head for the Lahaina shores, where the relentless rhythm of the ocean and the relative seclusion of a well-chosen spot can be counted on to do their part. In a historic and romantic return, she will submerge the bundle securely beneath the shoreline rocks buffeted by waves, where the fibers will ferment for up to two weeks in the salt-laden richness of the sea.

Those utilizing Japanese techniques for *washi* have their own rituals of preparation. In Japan, the bast may sit in the river or lie on snow, to be bleached with the action of the sun—or, as is more commonly done today, it will be bleached with chemicals. Because the sap-hardened stalks are harvested in winter, steaming is required to separate the usable bark from the stalk. The bast is soaked and stripped with a knife, then cooked in alkali solutions to disengage the darker, residual fragments of unwanted bark. Then the hand-filtering begins as laborers pick out the fragments by hand. "This is the suffering involved in making paper," Fujimori told his class at Temari last spring. "This is the part of paper-making that requires patience and commitment."

Most contemporary Japanese paper factories use mechanized wooden beaters, leaving the back-breaking process of pounding to the purview of traditionalists like Van Dorpe—or to the eager pursuits of Temari's students, who devoted the greater part of their workshop to cleaning and pounding the strands until they were transformed into pulp. The casting of endless strokes of the mallet onto mounds of resilient fiber has distinctively different roles in the making of kapa and *washi*.

Bea Krauss explains it this way: "In beating kapa, you're keeping the fibers discreet. But in making *washi*, you're reducing the fibers to a fine pulp." The kapa maker's beating refines the bark into ever thinner, wider sheets, each strip beaten into the next in a perfectly seamless expansion. The watermarking that distinguishes kapa from other types of

Polynesian paper is achieved again through pounding as the kapa maker wields a native wood mallet incised with a traditional design. It is the carefully orchestrated strokes of the mallet that etches the watermark into the sheet.

With *washi*, the finely beaten pulp separates into loose fibers that are stirred up in vats of water and mucilage, then scooped up in molded screens that shape the sheets to be dried. The papermaker determines the thickness and evenness of the paper in the scooping, dipping and sloshing motions that spread the fibers across the screen. The mucilage, or *neri*, is derived from a plant of the hibiscus family and possesses the quality of preventing the sheets from sticking together, so they can be stacked to be dried or dried individually.

"Today, there are only about seven people in Japan who still make papermaking frames," says Yoichi Fujimori. "They're made of cypress wood, to support the screens of thin bamboo. There are a certain number of bamboo sticks per centimeter on a screen. If you change the number of bamboo sticks, you get a different type and texture of paper."

The screen resembles a highly refined version of a bamboo blind or *sushi* roller. The sticks are held together with silk thread that's been treated with persimmon tannin, a necessary ingredient on the edge of non-existence. "There is one person alive in the world who prepares this silk thread," Fujimori explains with sadness and awe. "She is very old. There may be no one to replace her."

The implements of the kapa maker made their leap into extinction long ago. Were it not for the research and craftsmanship of woodcarvers who must work closely with the kapa maker, there would be no revival of the craft. Le Van Sequeira is such a craftsman, a Maui purist who has researched traditional Hawaiian im-

Van Dorpe wraps bast in ti leaves, in preparation for soaking in the sea.

plements and idols since 1962. He has carved full-sized and model canoes of unimpeachable authenticity. He is also the carver of Pua Van Dorpe's kapa tools.

"I kept running back to Le Van and saying, 'Could you go a little deeper on this design, could you lighten up there?'" Van Dorpe says as she displays her beaters, each one made of native wood. "We had to experiment all the time and redo the tools many, many times. We identified one eighteenth-century original by the way it was so crudely made. The kapa fibers showed us that the beaters weren't refined—it was before metal tools had arrived. You can see in the kapa fibers just when metal tools came. The fibers became finer and finer. Finally, the Hawaiians were able to carve the beaters so they got twenty-two ridges to an inch. It was that precise."

A round beater is used in the initial stages of beating and a square mallet, the ie kuku, for the refining and texturizing of the fiber. The ie kuku bears a different design on each of four sides, providing a tactile repertoire for watermarking. The foundation for the beating is the stone or wooden anvil, called the kua. In Van Dorpe's lau hala-lined halau in Lahaina, the anvils lie beside bast-filled calabashes and the stone mortars and pestles used for preparing the natural dyes.

There are vials of exotic potions and powders made from finely ground alaea, a dense red clay from Kauai, or from the black soot she collects by inverting a calabash over burning kukui nuts. The rich brown bark of kukui trees, the ground-up powder of coral, the skins and pulp of berries—all are ingredients in the wide-ranging palette for which Hawaiian tapa was renowned.

The Hawaiians achieved elegant pastels in blues, yellows and pinks as well as the primal blacks and browns that adorn all South Pacific tapa. Kapa was immersed after the beating

stage or stamped with specially carved bamboo markers. The markers were dipped in dye and applied in intricately prescribed patterns, and the colors were fixed with mordants derived from grasses or the gum of trees.

Van Dorpe has adopted with zeal the culture's pursuit of color. In the waning days of spring, she takes to the Maui wilds to comb the foliage for the bright red dots of akala, the wild Hawaiian raspberry that was the source of kapa pink.

"The akala season lasts only twenty-five days for the whole year," she explains. "In the old days, they had to be ready to use the akala in the short time it was fruiting. So I thought, this must have been the time of year, around spring, when everything was fruiting and at its highest, that the Hawaiians beat their kapa. They could beat the kapa and get ready for the makahiki in November, when they paid their taxes in kapa. And the patterns—going painstakingly, row by row with the bamboo markers, I had to realize how clever they were. The Hawaiians had no rulers, they had no tools for drawing lines, they got their dyes from the forest."

According to Bea Krauss, it was the ukiuki berry, another endemic plant, that provided the indigo and purple of ancient kapa. "The ukiuki extraction gave a purplish blue which disappointed me," she says. "I happened to have some soapy water nearby, and some of it fell on the dyed kapa by accident—it turned the color into a beautiful bright indigo.

"If you take the inner bark of noni and then add lime (from crushed coral), it will turn into bright red. Without the lime, it's a deep gold. And then there's the olena, or turmeric. What we use is the true root which grows exactly like the ginger we eat. Depending on its age, it could be a bright canary yellow, or if it's older it could be gold or mus-

tard. All these natural substances were used to dye kapa in pre-contact Hawaii, and they're the dyes we're using now."

Unlike kapa, contemporary *washi* is generally colored in its pulp stage, before the sheets are formed. After the sheet formation, the method of ornamentation could take any of numerous forms generally determined by use. As Japan is a culture of paper, the sheets produced by the papermaker may be destined for silkscreening, calligraphy, umbrellas, scrolls, lamps, baskets, purses and *shoji* doors. For Yoichi and Mieko Fujimori, the work ends with the coloring.

Mieko Fujimori is the colorist of the family, the wizard who mixes the dyes and dips intricately folded sheets in various patterns and colors to achieve any number of snowflake-like designs. In her workshop at Temari last spring, she demonstrated the versatile properties of chemical and natural dyes on handmade *washi*.

While chemical dyes will achieve the more brilliant, electric colors, she said, the natural dyes are used to produce soft, subtle shades. At the workshop, vats were prepared of logwood extract, black wattle, cochineal, onion skin and indigo, each with its own detailed method of preparation involving precisely measured ratios. Once the colors are prepared, they can be mixed and combined to create a plethora of other shades that will infuse flat paper surfaces or the sheer ribbons of cut *washi* to be twisted and woven into *shifu*.

Shifu is the Japanese treatment of paper as fiber, a process involving the laborious hand-twisting of individual paper strips into long, three-dimensional, cord-like ropes with a

different destiny. The strands are dyed, plaited and woven into textured mats and hangings with the patterns and tactile qualities of the finest of woven tapestries. This textural and dimensional exploration is one factor elevating *washi* from the realm of craft to the level of fine art.

Island artist Marcia Morse, who has exhibited substantially here and on the Mainland as well as in Japan, says her work involves exploring the flat surface of paper as a separate dimensional structure. "The forms I'm working with are tapestries, books, more dimensional things," she says. "My formal training is in printmaking, a medium that comes to rest on paper surfaces. I was working on lithography and etching and I was wanting other surfaces to print on. I realized that what you can go into the the store and buy is limited. I was looking for other qualities, and I wanted to be more involved with a broader image of the work."

Morse began experimenting by printing on good, commercially available paper, then began manipulating them as sheets, to be bended, flexed and folded into sculptural shapes divided into grids and space. Her recent works include handmade, hand-painted sheets of paper hanging sequentially on acetate rods and large, three-dimensional hangings and sculptures in which handmade paper has been cut, folded and sewn into orderly labyrinths of shape.

"I think this is a time of experimentation," she says. "At Temari, you make that experimentation possible, you support it and encourage it. And Hawaii certainly has the resources—the fiber and the water and the history. It's one thing to learn the tradition, to honor it—but then, what do you do with it? Do you maintain the pure tradition or find

other ways of expression? Just making a beautiful sheet of paper is wonderful in itself, but you can also consider how you want to go on for yourself."

It is a phenomenon worth considering, this co-existence of experimental papermaking with the pure allegiance of traditionalists like Van Dorpe. With one ear to the past and an eye toward new doors to be opened, each end of the spectrum upholds the precious legacy of Hawaii, a place where earth and sun and sea continue to serve as the source.

And while the galleries of today will house the innovations of Marcia Morse, there is that modern subdivision in Lahaina, where, at least 125 years since kapa making vanished from the Islands, you can hear an ancient, haunting echo as Puanani Van Dorpe gazes to the mountains and reaches for the past.

"Tracing the Art of Paper" was first published in March/April 1985. Pua Van Dorpe, Marcia Morse, Bea Krauss and the Fujimoris are all still active participants in the movement to perpetuate the ancient art of papermaking.

121

Shoreline rocks near the town of Lahaina serve as hiding places for Van Dorpe's precious bundles of bast.

TAKING SHOTS

122

He is gentle in manner and voice, but the statements he makes with his brush and watercolors are bold, witty and often acrid commentaries on the follies of modern-day society.

At age forty-six, with dark waist-length hair ribboned with white, Masami Teraoka is both a revivalist and an innovator. In striking images reminiscent of the ancient Japanese art of *ukiyo-e*, he turns a critical eye on such controversial issues as environmental pollution, widespread commercialism and destruction of wildlife. *Samurais* hoisting cameras and golf clubs, *geishas* licking ice cream cones, and floating condoms and Kleenex tissues are all part of the bizarre—and at the same time incredibly beautiful—settings in which Teraoka cleverly shares his observations.

Teraoka was born in Onomichi, Japan, the only son of a *kimono* merchant. He showed an interest in art from the time he was a toddler, and often amused himself by doodling while his parents minded the store. "I remember using chalk to draw on the cement floor at the shop," he recalled. "I remember using my *getas* as a table. I would prop my children's books on them and

AT THE SAMURAI

Masami Teraoka   *by Cheryl Chee Tsutsumi*

31 Flavors Invading Japan: French Vanilla IV

copy pictures off the pages. Customers would look over my shoulder and tell my father nice things about my drawings."

Teraoka's father was very supportive of his young son's creative ability, and provided the guidance and encouragement he had not received when he desired to pursue his own artistic goals. "My father wanted to become a musician," Teraoka said, "but my grandfather, who started the *kimono* store, insisted that he continue on in the business since he was the first-born son. Because of that, my father was strong in his decision to allow all freedom to me

to choose what I wanted to do in life. I was very fortunate."

Realizing that their son's talent needed refinement and direction, Teraoka's parents asked a local artist, Moemon Sugihara, to take the boy as a pupil when he was seven. During the two years he spent under Sugihara's tutelage, Teraoka mastered the watercolor technique, learning to produce precise, even brush strokes and rich, luminous tones from skillful layering of tints.

As a youth, Teraoka attended Kwansei Gwakuin University in Kobe, where his focus on aesthetics brought him a keen understanding

New Views of Mount Fuji/La Brea Tar Pits Amusement Park

31 Flavors Invading Japan: French Vanilla

of many aspects of art, music and literature. His search for more knowledge and a fulfilling role in the field of art took him to Los Angeles in 1961. He continued his education a few years later at the Otis Art Institute, from which he earned a master of fine arts degree, and became absorbed in abstract painting and the pop art movement that was emerging from the American art scene at that time.

The freedom of expression he discovered in America stimulated his artistic sense and opened the door to an exciting new range of creative possibilities. Said Teraoka, "When the soil is right for a seed, it grows. Los Angeles provided the right environment for me to grow as an artist. It is a place that accepts and supports new ideas, is more liberal. That is how an unusual format such as mine could become popular."

In 1971, Teraoka produced, in an erotic series titled *Hollywood Landscape*, the first of what was to become his artistic trademark—elements of *ukiyo-e* combined with a pop art approach. *Ukiyo-e* means "ukiyo picture." Originally a Buddhist term, *ukiyo* literally translates as "this wretched world" or "this world of misery," referring primarily to the transitory nature of human existence. It later came to mean the "floating world," in which fleeting worldly pleasures were valued. In the seventeenth-century novel *Ukiyo Monogatari* (Tales of the Floating World), author Asai Ryoi describes this notion as "living only for the moment, turning our full attention to the pleasures of the moon, the snow, the cherry blossoms and the maple leaves; singing songs, drinking wine, diverting ourselves in just floating, floating...refusing to be disheartened, like a gourd floating along with the river current..."

Conceived during sixteenth-century Japan, *ukiyo-e* portrayed the common people's world and was not considered to be a high form of art. Nevertheless, Teraoka was intrigued by the woodblock prints' flat two-dimensional qualities, clean fluid lines, sensitive treatment of color and spatial relationships, and earthy humor and symbolism. He quickly found it to be the perfect medium of expression for the messages he wanted to share.

"*Ukiyo-e* is the most unique artistic form Japan has created," Teraoka said. "Even though it was seen as no more than poster art, I was drawn again and again to this style. I learned a lot from Americans about aesthetics, but I realized I didn't have to throw away what I knew about Japanese culture. I realized I could use a traditional method to communicate a contemporary issue. The statement can be made more strongly that way."

There is serious reflection behind the absurdity and sheer beauty of Teraoka's paintings, which are produced in series, enabling him to elaborate on a particular theme. For example, *Fish Woman and the Artist I*, from the *Los Angeles Sushi Ghost Tales* series, is a cryptic look at ocean pollution. It depicts a courtesan with the face of a dead fish spewing out a condom, eerie red flames, and a black and green substance representing garbage and oil leaks. The recipient of this gross outburst is the artist himself, who is about to eat a morsel of *sushi* topped with *anago*. Teraoka explains that the woman is a ghost who is warning him of the poisoned fish on his *sushi*. To the right of the picture appears a menu in Japanese calligraphy, listing the specials of the day—*hamachi, uni, tako*...and free cancer.

Teraoka's popular *McDonald's Hamburgers Invading Japan* series explores one of his pet themes—rampant consumerism. In *Flying Fries*, a *kimono*-clad woman is shown with a bag of french fries flying out of her hand. The woman's posture and facial expression are exaggerated, creating a scene that is, at a glance,

McDonald's Hamburgers Invading Japan/Flying Fries

Samurai Business on the Way Home II

*McDonald's Hamburgers
Invading Japan/Chochin-me*

very humorous. On a deeper level, *Flying Fries* illustrates the spreading of the fast food industry across the globe and the loss of cultural identity.

"Fast food places produce quick, abundant and cheap food, but not better," Teraoka said. "People are more concerned now about making money than good products. Fast food also is replacing all the traditional delicacies of a country. If fast food takes over the world, we'll all be eating the same thing. It'll be boring, not enrichening." To further emphasize this point, he painted a small landscape in a corner of the work, replacing the customary *torii* with McDonald's golden arches.

The pitfalls of commercialism is a topic Teraoka makes reference to again in his *31 Flavors Invading Japan* series, a satire on the Baskin-Robbins ice cream business with erotic overtones, and in his most recent *Tampon* series. Discussing the significance of the latter, he said, "Industry experiments at the consumer's expense. New products are released and then later, they are found to be dangerous to the health. It happens all the time."

A figure that appears repeatedly in Teraoka's paintings is the *samurai*, usually armed with golf clubs and a camera. To him, these are status symbols—items "every successful businessman in Japan owns and keeps to maintain his image." He pokes fun at this materialism in *Sinking Pleasure Boat* from the *New Views of Mount Fuji* series. In the painting, a group of merrymakers is gathered on the bow of a sinking vessel. Everyone seems either unconcerned about their hazardous situation or determined to enjoy themselves to the very end. One *geisha* photographs the calamity while a *samurai* pushes another *geisha* aside in his attempt to rescue his golf clubs from the overpowering waves. Said Teraoka, "Part of the

New Views of Mount Fuji/Dolphins and Samurais

message is that he would rather save his possessions than the woman's life."

Kleenex is another commonplace object that holds much meaning for Teraoka. "It represents the irony that exists in society today," he said. "We know we need it, yet on the other hand, it's the cause of environmental unrest. We're cutting down trees, destroying forests to manufacture it. In Japan, the paper company causes more pollution than anything else."

With graceful lines and harmonious blends of color combined into scenes of engaging and thought-provoking fantasy, Teraoka's paintings exude a refreshingly unique quality. His work has appeared on the cover of *Time* Magazine (March 30, 1981) and enlivens the private collections of art connoisseurs around the world. In America, he has found the perfect incubator for his creativity. "I'm enjoying living in America because I don't have to worry about the way I look, dress and respond to people. In Japan there are rigid rules. Everything must be immaculate. Cars always have to be polished and in good shape—nothing hanging from the bumper, nothing broken. Here we can be ourselves and it's much more relaxed. Japan is a conformist soci-

ety. In America, I can do what I want to do and say what I want to say."

Although his subjects and art form are decidedly Japanese, Teraoka says he is painting from a Western point of view. He has never exhibited his work in his homeland. "The Japanese people may not be ready to accept what I'm saying," he said. "Take pollution, for example. They are still trying to be Western; industrialization is beautiful to them. They wouldn't want to hear what I'm saying when I tell them industry makes the air and the water bad. The Japanese government is promoting industrialism. Also, the people would see that I'm reviving the traditional *ukiyo-e* style, but would miss the point of the paintings. They would not like to identify with anything traditional."

It takes Teraoka several months to complete one painting, a tedious process that often involves more than 100 preliminary drawings and countless hours of careful thought. It is not unusual to find him working fourteen hours a day on several different projects.

Teraoka's work is handled exclusively by Space Gallery in Los Angeles. He spends several months out of each year working in his Los Angeles

studio, but considers Hawaii his home now, having moved here two years ago to "escape the smog and pollution of the big city. Hawaii has a different environment than Los Angeles, but it also welcomes artistic freedom. The tropical atmosphere and the cultural mix here can add another dimension to my work. I feel I have another 'seed' planted here that can grow and expand into new ideas and new forms of art."

In an unpretentious house near the beach on the windward side of Oahu, Teraoka lives and enjoys the life of a recluse. His home is sparsely furnished, and, surprisingly, not decorated with any of the fanciful images that have won him critical acclaim. His explanation, like the life he has chosen to lead, is simple. "Without paintings on the walls, I can imagine more."

127

"Taking Shots at the Samurai" was first published in November/December 1982. Masami Teraoka still works out of his rural Oahu home, although the subject matter of his intriguing paintings now focuses on such controversial current issues as AIDS.

SUSAN MCGOVNEY HANSEN
STROKES OF SUCCESS
BY BETTY FULLARD-LEO

Tea With Gauguin II

T here were certain unavoidable frustrations for Susan McGovney Hansen when she resumed painting after a self-imposed hiatus to raise her family. "I would be working on a painting, and I'd realize it was 4:30 P.M., and I'd have to stop to fix dinner and I'd be mad. I'd be (in the kitchen) banging pans around and no one would know why I was mad. Who could be mad, because they had to quit painting?" she interrupts herself to ask logically. "I don't think most people know the place that artists get to as they're painting. To come back to the real world takes a lot of adjustment. I found myself resenting that more and more."

McGovney Hansen is, today, on her way to renown as a leading pastel and watercolor artist of Polynesian women and still life scenes. Her work is well-respected by the local art community for its artistic beauty as well as its sound technical rendering. Depending on size, her watercolors command prices from $800 to $4,000, while her etchings are in the $50 bracket. And despite the fact that McGovney Hansen handles most of the distribution and business details of her own career, her paintings are in such demand that she has difficulty filling all the requests.

For McGovney Hansen, however, the road to success and self-sufficiency has not been easy, nor was the decision to embark on it made at an early age. Art, as a matter of fact, is a second career for her, falling distinctly behind motherhood.

The soft-spoken artist lives in windward Oahu in a tree-shaded house overlooking the sea which she and her former husband bought twenty-five years ago. Her peaceful Lanikai home is conducive to artistic inspiration, with picture windows framing the Mokulua Islands situated beyond a broad expanse of emerald lawn and turquoise sea.

McGovney Hansen has been di-

South Seas Figure I

vorced for eight years, and she says of the adjustment, "(At the time) I was as afraid as I was at twenty, when I thought, 'I can't take care of myself; I'm never going to make it.' The divorce was the catalyst that brought me to make my living through art."

She continues, "I would like other women to know how things developed for me, and that it is possible to develop a career later in life. Before I was divorced, I had begun to get back into my artwork. I'd started taking classes, entering art shows, working on it, but always holding back because of my family. When I was very young and got married, I had decided not to try to do my artwork and raise a family at the same time, because I knew I'd be frustrated."

McGovney Hansen makes it clear that she never regretted putting aside her artwork for the homemaking career she considered a higher priority. "Raising children was very important to me. I thought, 'This is my

job,' so I put the artwork away. I knew that I would come back to it."

She has a sound background in art and even before her traumatic teenage years, she exhibited a glimmer of talent that her parents were wise enough to recognize and nurture. Her mother died when she was ten years old, and her father, an orthopedic surgeon who served from 1941 to 1946 in the Army Medical Corps based in Los Angeles, found it necessary to send his three daughters to boarding school in Santa Barbara, California.

Looking back, McGovney Hansen says, "Going to boarding school gives you a whole different outlook and a whole new set of circumstances to deal with that a lot of people don't have. Instead of sharing your feelings, I think you learn, or at least I did, how to handle things inside yourself. You're on your own, really."

The family was reunited when

her father married again. He reestablished his private practice in Santa Barbara and sent his daughters to public school. But McGovney Hansen was not a dedicated student. A socializer who lacked direction, she did well only in classes that appealed to her. In a family of educators and medical people, she felt she was a disappointment. "There wasn't an artist in the lot," she says. "In addition, my two sisters would come home with all kinds of honors and prizes and good grades, but it always said on my report card, 'Not working up to her capabilities.' My father knew I could do better."

When he insisted she transfer to Laguna Blanca, a private day school, she resented leaving her friends in public school, but her grades improved. During this time, it was a matter of course that every Saturday morning, she went to private art

Tea With Gauguin I

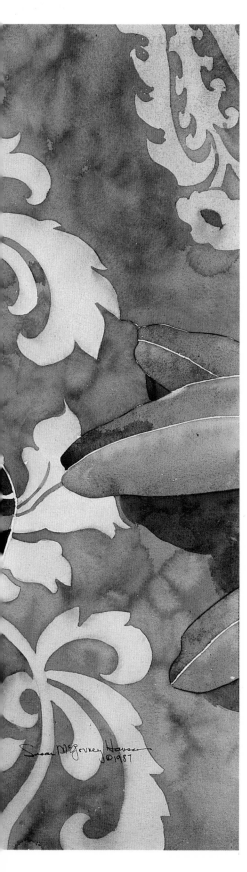

classes taught by a Santa Barbara artist, Ann Louise Snider.

In retrospect, McGovney Hansen says, "I knew art was what I wanted to do if I did anything, but I don't think I had dreams of having a big career because I think my self-esteem was such that I couldn't handle that." When she graduated at sixteen, one of her teachers chose this quote to appear under her picture in the high school annual: "The secret of success is constancy of purpose." Whether it was meant as an admonition to an unambitious pupil or as a prediction of things to come was never explained.

There followed two years at UCLA, and then a sorority sister talked her into transferring to Art Center College of Design in Los Angeles. "I was just in heaven," McGovney Hansen says, "because it was all art classes." She completed two years, majoring in illustration before dropping out to marry.

McGovney Hansen's three children were born in Tacoma, Washington. After she had her first child, she took a job in a print shop. "It bothered me so much to leave my first child, I immediately got pregnant. That's how I stopped that (job)," she says wryly. The family moved to Hawaii in 1963, accompanied by their three children, aged two, six and eight.

McGovney Hansen immediately felt an affinity with the sun, sea and Island people. She had long since put away her brushes and palette. "But I knew I would come back to (art)," she admits. "Every once in a while I'd do a little drawing of the children. I started taking an art class so I could get out of the house, but I knew if I started working at home, I would get too involved."

As the children grew older, she began to dabble again in art, taking a life drawing class, entering an oc-

casional show. Even her choice of a medium reflected her concern for her family. She says, "When I wanted to do some painting at home, I set up on a corner of the lanai. I wanted to work in a medium that didn't smell like oils and turpentine—which I love—but I didn't want the smell to be a problem for the family, so I chose watercolors."

Additional study followed. McGovney Hansen joined the Hawaii Watercolor Society and took every workshop that was offered by visiting artists. Later she taught at the Young At Heart Gallery in Kailua and then briefly at the Bishop Museum and the YWCA on Richards Street in downtown Honolulu. When the Honolulu Academy of Arts needed an instructor for its workshops, she was confident and eager to share her knowledge. She taught there for several years.

McGovney Hansen laughs as she remembers the thrill of selling her first painting in the early seventies. "Here was a person who had never earned a thing in her life herself, so to think that I actually sold something that I did and that somebody actually wanted it enough to spend their own money for it—it was a real turn-on, let me tell you. One of my neighbors, a dear friend who has been a client over the years, bought a picture for sixty dollars. I was so thrilled that I could earn money doing something other than baby-sitting! I've become a little more of a businesswoman since then."

Her transition from housewife to self-supporting artist was accelerated during three hectic months in 1979. That summer, her older daughter got married, her younger daughter graduated from high school, her son graduated from college, and she and her husband "parted for the last time." Then, in the fall, she won her first "best of

show" award in a Hawaii Watercolor Society exhibit.

McGovney Hansen knew the statistics. She knew that nationally only one or two percent of all artists earn their living by painting. She told herself she had to be in that one or two percent. She had participated in a few shows by then. In 1976, she had had twenty paintings in a show at City Hall, and the State Foundation on Culture and the Arts had purchased some of her work. She was represented by a reputable dealer, Greg Northrup, and she had determination on her side. "I just have an inner core that I know I can get through things. I decided I would do this and not go to lunches. They break up a day."

In 1980, she was chosen to do the cover illustration for the upcoming Honolulu telephone directory. She credits this commission with initially getting her name known throughout the state, as the phone directory finds its way into nearly every household in Hawaii, but she says, "It still surprises me that people know me. I don't blast out with a lot of advertising. I want people to come across one of my paintings and say, 'Wow, I would like to have one like that'—a more personal kind of thing, to discover me on their own. I can only do so many paintings, so I can't get too many clients. I am kind of a one-woman band around here. I take things to photographers, to the framers, do all my own ordering, delivering and picking things up. I make decisions on my career myself—possibly because I don't know anyone else who cares about my work as much as I do, and I want to keep up the quality."

The Village Gallery on Maui, which featured McGovney Hansen's watercolors in a one-woman show last October, represents her, though paintings may be purchased directly from the artist as well. One of her biggest problems is keeping the gallery supplied with canvasses to sell. At most, she can create about fifty paintings in one year, and she prefers to limit mass production of her work though she has done a set of illustrated notecards and three commissioned posters (one for the Lanikai Canoe Club, one for the Hawaii Opera Theater and one of the Salvation Army's Waioli Tea Room), and two posters on her own (titled *Maui Dancer* and *Na O Kika O Hawaii*).

In the fall, she completed a series of watercolor still lifes titled *Tea With Gauguin,* who is one of her favorite artists. "The idea came to me to have the cattleya (orchid) seem almost inconsequential in (each of) the paintings. I was fascinated with the way the leaves grew, but I wanted to get other patterns going in the painting, so that you almost come across the orchid unexpectedly when you are looking. My paintings have to have some kind of depth to them so people can discover things over the years. They are carefully thought out as far as composition and structure, so at another level, there's a lot going on, not just subject matter. Each one is individual to me. I don't have a formula."

She displays a painting she is in the process of completing. The vivid, intricate patterns of Tahitian *pareu* cloth cover a table where someone apparently has just stepped away from drinking tea while reading or writing postcards illustrated with Gauguin reproductions. A delicate lavender orchid is part of the tableau. The perspective of the painting is unusual—it is as though the viewer is standing above the scene, looking down on the table.

The artist's studio, with its peaceful, beautiful ocean view, seems to have been dropped into this same sort of idealistic setting. McGovney Hansen shares her home with her older daughter, son-in-law and three-year-old grandson, who live in the upper level of the two story house. Her lower-level studio has just enough space for a modeling platform, an easel and a few chairs. It is here that she arranges still life scenes or poses the model she has been working with for the past ten years. Mihana Aluli Souza has classic Polynesian features and will be the first portrait model for a new series in oils. McGovney Hansen has always avoided painting portraits on a commission basis because she feels she might "see" a subject differently than the person who hires her, so she says, "I want to do portraits just for myself—not for others."

Because she is already known as a watercolorist, she says, "That's what people want (to purchase), but I am a painter. That's how I consider myself. I keep trying to do my oils and probably haven't hit my stride in them yet because I haven't concentrated on them. My 'soul' kind of painting, I think, is oil, because when I dream, I am at my easel and I'm painting in oil. It might be that these oil paintings are not going to sell, they might not be what people like, but they are more my soul."

According to McGovney Hansen, watercolor and oil are such different mediums, they can barely be compared. Watercolors use the whiteness of the paper as part of the picture. For her watercolors, which, unlike oil, soak into the paper, she first draws a scene with pencil. She applies a background wash in the lightest overall color, leaving the white areas dry, since the white of the paper becomes any white that shows in the picture. With oils, she says, "You paint in the white color. Oil stays on top of the canvas and can be built up, so it's a whole

Awapuhi Series—Haumea II

different process. You use the same basic structural ideas as far as line, texture and space, but the quality is completely different."

McGovney Hansen is planning new directions for her work as well. She just completed her first etching in conjunction with a printer; she did the drawing on the plates and etched the image in acid, then the printer ran off the prints. She also recently started a sculpture class with Hawaii sculptor Sean Browne. She is

confident of her ability to master the new medium, explaining, "I think three-dimensionally when I do my paintings and I know a lot about the figure. I have in mind to do Hawaiian dancers, kind of like Degas did ballet dancers. You do them in clay and then you make a mold and cast them in bronze. I don't know why I'm adding another medium—it just happened that I wanted to try something else."

When McGovney Hansen looks to the future, she thinks in terms of

Maui Dancer

Red Orchid with Striped Cloth

art and is pleased that hers is a profession in which retirement is not mandatory. She is well aware that many artists do their best work in their later years. She aspires to becoming a better artist, knows she will take time off for travel whenever feasible and is not averse to finding a "life partner," though she says, "It would take a special kind of person to understand how much time goes into art, especially if you're a perfectionist about your work, as I am. If I could figure anything out, it would be how to work faster without compromising the quality of my work."

A typical working day for McGovney Hansen begins at 8:30 or 9:00 A.M. After a midday break for lunch and a possible walk on the beach, she continues to paint until 4:00 P.M. She has learned to balance her passion for painting with a businesslike approach. "I don't know whether I'm getting more aggressive," she says. "I don't know that I have a goal of being famous. I'm certainly learning, because you never stop learning. I know I have to continue to earn my living at this, and I'm probably getting better at that, but I have a goal of getting better and better in my art, too, and that's probably only judged by me"—and perhaps by some teacher in her past, who smiles every time she thinks of young Susan McGovney who simply needed a little "constancy of purpose" to succeed.

"Strokes of Success" was first published in July/August 1988. Susan McGovney Hansen remains a highly respected figure in local art circles.

Fumagalli

AN ARTIST'S MAGNIFICENT LOVE AFFAIR

by Rita Ariyoshi

134

"Painting?" Luigi Fumagalli pulls on his pipe, thinks, smiles and his eyes dance the way I remember the eyes of the men in Rome when I was a young student. "Painting is like making love. I put so much intensity into it. It's like loving all the women that I can't have. Creating is making love, you know. When I'm working on a painting, I let it rest awhile and then when I'm almost finished with it, I have to smoke a cigarette. I have to delay that last stroke." He laughs, warmly and with appreciation. "It's such pleasure to finish a beautiful woman."

His wife, Noriko, whom he calls Maggie, is smiling, too. Looking at her sitting at his feet, demurely, with bowed head and lowered eyes, as she appears in so many of his paintings, he adds, "Painting a woman is like getting involved." He finishes with rowdy Latin laughter, "Then, I love them and leave them." It's on to the next painting, the next woman, the next fantasy.

Maggie says, "I sometimes select the model for him. I look for somebody who has inner beauty. You can see on canvas immediately about that person. A camera can fool you, but when you paint, you have to know the essence of the person."

Visions of Maggie are everywhere in Fumagalli's studio. Speaking of her, the artist says, "I know her so well. I really know her—and still it's a mystery. I can paint her in a million different ways and just when I think I know her—zap—another painting."

Maggie was an art history student from Japan when she met Luigi. "I fell in love with his work and it drew me to him. I thought he was the greatest artist alive." She agreed to pose for him. "I wanted to help him. I did it out of love. I still feel embarrassed. I don't like to look at myself on canvas. I want to hide."

Fumagalli immediately leaps from his chair and rushes for a stack of

135

Under the Cherry Blossom

Maiko (Dancing Girl)

paintings. "Here, look at this, Maggie, just look at this."

She glances shyly at her portrait.

He urges, coaxes, "Aren't you proud of that?"

She nods and smiles, saying indulgently, "He's more settled now."

Fumagalli is perhaps best-known for his bold paintings of horses and his primitive, cubistic women. His idol was the Italian cubist sculptor and painter, Marino Marini. "I modeled myself after him. I also admired Picasso, Dali."

Marini had a studio in Monza, the town near Milan, Italy, where Fumagalli was born and raised. "He (Marini) was so famous. 'Maestro,' I called him. Because of him, I am what I am now. He inspired me. The control of color, movement—something clicked when I saw his work. Inside me there must have been something that said, 'You're going to be like that.' When something like that happens, from then on, you're a slave."

The young Fumagalli began to sing to buy canvasses and paints—"and to eat." That launched a parallel career. It was his voice that got him out of his small Italian town and off to the Hong Kong Hilton, and it was his voice that landed him his first job in Hawaii, singing at the Waikiki restaurant Trattoria, where, seventeen years later, he still sings and plays the guitar every night but Sunday.

Thinking back on his offer to go to Hong Kong, Fumagalli says, "My mother didn't want me to go. It was a different world. I went to the library—and wonder of wonders—there were books on *Kabuki* and the whole Orient—and I said, 'God, I'm going to do it.'

"My first impression of Hong Kong—I took the Star ferry from the Kowloon side—it was like ecstasy. It was 1964. I'm sitting on this ferry all by myself, afraid to talk. I had never been anyplace. I was like a child. I looked at the beautiful skyline—here I am in the heart of the Orient. It was like being in a dream. 'Now—from now,' I told myself, 'I start living.'

"I entered a world of luxury—the Hong Kong Hilton. I had a contract to entertain for six months and stayed six years. I fell in love with everything Oriental—junks, *cheong-sams,* babies in baskets. I did a lot of paintings—the lights, colors—red, green, gold. Hong Kong is to a canvas what a piano is to a concert—it is a living canvas. I'd go to Aberdeen and throw coins to the kids and I'd try and get them to stay still and I couldn't. I painted junks till I was bored with them. I painted a woman in a *Hakka* hat and her baby in a basket on her shoulder pole with some food in the balancing basket."

When it was time for Fumagalli to move on, Hawaii was meant to be "a halfway house" between the Orient and California or New York. Instead, "I fell in love with the Islands—the beautiful women, beautiful weather and I thought, 'Here we go again—another six years.' I didn't intend to stay all these years!"

Slowly, his art began to change. "I started to experiment with Hawaiian folklore, but I was still doing it very primitive, massive, cubistic, but the more I got involved with Island life, I realized I was attracted more and more to the beauty of the women of the Islands. I think 1980, yes, 1980, was the turning point. I had a Latin temperament and I be-

Lei Aloha

Equestrian

gan to slow down. Before that, my horses (his series of horse paintings) were almost violent—a lot of red, a lot of frustration."

His horses, however, are not abandoned—merely put out to pasture in favor of his *Kabuki, geisha* and new Hawaiian themes. Between new styles he always returns to his fantasy horses. "When I paint horses—beginning to end, it's just emotion. I finish what I start if it takes all day and all night. It's like dreaming with your eyes open. I stare, I squint my eyes and—aha!—I reach a form and movement that's pure fantasy. It's a buildup of changes coming from inside me.

"This, now"—and he gestures toward an unfinished canvas of two young hapa-haole women in *pareus*—"is more contemplative. The details. The *kimono* has so many surprises in the way you fold it, it is so full of details. Now I discover surprises in the folds of the *pareu*. I buy twenty-foot *pareus* and drape them every way. This is exciting—another couple of years of madness."

Maggie says, "He goes through phases."

Fumagalli jumps in, "If you stop inventing, stop doing something new, you become a production worker—we know artists like that, right? A flower here, a flower there. Nothing new. I might as well be a dog or cat, eat my Friskies and go to sleep."

His earliest painting was a Madonna and child, done for the nuns who taught him in school. He was eleven and remembers, very clearly, his careful penmanship and pride when he put his name on it. "Before that it was graffiti. Every white surface was in trouble."

The most famous walls Fumagalli has painted are the massive murals at the Hawaiian Regent Hotel and First Interstate Bank on South King Street.

The walls of his studio support canvasses from his several stylistic phases. He says, "I have some paint-ings I've been working on for twelve years. They're always in danger. Right now, there are ten or twelve of them. They're in jail. They're not safe until they're signed. When it's signed, I hide it and don't touch it."

Usually, once a Fumagalli painting is signed, it's sold. Of the signed works in his studio, there was not one left from the time of the first interview until the second—and perhaps six weeks had elapsed.

When he had a showing at the Foundry gallery in Kakaako in 1973, it was a sell-out. "A guy from Chicago came in blue jeans, unshaven. At first I didn't want to waste time with him...He asked me how much for a painting and when I told him, he said, 'Alright, I'll take this one.' He bought the whole show—thirty-two out of thirty-five works—and I never heard from him again." Fumagalli's paintings have also been purchased by film and political celebrities.

Naturally exuberant, Fumagalli smiles readily, sits back confidently, then leans forward and says earnestly, "I want to know the mystery of everything. Zillions of things."

Asked how he sees his work changing in the future he says, "If I moved from the Islands, I wouldn't paint this way (referring to his soft and innocent women). It is so exquisitely suited to the Islands."

The Fumagallis plan to travel. He says, "I always say yes, and then I begin to paint and we don't go."

Maggie smiles, "He's become Hawaiian."

Art, marriage, Hawaii, women—for Luigi Fumagalli they are all components of his intense love for life, sometimes expressed boldly and with fury and at other times with a precise delicacy and exquisite grace.

"An Artist's Magnificent Love Affair" was first published in September/October 1987. Luigi Fumagalli's latest works include a striking series of abstracts.

Soaring Eagles

YVONNE CHENG
DYEING FOR A LIVING

BY BETTY FULLARD-LEO

Yvonne Cheng's big, beautiful Hawaiian earth mothers have been gazing from the walls of homes and public buildings throughout Hawaii since the early 1970s. In a surprisingly short time, Cheng's powerful batik paintings have established a widely recognized identity, unusual for a Honolulu artist. Today, her pieces sell in the $2,500 range, and she is often compared with Madge Tennent or Pegge Hopper, two artists who are also known for their magnificent renderings of massive Hawaiian women.

Cheng was born in Indonesia in 1941, which in a way made batik a natural art for her to pursue, since folk craft batik art was part of the culture in which she grew up. "They train young children (in Indonesia) and when they're adult, they are masters, but a lot of them are illiterate," she said. Cheng did not attempt the craft until she came to Hawaii to live.

Attractive, trim and young in appearance, she is the daughter of a relatively well-to-do Chinese father and a mother who is half-Dutch, half-Indonesian. Raised by her father and stepmother from the age of two, Cheng did not see her mother again until five years ago when she was forty years old.

"It's kind of a soap opera story," she mused. "When my father married my stepmother, she didn't want to have anything to do with the past, so she tore up all the photos and I was not really allowed to talk about my mother. It was unusual at that time that I had gone with my father, so I kind of always felt that she had abandoned me." Through the years, Cheng's mother attempted to make contact with her, but was not encouraged because of the new stepmother. Finally, her mother obtained the address of Cheng's best friend from the Indonesian Embassy in Holland and wrote to her in New York. The letter was forwarded to Cheng.

Cheng learned of the existence of a half-sister, who subsequently came to visit her. In 1981, Cheng flew to Holland where her first glimpse of her mother was through the plate glass windows of Schiphol Airport. "It was strange, I could immediately recognize my mother. I was looking at myself twenty years from now. Not only that, our personalities turned out to be identical. When we looked at each other, I cried, but just for a few minutes. Then we started laughing and all those years fell away. All through my stay, my sister and her husband couldn't get over it, because we would be somewhere and (my mother and I) would say exactly the same thing about the same person. She has this looney sense of humor. We both like to comment off-the-cuff."

Cheng added, "At the time we met I was very insecure about my future because art was my sole income, but my mother also had had only a high school education and had led a much harder life than I. I could see such eerie similarities between her life and mine, and now she's very settled, so it gave me a lot of faith.

At the time of the divorce, Cheng's mother had custody of her daughter, but had realized she would have a better life if raised by her older, financially comfortable father.

As a child, Cheng was educated in Dutch schools in Indonesia and though her teachers singled her out for advanced tutoring in art, her stepmother did not encourage her to pursue her talent. Many of her cousins were studying to become doctors, lawyers and professional

Multi-media, 25 X 19 inches.

people. Cheng said, "I loved art, and I never had any other idea than becoming an artist since fourth or fifth grade. I dreamed and I wanted to do it, but my stepmother was dead set against it because it wasn't the 'proper' thing to do. Her final lament to me was, "Couldn't you at least become a vet?'"

Cheng finished high school but had no desire to continue her education. "I lived with my parents and I designed clothes. I had a seamstress, but it was all fun and games," she said. She still designs as a hobby and on this day she wore a chic pants outfit that she had created from antique *kimonos.* For years her artistic talents lay dormant, although she did teach art in a Catholic school prior to leaving Indonesia in 1966. "They just took me," she said, "because I could speak the (English) language." The country was in a state of flux as the Indonesian people

Batik, 70 X 42 inches.

142

demanded independence from the Netherlands. "I'd come to know my husband, but we hadn't married yet," Cheng explained. "He was a high official with President Sukarno, so when Sukarno was toppled he had to leave the country since he was known to be very close (to the president)."

Eight months later, she joined him in Cambridge, Massachusetts. They married and she assumed the responsibility of motherhood, caring for her husband's two preschool children by a former marriage. The few other times she had been out of Indonesia were on brief vacations to the Orient. "It was a cultural shock

coming from a third world country. I grew up with servants, and now I had a two-bedroom apartment to take care of. My idea of cleaning was to throw everything in the closet and just close it," Cheng said.

In 1967, when her husband decided he would rather live in Hawaii where he had often visited, the family packed a few suitcases and moved to the Islands. In another year, their son, Tony, was born, and Cheng stayed home to care for the three young children while her husband worked in real estate.

When the two older children began to attend school, she took a few

painting classes at the YWCA. At one point she showed a painting with the Artists' Group, but she wasn't comfortable with oils. She switched to ceramics only to find she was allergic to the clay. The quest for a fulfilling art form led her to a batik course at the Bishop Museum. "It took me a year to figure out what I really wanted to do, because my teacher was doing mostly abstracts. Since I always liked to draw figures, I started doing figures," Cheng explained.

Her first batik piece sold against her will. A friend saw her working at her "hobby" and asked to buy the

piece when it was finished. "I said, 'Are you nuts?' I finished it and never really let her know. She caught me and said, 'Why didn't you call me?' This one was my first Hawaiian woman and she bought it and I thought, 'My God, she paid $125,'" Cheng said. Up until then she had done only a few small Indonesian figures in batik for gifts and pillows.

In the early 1970s she walked into the Downtown Gallery which used to be on Merchant Street, asked to speak to the manager, Greg Northrup, and said, "I would like to have a one-man show." He hedged a bit, but promised to present her work to the board. As the summer went by and there was no word, Cheng worried that he hadn't liked her work, but eventually she summoned enough courage to call him. Initially, a few of the batiks were shown in the gallery; when they received enthusiastic approval, Cheng was granted her show. Her first batik paintings sold for $375. Three other shows followed, each a year-and-a-half apart. As her success grew, Cheng gained confidence and began to develop her own interests and friendships.

Of her relationship with her husband she said, "We were opposites to start out with, but it was fine because I was a nice Oriental housewife, but suddenly I realized that people were really paying attention to me. It opened a whole new world to me. I had to go to meetings with architects; businessmen wanted my opinion. I realized I didn't always have to do what (my husband) wanted me to do."

She was divorced in April 1977, and her fourth show opened at the Contemporary Arts Gallery the following September. She felt pressured adjusting to her new single status while simultaneously meeting the show deadline, but she also felt freer than she ever had, and the new attitude reflected in her work. "It was the first year I was showing bare breasts. I guess it had something to do with the fact that I really felt a sense of freedom." Cheng, who was raised a Catholic, said she was taught that it was sinful to draw attention to the body, but she began to realize that was not necessarily true. She sees her massive Hawaiian figures not so much as bodies, but as beautiful sensual shapes.

At one time, most of Cheng's paintings were commissioned for private homes; today most of her work is purchased for commercial buildings. One of Cheng's typical batiks on 100 percent Belgian linen might measure forty-four by sixty inches. Her biggest undertaking to date is a series of five panels, each five feet long, that hang at the Ala Moana branch of Bank of Honolulu.

As well as furnishing a means of support, Cheng's work is a labor of love. "It used to be very hard for me to give up the finished piece," she admitted. She maintains a disciplined working schedule in the peaceful, airy home that she and her son, now eighteen years old, share in Kaimuki. Each morning from nine o'clock she works in her studio, which is filled with brushes, sketches, handmade paper and other artistic paraphernalia. When she is ready to work on the dyeing process of batiking, she pulls on rubber gloves and moves outside to a cobblestone courtyard. Here, with the birds singing and gentle breezes ruffling the leaves of a nearby mango tree, she finds art a complete escape. "For me to create, it doesn't have to be beautiful. For me, I need peacefulness," she said. She works until five in the afternoon with a break for lunch.

The batik process begins with an idea which Cheng draws on paper before sketching the outline with charcoal on her linen canvas. She creates the picture using a wax and dye resist method, meaning that whatever area of the cloth is coated with wax will resist the dye. Wax is applied first to the area that is meant to stay the lightest in color with paintbrushes of pure bristle. Brushes of man-made material melt in the hot wax. After each wax application, the linen is dipped in dye baths, progressing from the lightest to the darkest in color. The darkest portions of a finished picture are those spaces that have never been waxed, because they absorb the most colors.

Cheng uses ten or more layers of wax and nine or more dye baths for each picture. She signs her name using a *tjanting*, an ancient Javanese tool with a reservoir to hold hot wax, which is directed through a small pointed spout in order to draw detailed patterns.

Batik is so old a craft that its true origin has never been determined. Archaeological findings suggest that 2,000 years ago, the people of Egypt and Persia wore batik garments. In Africa, batik takes on tribal patterns; in the Orient the designs are more delicate. In Indonesia, some classic patterns can only be worn by the nobility. Cheng's batiks, though created by a method similar to that used in Indonesia, are completely different, bringing alive the Hawaiian figure.

It takes her perhaps three weeks to complete a piece. She uses photo sensitive dyes that are affected by the sunlight, so if it rains, she cannot do the outdoor work. Because the dyes are earth-colored in their original form, the final shades of color are sometimes a surprise. Cheng repeatedly irons the completed picture between pieces of clean newsprint to remove the dye. Finally, she soaks the piece overnight in water and detergent, dries and irons it again, and then it's ready to place on a stretcher for showing.

With fifteen years of creating beautiful batiks behind her, Cheng no longer finds it difficult to give up a newly dyed piece. "It must be a growing thing," she said reflectively, "because a couple of years ago I started doing abstract collage, and it is hard to give those up." She realized she was walking around with ideas in her head that she could not express in batik. Because she was trained in representational art, she has found the transition to abstract art a challenge. She sold her first multimedia collage in 1981. She explained, "Abstracts are more difficult because you have to peel away all the outer layers to get to the core. It's more emotional than theory. Of course, there's a matter of balance, the matter of color. I'm still fascinated by textures. I start with an overall idea like a shell. It's something that I've seen and I just want the essence,

the meaning."

A set of two dark blue matching abstracts rested on an easel in her studio. Cheng layered bits of paper, handmade locally, with coats of color. She called it a frustrating process. "Sometimes I change midway, sometimes I just have to walk away from it for a week."

These are the times she escapes to yardwork for meditation. "My mind keeps racing all the time. I need to do something to really calm me down," she said.

Cheng's paper and paint collages were destined for a wall above the sofa in her living room. The house was bare of any of her batik paintings and she explained, "It's the deeprooted Oriental in me. I guess it's my stepmother. She said, 'If you hang something of your own, it's quite arrogant. Do you think you are that great?' I'm getting a little bit out of it, but I still have it."

Cheng drew attention to another medium she enjoys: a small, peaceful watercolor with a wash effect. It seemed a representation of her life at that moment—pleasant and softening at the edges, but moving so quickly it was almost blurred.

"The other day," she said, "I came to the conclusion that I haven't been bored for so long, I don't remember the meaning. At the end of every day I think, 'Oh, God, if I just had ten more hours.'"

"Dyeing for a Living" was first published in November/December 1986. Yvonne Cheng continues her extraordinary work in batik.

KEEPERS OF THE ANCIENT HULA

BY CHERYL CHEE TSUTSUMI

144

*N*ana I Na Loea Hula (Look to the Hula Resources) documents the role of the Hawaiian dance in the lives of seventy-six Islanders, who have each earned, through demonstration of their knowledge and expertise, the coveted recognition of kumu hula or master of the hula. The book is a compilation of their stories in their words. The essence, the heart of the hula, is revealed through these narratives as a dynamic force that only begins to show itself in the grace and beauty of the motions. The kumu range in age from twenty-nine to ninety-three, and their experiences and philosophies about the hula represent as broad a spectrum. There is conflict in their reminiscences as well as contentment, trial along with triumph. And though their thoughts are expressed in language that is simple and direct, the concerns they raise are far more complex. If the hula kahiko is indeed a sacred, historical record, should strict boundaries be placed on its structure, or should it, as a creative art, be allowed total freedom of individual interpretation? How are contemporary attitudes toward the dance going to be reconciled with the traditional teachings of the kupuna? What is hula's place and future in a modern setting that grows more distant from the old Hawaiian way of life with each passing day? The excerpts we share from the book, even in their brevity, are poignant, powerful, profound. *Nana I Na Loea Hula* is an inspiring, moving tribute to a truly great art form and the gifted men and women who have dedicated their lives to perpetuating it.

145

Diane Ahrens-Obedoza dances at Halemaumau Crater, Hawaii Volcanoes National Park, island of Hawaii.

Mae Loebenstein and her granddaughter, Maelia.

For Wendell Silva, the completion of *Nana I Na Loea Hula* is but a beginning—a cornerstone for the Institute of Hawaiian Dance and Culture he hopes one day to establish in Hawaii. Developing such an organization to revive and nurture the Islands' fading traditions is Silva's fervent dream and a task he has assumed as his personal responsibility.

Silva is the executive director of the Kalihi-Palama Culture and Arts Society, which published *Nana I Na Loea Hula.* The nonprofit group was founded in 1970 "to enrich the lives of (the) peoples of Hawaii through cultural and educational arts-oriented programs." It is a directive that also governs Silva's life. "I could foresee the loss of so much of our resources and culture," he said, his words punctuated by an unmistakable sense of urgency. "What we do have left, I think, are remnants compared to the vastness of knowledge that once existed. We of Hawaii have no place else to go, as far as our culture is concerned, but within ourselves. Chinese people have their roots in China; Japanese can go to Japan and find a lot of their culture still alive there. Hawaiians have only the resources here. And unless we know who those resources are, we won't know who to turn to."

Prompted by that realization, Silva was determined to compile a record of hula resources. He and three young associates—Columbia University English major Alan Suemori, photographer Shuzo Uemoto and graphic arts designer Milton Chun—devoted hundreds of hours to the planning and production of *Nana I Na Loea Hula* with no financial compensation. Three years in the making, the book exceeded all of their expectations. What Silva had initially proposed as a directory of kumu hula with small, passport-type pictures emerged as a publication of the highest quality, with dramatic, full-page portraits and stirring narratives that define the hula in its purest sense and describe the sacrifices expected of all those who truly commit themselves to the dance.

Said Silva, "What it will do is immortalize a lot of people. In the seventy-six stories you'll find similarities—you'll find people undergoing similar experiences, similar frustrations, similar training techniques. It also shows a polarization. It shows a concern for the survival of the art, a very deep concern that is dividing the hula community. I think the book will help some of these hula people resolve questions that they had before found difficult to answer in themselves."

For Suemori, Uemoto and Chun, becoming closely involved with the hula was a source of enlightenment and rejuvenation in itself. Although they are all "local boys," none of them had been extensively exposed to it, and participating in the project was an experience of immeasurable value.

Using a questionnaire he and Silva had developed, Suemori conducted the majority of the interviews with the kumu. "We asked them about their background, how long they had been teaching, who their kumu hula were and how they thought the hula had changed during their careers," Suemori said. "What we wanted to do was to create a platform for them to share their ideas, to get everything out in the open, to help them realize that they have so much in common. They have differences, but what they have in common is so overwhelming. The need to have the Hawaiian culture perpetuated overrides any other differences."

The hours Suemori spent talking to the kumu were emotion-filled lessons. "Just meeting all those great people was a reward that was more than adequate for the time I put in," he said. "There were several people that touched me very deeply and educated me. They were down-to-

Tattooed member of Hui Hooulu Aloha.

Warrior, Hula Halau Ka Ua Kani Lehua.

A dancer from Na Pualei o Like Lehua patiently waits for her turn to perform. All photographs taken at the Merrie Monarch Hula Festival, Hilo, island of Hawaii.

147

Speaking of the heavens.

148

earth, very warm and giving. That was their greatness. There were many times when people broke down and cried. There were times when I felt a special spirit coming from them, something bigger than any of us. I remember seeing Hawaii in a totally different light than I've ever seen it before. Driving along the road, I'd look at the high-rises over Punchbowl and the mountains of Kualoa. Comparing the two, it struck me that there was once a great civilization and culture here, greater than any high-rise we could ever build today. So much of it is being lost, and I don't think people realize how profound a loss it really is."

Since work on the project began in 1981, six of the kumu who appear in the book have passed away—Maiki Aiu Lake, Bella Richards, Luka Kaleiki, Sam Naeole, Eleanor Hiram Hoke and John Watkins. The importance and timeliness of *Nana I Na Loea Hula* thus becomes even more evident: With the passing of each kumu comes the loss of irreplaceable knowledge and experience; with each death, one more cultural link is broken in the already tenuous bond modern-day Hawaii has with its past. Said Silva, "In some cases, ours is the last picture taken of the kumu before their death."

The portraits in the book are sensitive images, expressive storytellers in themselves. They project an aura of dignity yet humility, gentleness yet intensity. Photographer Shuzo Uemoto, noted Silva, "took his assignment into an artistic dimension that's incredible."

Said Uemoto, "I was trying to find a definition of what was Hawaiian to me. I was searching for that poignant side of 'alohaness' that needs to be remembered in our modern world...Pictures of people can be as breathtaking as those of nature. Portraits are human landscapes—every face is different and intriguing."

To preserve the integrity of the

negatives, Uemoto used a large four-by-five format camera, which necessitated manual loading of each shot. He took the photos of the kumu on weekends, and developed the film himself on weekdays at PhotoPlant, where he works full-time as a lab technician. Suemori, who usually had completed the interviews sometime prior to the photo sessions, accompanied Uemoto to make introductions and assist where needed.

"We'd leave at 6:00 A.M., have breakfast at King's Bakery and be on the road by 7:00," Suemori said. "We'd hit the first house by 9:00. We set up the appointments according to the kumu's schedules, so we'd maybe have to drive out to Waianae for the morning shot, drive into Kaneohe for the midday shot around noon, and have to be in Kalihi somewhere for the late afternoon shot at 3:00. The hours were long—we usually wouldn't head for home until six in the evening."

A perfectionist, Uemoto once invested five hours in a shot before he captured the exact mood and moment he envisioned. "I wanted to create photographs that expressed the feelings of the people involved in the hula. Before I took their picture, I tried to establish a rapport with them—I talked to them and explained what I was interested in getting. I wanted a very quiet, thoughtful, but pleasant expression. I often asked them to think about some happy times in their lives that made them feel good...Sometimes they talked about their chants. Some of them even sang and chanted for me—I got chicken skin. When they chanted about certain areas of the Islands, the beauty of the mountains, rain and mist, I really felt a closeness to nature. When they chanted, it was something beyond reality...The size of the pictures in the book is large—a full page—and that's what I wanted. I wanted people to be in the presence of the kumu when they read their interviews."

Nana I Na Loea Hula emanates a special magnetism, a quality that is almost spiritual in nature. "Throughout this entire project there has been a direction, a guiding force," Silva said. "It was interesting, many of the kumu said when we met them, 'We know of you. We've long awaited your arrival and now that you are here, we greet you.' It was almost like the promised Messiah had come."

A major concern of the kumu was that the book would turn into a commercial venture, that "somebody would pick their brains and make money off of them," Silva said. "They had seen too many beautiful por-

The littles ones are the big stars at the Keiki Hula Festival, Honolulu.

149

Pukalani Hula Halau is a vision of grace.

Mapuana DeSilva

MAPUANA DeSILVA

I am learning to hold true to the spirit of what my teacher gave me. I think now that this spirit comes in two parts. First, it is my duty to respect and preserve the traditional dances. If I inherit a holoku from my grandmother, I don't chop it into a miniskirt just because fashions have changed. The same is true for the chants and hula that have been given to me. They are priceless gifts; I shouldn't be so presumptuous as to fiddle with them just to keep up with what is fashionable. Secondly, it is also my duty to create. I am a keeper of the record of my own time and of my own place. I've tried to keep and honor what was passed on to me, and I've worked hard to build through creation and recreation, a tradition of my own. I think that there are boundaries to creativity and they are based on common sense. If you're going to create a traditional hula you shouldn't wind up with a square dance. You have to know your text, you have to feel the magic of the language and you have to be well-versed in hula's traditional vocabulary of motions. Only then can you conscientiously experiment and innovate.

A talented young performer from Halau Hula Kawaimaluhia.

150

traits of alii used on postcards and liquor bottles. They wanted the material to be properly used and administered for educational purposes. They wanted to ensure that the value of their knowledge as a legacy to the people of Hawaii would be respected and cherished."

Nana I Na Loea Hula shares a message of caution and encouragement. Silva sees it as a way for the kumu to "gain insights into the thoughts and feelings of one another, to help them understand each other's points of view and relate to each other even without conversing. It clarifies the different perspectives on the hula and offers suggestions on how they all can function within the art form."

Said Chun, "It was the most meaningful project I've ever worked on. The book is not just a bunch of words and pictures. I think it's going to take a long time before people fully realize what the book really means."

Puluelo Park

PULUELO PARK

Today's kahiko is what the modern audience wants it to be but it's not necessarily the hula of old...Lokalia (Montgomery) taught me that the old way is not the only way and that as a teacher, you must be creative, but I feel this creativity has gotten out of hand. The older kumu have to step forward and draw the line of what is traditional.

MAIKI AIU LAKE

As far as my family was concerned, the hula was a closed book. I came from a straight-laced Christian family and most anything Hawaiian was not condoned. But in my family was a grand aunt named Helen Correa and to her, the hula was great people accomplishing heroic deeds in everyday life. My tutu taught me the mannerisms, the attitude and the gentleness of the actual dance performance but my first formal teacher was Lokalia Montgomery. As I studied under her, I learned that the kahiko could be performed without all the rituals. I didn't have to be afraid and I didn't have to compromise my Christian faith. Sometimes everyone forgets what the hula is all about. But you come back and remember. I've forgotten many times what it really means but as you get older, you find that it's real and it's there. The spirit of the kupuna will always be there.

JOHN LAKE

My first kumu in the formal training sense was Aunty Maiki Aiu Lake...She taught me that the beauty of the hula is to come to terms with the essence of one's self. She said that the Hawaiians call your inner light the manao and it is the real source of your dancing. Your body is simply an expression of your manao.

ROSELLE BAILEY

I think the qualifications for a kumu are tremendous...A true kumu has to be a psychologist, psychoanalyst, historian, naturalist, priest, choreographer, nurse, sister and mother.

KAULANA KASPAROVITCH

My goal became to bring back as much as possible the expression and love in a dancer's face and movement so that a haumana can dance in place and emulate through the face and heart the entire dance. That is a dancer. Anybody can perform or teach technique but to draw an audience into the emotions of the dance is something else.

ROSE LOOK

My advice to a young dancer is you have to be beautiful inside to do anything well. Beauty starts from within. You can have all the steps, all the physical attributes, but unless you have an inner beauty you are just a person moving from side to side. Hula is beautiful and to portray it you must have a humility and respect for people.

KENT GHIRARD

When I first saw hula performed I was attracted to the groups that relied on a very simple style. I felt it gave the dancer more of an opportunity to express emotion without being able to rely on the gimmicks of a fast pace and complicated motions...The new kahiko of today is exciting and vital, and I'm all for it,

but it should be classified in a category all its own, otherwise what has been passed down from generation to generation and what has been created last month will become hopelessly muddled. I never had a wealth of knowledge of Hawaiiana. What I brought to the hula was all heart and a love for the music and dance...My greatest thrill still today is to perform in front of Hawaiians and be accepted although I am haole.

GEORGE HOLOKAI

One morning Tom Hiona (a well-respected kumu hula) woke my mother up at 4:00 A.M. and said he wanted to go down to the studio before the sun came up. We got to the studio at 5:00 A.M. and he told my mother he was going to make me his assistant. My mother was hesitant but he told her he knew what I could do. Furthermore, he said he would proceed, with my mother's permission or not. He said that I may be my mother's son but my life in the hula had already been chosen for me...In 1955, a woman walked into the studio and told my mother that she wanted me to be her student...Her name was Lillian Makaena and she said she had dreamt of me and had spent months searching the city to find me. She said she didn't have very long to live but she wanted to teach me whatever she knew as fast as she could. Like Tom, Mrs. Makaena expected me to learn strictly by listening. There were no papers or notetaking allowed. Mrs. Makaena told me if I drank I had to quit and if I had a girlfriend I had to give her up as well. I was told I could never get married. She said these were my kapus and if I broke any of them I would lose all of the knowledge that she had shared with me...I would be taken frequently to the Blow Hole and she would stand on one side of the cove with me on the other side and she would instruct me

George Naope

Olana Ai

to chant. Without shouting, I would have to make my chanting voice heard over the wind and the waves of the ocean.

Pearl Keawe

Alice Namakelua

WINONA BEAMER

My first kumu were my great-grand-mother, Isabella Desha, and my grandmother, Helen Desha Beamer, whom we called "Sweetheart Grandma." She was a great inspiration to me. She was always trying to train us to have the right feelings within ourselves so that we could experience the calmness that was all around us. When we walked into a room we had to walk as if our feet weren't touching the mat. If she heard your feet scuffling the mat, you would have to go out and come in again. Sometimes she would train us outside and the fragrance of the leaves and the mangoes would be all around...My grandmother would give each of us a ti leaf and talk about faith and hope and love. She would tell us the chants of Laka and she would tell them as if Laka was right there. While she talked she would tell us to feel the shape and the texture of the leaves and to put them up to our faces and feel their smoothness. She would talk of the mist over the mountains being the spirit of Laka and so everything that we do and say should be pleasing. So of course we would try our very best since we had a spirit watching over us.

ROBERT CAZIMERO

I consider myself a contemporary kumu and I like being a teacher of today. To me, hula includes the sounds of jackhammers, cranes, buildings going up, traffic. I see hula in all of these things...When I started in hula, one thing that I had made up my mind to do was prove that men could dance. That you didn't have to just get up on stage and stomp around with a spear while hitting a paddle against a canoe. There is such a thing as manly grace.

Eleanor Hiram Hoke

ELEANOR HIRAM HOKE

I was taken at birth by my grandmother, Katherine Keakaokala Kanahele, to be the chosen one for the hula kapu. I was reared in the area of Marconi Wireless Station in Kahuku, and it was there that I received my hula kapu training until age eight...For eight years, all I did was live the hula. Hawaiian chants were chanted to me like nursery rhymes are sung to other children. Throughout the day and the night all I did was practice and study chants...I could not be touched by unclean hands and my meals had to be prepared at the kuahu in the halau by Tutuwahine alone. The mullet that I ate had to come from a pond in Marconi Wireless and not from the ocean. The pigs that were fed to me could not be fed swill but only the best of grain. They also had to be spotlessly clean...When I came of age, I was taken to school. I was not allowed to share any part of my lunch with my friends nor was I allowed to exchange any food. Because of my kapu training I was not allowed to play with the neighborhood children...The reason my knowledge of the hula has survived is the hula kapu. Nothing was written down yet I can remember every mele, every hula motion, every chant that I learned at the kuahu.

Frank Hewett

FRANK HEWETT

When I dance, I offer certain evocations, to ask certain spirits to become a part of me so that they may be happy again in coming back to life through me...Hula is a religious ceremony to the Hawaiian gods and goddesses of our ancestors...Each movement symbolizes something important and if they are embellished, then we have blurred the lines of our history.

ALICE NAMAKELUA

In 1945, I was offered a job with the Department of Parks and Recreation to teach hula ipu...I basically taught auwana and I asked all my students what my uncles had asked me when I began. Did they want to become an instructor, an entertainer or did they just want to do it for fun? I taught them the mele, then the translation of the mele, and then I trained them on cowboy handkerchiefs. If you can dance on a cowboy handkerchief you can call yourself a dancer. You must be able to perform everything on that space...Today it seems we are losing almost everything Hawaiian about our culture—our language, our dress, our religion and now our arts. I don't consider what is being done today as the Hawaiian hula. There is not much remaining that people my age enjoy and recognize. It is only exercising. It exists today only to keep modern audiences happy. I don't see the hula being Hawaiian in the years to come...There are no boundaries or definitions anymore. You make the cake the way you want, I make the cake the way I want.

KAMAKI KANAHELE

I didn't realize I was interested in the hula because I was already doing it as a part of my everyday life...My mother and grandparents were my first teachers and we were raised to move, sit right, stand right and speak correctly—to understand these things as an important part of life...Grandma Lokalia Montgomery...finished my formal training in the hula kahiko...She was hardnosed, no-nonsense...She would summon me at any time of the day or night...I learned that the hula is not just merely getting up to dance or to perform. Instead, every time you stood to dance or sat to chant it was your responsibility to summarize life and hint at its happiness and sadness. Describe the good and the bad, make a beginning and end it with pride. The dancer becomes an alii, a god, a shark or a dog. They can be beautiful or arrogant, handsome or ugly. You give the human being a glimpse of his time on earth with a repeat of these reminders each time he comes to the floor...Hula must always have its piko, its center of balance. It is a living energy and a beckoning force. There will always be controversy about what is proper and correct, but a demonstration of the unity of hula in our time can only solidify the remnants of what is left of a great heritage.

HOOULU CAMBRA

I regard the hula as an art, specifically a living art that must be worked at and prepared for constantly...Hula is a way of life, it is a people's inspiration. It is the Hawaiian's connection to the universe around him.

KAAIIKAWAHA KALAMA

I consider myself a contemporary hula teacher and not a kumu hula. I think the word kumu is used too loosely today...My teachers were the real kumu. To be a real teacher you cannot have two lives. You cannot be married or have a family because your life has to be dedicated to your students.

KEVIN "CHUBBY" MAHOE

(My) endeavor is to worship God in the beauty of his Holiness. The hula is Hawaii's most beautiful art and can certainly be used to display His magnificent handiwork...The hula that I do today—the interpretation, the motions—are all inspired by God.

KAUI ZUTTERMEISTER

My uncle told me the only way the culture is going to live is if the dance is kept pure. Hula kahiko is all that we have left of our kupuna. It is the only reflection of Hawaii's past...What I enjoyed most about my uncle was his instruction in chanting. He taught us the proper way to breathe and the proper time to breathe. There were many times when the instruction made me feel frustrated and bored. My uncle would put me in front of him and he would say a word from the chant and I would have to repeat it the exact same way he said it over and over again until he was satisfied. One day I asked him why we had to go over one word or one motion sometimes for three hours. He replied that this was how a kumu passed on his manao and power to a haumana. When I imitated him, I was accepting his mana. Moreover, he had taught me my first real lesson in the hula which was humility. In every art, in every profession, you are taught humility through discipline, and the hula is no different.

JOHN R. KAHAI TOPOLINSKI

Mrs. (Kawena) Pukui told me that hula is not only for our people. It is for anyone who has the desire. You do not have to be Hawaiian to dance. If you want it to live, you must give it to everybody.

John Kaimikaua

Leiana Woodside

JOHN KAIMIKAUA

What is sorely missing in the ancient hula today is the purity of spirit within each individual kumu and dancer. Ancient hula is spiritual. When we perform, we are indeed reenacting the past life of our forefathers, and we must be clean from the inside out in order to spiritually satisfy and represent the hula according to tradition. The hula was held sacred and was a means of expressing the lifestyles and culture of our forefathers. It was not entertainment but their way of communicating effectively our whole Hawaiian culture: its lifestyles, government, temple ceremonies, genealogy and interests were preserved in these chants...The hula is the inspiration that will enable the Hawaiians to rise up from the dust of obscurity. It is the last hope that can make us feel Hawaiian and remember our culture and forefathers. The dance will thus be the last of our cultural strongholds that may well preserve our dying heritage.

"Keepers of the Ancient Hula" was first published in November/December 1984. Since Nana I Na Loea Hula was released that year, ten kumu hula have passed away. Jan Itagaki, the current director of the Kalihi-Palama Cultural and Arts Society, reports that her organization's crusade to preserve and perpetuate the hula goes on; a sequel to Nana I Na Loea Hula, in fact, is presently in the works.

153

For Mieko and for all of us it was *kimono* day once again and we watched the dawning skies anxiously, even though Mieko confidently expected sunshine and quiet. She was right every year. And every year this increased my awe of her, and of her Buddha—so unfailingly gracious.

On this morning I watched my always-in-a-hurry father as he eased the old Hudson sedan out of the garage and drove so slowly down the sandy driveway that no puff of dust was raised. My mother walked after the car, dragged both screeching wings of the tall iron gate closed,

KIMONO DAY

BY BARBARA ROBINSON

clanged the long bar down and locked it with a filigreed iron key. For this one day of the year, no cars would come farther up the road than to Aunt Winnie's house. Furthermore, all tricycles, scooters and balls were locked up in the storeroom. Not a single speck of dust was to be stirred up today.

Mieko's husband, Rokuro, had the day off even though the summer pineapple canning season was in full swing. The neighborhood children on this one day were kept away. But my sister and I had permission to watch from the kitchen sidewalk, knowing that if we put even one toe off that freshly washed walkway we'd be sent straight indoors. We could watch from the upstairs windows to be sure, but there was more to this affair than just watching.

In the dim dawn, two of Rokuro's brothers and their wives arrived and parked their car outside the gate. Quietly, the brothers stretched long ropes between our house roof eaves and a tall kiawe tree across the lawn. Mrs. Andrews, Mrs. Rowan and my grandmother arrived through the hedge carrying rolls of

155

grass mats from their bedrooms, and the two brothers laid them out under the lines and over the lawn, creating a patchwork quilt effect of lau hala mats and *tatami* matting from all our houses. Not an inch of our sloping front lawn was left uncovered, and a long path of lau hala matting led to the door of Mieko's and Rokuro's cottage.

Great-aunt Winnie and my mother turned on garden hoses and wet down the ground in Aunt Winnie's garden and in our chicken pens and papaya grove. Mr. Douglas next door turned on his sprinkler over his sandy backyard where no grass grew, and Rokuro and his brothers went into the garage and brought up, one by one, three great pine chests with rope handles and brass fittings and placed them in a long row on the mats. Then Rokuro and his brothers went, skipping carefully along the lau hala path, into the cottage.

As the clouds were turning pink over Iao Valley they came out again, dressed now in traditional dark *kimonos* with tight black sashes. Next, Rokuro's sisters-in-law emerged from the cottage. They were dressed in beautiful gray *kimonos* with *obi* sashes of red, orange and gold patterns on white satin. Silently they held the door open and quietly Mieko appeared.

Each year at this moment she became transformed once more into a distant mysterious other self—someone, we eventually learned, who appeared on this day once again as the person she really was—the daughter of a noble family in Hiroshima. She had arrived in Hawaii with her husband, a political refugee, to become at the age of forty, a servant in a foreign household.

Mieko never clashed with anyone. But no one ever argued with her either. Even with broom or vegetable peeler in hand, she was never ordinary, never without dignity. (As my grandmother said, "A real lady never needs to say she's a lady.")

And now Mieko stood in the early sunlight, regal in her sweeping court robe of gold, red, silver and black. There she stood, framed by pink oleander, hibiscus hedges, the garage wall, chicken pens, jacaranda and kiawe trees, green lawn and lavender sky—Haleakala Mountain on her left, the West Maui Mountains to her right. Aunt Winnie's best lau hala mat was under her feet. Before her ran the soft padded paths connecting her with these families of Japan and England and Hawaii and America who now stood waiting before her.

Aunt Winnie stood near a hibiscus bush that marked a dimly remembered boundary between her yard and ours. She held four quilted coat hangers. I knew she kept those big hangers specially for her San Francisco clothes, and that right now those coats and dresses were draped over a chair in her bedroom. My mother also waited, also holding her best hangers—wooden ones covered with my grandmother's crocheted wool webbing. Mother's party dresses were tossed on her bed today, as were those belonging to Mrs. Rowan and Grandmother.

Mieko looked over her court—a far cry from the hundred servants and the gardens of her family estate in Hiroshima. No one spoke. No one moved. It was a sad, grand moment for all of us.

At last Mieko moved up the gently rising slope to where the three men waited. She gave her husband a tiny nod. Then Rokuro and his brothers bowed in old-fashioned style to her, turned to the first big chest and lifted the heavy creaking lid. Perfumes of spices and camphor rose and flowed around us, min-

gling with the ever-present scents of lantana and gardenia.

The two sisters stepped closer. Rokuro stooped and lifted out a glimmering roll of red and silver brocade and laid it carefully across the outstretched arms of the two sisters. Slim tubes of soft packing were drawn from inside the roll, which, unfolded, became a magnificent *kimono*. This *kimono* was set upright, so stiff with silver thread embroidery that it stood alone, unsupported, brave and unsagging before Mieko.

After a long pause, she walked slowly around it, inspecting without touching it. Returning to her position facing the robe, she nodded again to Rokuro.

Carefully, he slid his hand through a cuff, drawing the wing-like sleeve, collar and other sleeve up toward his shoulder until the *kimono* hung like a banner from his extended arm. He paused, swayed left, swayed right, then with smooth powerful grace he turned himself in wide circles, and the robe, rising like a heavy crimson kite, sailed rustling and sparkling in the slanting sunbeams, filling the morning air with the scent of cedar. It seemed alive—a great slow-flying moth.

With gentle precise movements, Rokuro brought it to rest poised on his arm. He glanced toward Aunt Winnie, and she put a soft cushioned hanger in his hand. Swiftly, lightly, Rokuro floated the *kimono* onto the hanger and again lifted it high. The two sisters fixed big ivory fasteners to close the front, and the robe was hung up on the pole-braced rope line to sway in the breeze.

At a nod from Mieko, another *kimono* was lifted from the chest. This was pink with silver embroidery, lined with darker pink. After a flight on Rokuro's arm it was arranged on one of mother's quilted hangers and hung up on the rope,

two arm-span's distance from the first.

As each marvelous *kimono* was lifted from the chest, its rolls of inner padding were carefully arranged on the open lid. The silk box lining was lifted and draped over the edge, and the chest and its trays were left open to the sun.

One by one, each shimmering *kimono* was lifted out—patterns of butterflies, peacocks, bamboo, plum blossoms, leaves, buds and chrysanthemums in crimson, lavender, green, rose, ivory and black—each *kimono* stiff with the weight of silk, gold and silver thread. Twenty noble garments were taken from the chests, placed erect and separate on the mat, lifted, floated, and set to sway and swoop on the long pole-braced lines.

The sun rose higher and a breeze swept up from the plains of Kahului. Mr. Douglas turned the sprinklers higher over his sandy yard. Aunt Winnie and Rokuro's two brothers walked through the hibiscus hedge to her lanai and brought back her tall curvy peacock chair. The chair was placed in the shade of the kiawe tree and Mieko was seated. A yard-square flat cushion was placed under her feet. Her sisters brought her tea in tiny cups. Her treasured garments from her child-home past swayed like courtiers before her.

And all that day Mieko dreamed, until the evening shadows of the West Maui Mountains rose inexorably up the pink slopes of Haleakala, and her families came again, wrapped each *kimono* in silk once more, and lowered them into their chests. The chests were closed and carried down the sloping lawn to be stacked again, one on top of the other, against a wall in our garage.

157

"Kimono Day" was first published in May/June 1981.

THE CHRISTMAS SHIPS

BY STEVEN GOLDSBERRY

ILLUSTRATION BY SANFORD MOCK

Most people think you can't do much with walnut shells, but when I was a kid my dad used to turn them into sailing ships. Other kids' fathers could do this, too, once they'd seen that all it took was a little melted candle wax in the bottom of a halved shell, a toothpick for the mast and a square piece of paper for the sail. "Hell, anyone can make these things," my dad would say.

He'd rattle through the walnut bowl looking for the biggest nut, crack it slowly, dig out the meat with those slim silver picks that came with the nutcracker set but which no one else ever used, and he'd hold up the best hull you could imagine: prow pointed, keel deep, stern bridged by the last bit of thin interior shell.

He'd send one of us kids to the hall closet for a spool. "It has to be brown thread. Light brown is better." And he would cut a length of it, push the middle down into the bottom of the shell and drip wax over it. The wax would cloud and the thread would disappear, except for the ends fore and aft, the starts of the rigging. "A frigate," my dad would say, taking scissors and trimming down three toothpicks—the shorter masts and the jib boom—so they wouldn't have ragged ends.

He'd drip more wax in. "Not too much or the thing won't float." When the wax jelled enough, he'd slip in the masts. They would already be fixed with square sails, pushed down to crescents to appear filled with wind. He would cut the spanker and jib sails to the proper shape and glue them to the spars. The wax had to be cold, as hard as a candle again, before he would finish the rigging, tying thread to catch the mast top, then quickly snipping off all the loose ends.

This was always around Christmas when there were several large bowls of nuts in the house, and more still in bags in the cupboards. When he was done making three ships, one for each of his boys, my dad would want them painted. Gold, always. We would search our model paints and bring out the bottles. It took two coats to cover the hulls. Once or twice we spray-painted the ships, sails and all. Then he would hang them on the tree.

"Dad, we want to sail them," I'd say.

"We can make some others to sail," he would tell me.

The ships were beautiful on the tree, floating above the thin glass globes and colored lights. Flying ships like Captain Hook's, dusted gold to lift them into the air.

But ships are meant for sailing, and every boy is a sailor. The golden frigates would end up at the bottom of the tub, each hull weighted down with a marble for a cannonball, masts and sails broken and bobbing on the surface. Five years, maybe, my dad had patience enough to build these ships for us, three to be sunk before Christmas, and three right after.

I have my own son now, and a daughter. Six and five. I tell them tonight about the Christmas ships. We start cracking and sorting the shells. My wife lights a candle. The sails are cut and the box of toothpicks discovered behind the spatulas in the drawer. My son is louder and more enthusiastic. He thinks the first ship is for him. My daughter has been taught that girls are still first. I know that into whichever little hands this homely craft is bound, it is doomed. Both of my children hold the glint of determined foundering in their eyes.

But it doesn't matter. Nothing matters but the building, I realize. I start singing a Christmas song that is not about sailing. I watch the wax drops cloud in the bottom of the shell. For all those ships my dad built for me, I build this one for him.

"The Christmas Ships" was first published in November/December 1986.

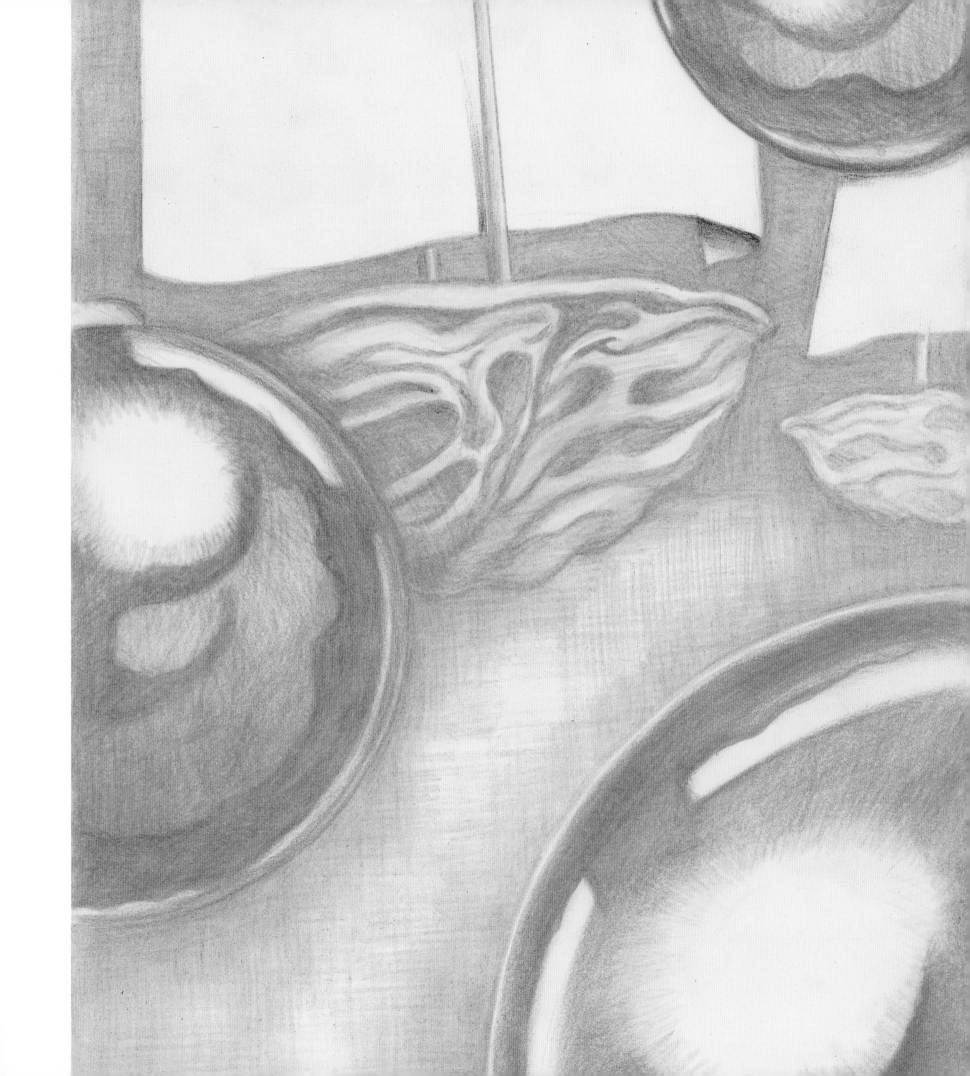

Silkies brighten a fifties scene at Alex Drive-In, Kapahulu. Inset: The ubiquitous aloha shirt.

THE ALOHA SHIRT

A COLORFUL SWATCH OF ISLAND HISTORY

BY DeSOTO BROWN

Elvis Presley had an entire wardrobe of them in the sixties films, *Blue Hawaii* and *Paradise, Hawaiian Style.* During the fifties, entertainer Arthur Godfrey and bandleader Harry Owens often sported them on television shows. John Wayne loved to lounge around in them. Mick Jagger felt compelled to buy one on a visit to Hawaii in the 1970s. Dustin Hoffman, Steven Spielberg and Bill Cosby avidly collect them.

From gaudy to grand, from tawdry to tasteful, aloha shirts are Hawaii's gift to the world of fashion. It's been more than fifty years since those riotously colored garments made their first appearance as immediately recognizable symbols of the Islands.

The roots of the aloha shirt go back to the early 1930s, when Hawaii's garment industry was just beginning to develop its own unique style. Although locally-made clothes did exist, they were almost exclusively items for plantation workers which were constructed of durable palaka or plain cotton material.

Out of this came the first stirrings of fashion: Beachboys and schoolchildren started having sport shirts made from colorful Japanese *kimono* fabric. The favored type of cloth was the kind used for children's *kimonos*—bright pink and orange floral prints for girls; masculine motifs in browns and blues for boys. In Japan, such flamboyant patterns were considered unsuitable for adult clothing, but in the Islands, such rules didn't apply, and it seemed the flashier the shirt, the better—for either sex. Thus, the aloha shirt was born.

It was easy and inexpensive in those days to have garments tailored to order; the next step was moving to mass production and marketing. In June 1935, Honolulu's best known tailoring establishment, Musa-Shiya, advertised the availability of "Aloha shirts—well tailored, beautiful designs and radiant colors. Ready-made or made to order. . .95¢ and up." This is the first known printed use of the term that would soon refer to an entire industry. By the following year, several local manufacturers had begun full-scale production of "aloha wear." One of them, Ellery Chun of King-Smith, registered as local trademarks the terms "Aloha Sportswear" and "Aloha Shirt" in 1936 and 1937, respectively.

These early entrepreneurs were the first to create uniquely Hawaiian designs for fabric as well—splashy patterns that would forever symbolize the Islands. A 1939 *Honolulu Advertiser* story described them as a "delightful confusion (of) tropical fish and palm trees, Diamond Head and the Aloha Tower, surfboards and leis, ukuleles and Waikiki beach scenes."

The aloha wear of the late 1930s was intended for—and mostly worn by—tourists, and interestingly, a great deal of it was exported to the Mainland and even Europe and Australia. By the end of the decade, for example, only five percent of the output of one local firm, the Kamehameha Garment Company, was sold in Hawaii.

World War II brought this trend to a halt, and during the postwar period, aloha wear really came into its own in Hawaii. A strong push to support local industry gradually nudged Island garb into the work place, and kamaainas began to wear the clothing that previously had been seen as attire for visitors.

In 1947, for example, male employees of the City & County of Honolulu were first allowed to wear aloha shirts "in plain shades" during the summer months. Later that year, the first observance of Aloha Week started the tradition of "bankers and bellhops…mix(ing) colorfully in multi-hued and tapa-designed Aloha shirts every day," as a local newspaper's Sunday magazine supplement noted in 1948. By the 1960s, "Aloha Friday," set aside specifically for the wearing of aloha attire, had become a tradition.

Most of the Hawaiian-themed fabric used in manufacturing aloha wear was designed in the Islands, then printed on the Mainland or in Japan. The glowing vibrant rayons of the late forties and early fifties (a period now seen as aloha wear's heyday) were at first printed on the East Coast, but manufacturers there usually required such large orders, local firms eventually found it impossible to continue using them. By 1964, ninety percent of Hawaiian fabric was being manufactured in Japan—a situation that still exists today.

Fashion trends usually move in cycles, and aloha wear is no exception. By the 1960s, the "chop suey print" with its "tired cliches of Diamond Head, Aloha Tower, outrigger canoes (and) stereotyped leis" was seen as corny and garish, according to an article published in the *Honolulu Star-Bulletin*. But it was just that outdated aspect that began to appeal to the younger crowd, who began searching out old-fashioned aloha shirts at the Salvation Army and Goodwill thrift stores. These shirts were dubbed "silkies," a name by which they're still known, even though most of them were actually made of rayon.

Before long, what had been fifty-cent shirts began escalating in price, and a customer who had balked at paying $5 for a shirt that someone had already worn soon found the same item selling for $10—and more. By the late 1970s, aloha wear designers were copying the prints of yesteryear for their new creations.

The days of bargain silkies are now gone. The few choice aloha shirts from decades past that still remain are offered today by specialized dealers for hundreds of dollars apiece. The best examples of vintage aloha shirts are now rightly seen as art objects worthy of preservation for the lovely depictions they offer of Hawaii's colorful and unique scene.

"The Aloha Shirt: A Colorful Swatch of Island History" was first published in September/October 1987.

UKULELE: THE STRINGS THAT BIND

BY CHERYL CHEE TSUTSUMI

On the afternoon of August 23, 1879, the vessel *Ravenscrag*, carrying 419 Portuguese immigrants to their new home in Hawaii, laid anchor in Honolulu Harbor. It had been an arduous, 15,000-mile, four-month journey from Madeira, and in celebration and thanksgiving for their safe arrival, young Joao Fernandes borrowed his friend's *braguinha* and began playing folk songs from his native land on the wharf. Bystanders were delighted by the lilting sound of the tiny four-string guitar, and immediately adopted it. Soon every Island music-lover was strumming a local version of it—from farmers and fisherman to kings and queens.

The Hawaiians named their new instrument ukulele, or "jumping flea," because, according to one the-ory, the fingers of a skilled player conjured up that image when they moved nimbly across the frets. Queen Liliuokalani is said to have favored the ukulele's more poetic translation, "the gift that came here"— from uku, defined in some contexts as "gift or reward," and lele, which also means "to come." Another account says the instrument was initially called ukeke lele or "dancing ukeke," after the Hawaiians' three-string musical bow. The name, so the story goes, was mispronounced and gradually changed over the years to ukulele.

It is difficult to determine which explanation is the most accurate, but one fact is certain: the ukulele quickly became entrenched in the Hawaiian lifestyle. From pau hana jam sessions to elaborate galas at Iolani Palace, there was seldom an occasion in the Islands that wasn't brightened by a song or two on the ukulele. By the turn of the century, few people would

Wooden molding forms, well-used tools, glue and skill transform rough koa into gleaming instruments at Kamaka Hawaii.

remember that its origins were rooted halfway around the world in Portugal.

Among the immigrants who arrived in Honolulu on the *Ravenscrag* were Augusto Dias, Jose de Espirito Santo and Manuel Nunes, woodworkers who had earned reputations in Madeira as makers of fine furniture and musical instruments. Most historians credit Nunes with developing the Portuguese *braguinha* into the ukulele we know today. He increased the size of the instrument, slightly altered its shape and changed its steel strings to gut strings so that picks no longer were necessary to play it. He also tuned it differently, allowing for less complicated chord fingerings.

The Hawaiians adored the ukulele because it was simple to play and tune, and, being small and lightweight, it was portable. By 1884, in response to the growing demand for instruments, both Nunes and Dias had opened ukulele manufacturing shops in Honolulu. Four years later, Santo was also listed in the *Honolulu City Directory* as a guitar and ukulele maker. All three crafted exquisite instruments out of koa, some featuring intricately carved decorative touches, others inlaid with gleaming mother-of-pearl. These early ukuleles sold for $3—an amount equal to a sugar plantation laborer's monthly salary. Those who couldn't afford the price made their own instruments out of halved coconut shells, cigar boxes and other materials.

The alii, who were ardent lovers of music, enjoyed listening to and composing songs on the ukulele. In fact, it was King David Kalakaua's favorite instrument. He played, designed and even made his own ukuleles under the tutelage of Augusto Dias. As one of Dias' most loyal patrons, Kalakaua gave him permission to stamp the royal crown as a trademark on every ukulele that he made.

In the late 1800s, Island bands on tour introduced the ukulele to Mainland audiences. By 1910, Hawaiian music—and the ukulele—were enjoying phenomenal popularity all across the United States. A 1917 issue of *Paradise of the Pacific* observed, "Hawaii has captured America. From every phonograph shop comes the strains of the 'Hilo March'...The boy in the street whistles 'Hello, Hawaii, How Are You?' Our music teachers have closed the piano and put aside the violin—in order to live, they advertise lessons on the ukulele..."

Competition increased for a slice of the lucrative ukulele manufacturing business. Ukulele production even began on the Mainland, the best-known operation being C.F. Martin Company of Nazareth, Pennsylvania, which was founded by German guitar maker Christian Friedrich Martin. Backed by an undisputed reputation as the finest manufacturer of guitars and mandolins in the world, C.F. Martin produced its first ukulele in 1916—based closely on the Nunes design. Today, Martin ukuleles, usually fashioned from mahogany or rosewood, must be custom-ordered at a cost upwards of $700 each.

Leslie Nunes, the great-grandson of Manuel Nunes, is probably the foremost authority on the ukulele. He has been researching the instrument for thirty years, and is currently working on a comprehensive book on the subject. He also boasts a rare collection of more than 100 ukuleles, including what is believed to be the oldest one in existence—an 1885 koa instrument made by his great-grandfather.

In August 1979, Nunes spearheaded a celebration at the State Capitol to observe the ukulele's centennial. He also helped design a special koa "centennial ukulele," patterned after Manuel Nunes' popular 1910 series. The centennial was marked by the completion of a book entitled *The Ukulele: A Portuguese Gift to Hawaii*, which Nunes authored with the assistance of John Henry Felix and Peter Senecal, two leaders in the local Portuguese community. The sixty-three-page book, containing a history of the ukulele along with numerous historical photos, was released in April 1980 in conjunction with the opening of a nine-month ukulele exhibit that Nunes organized for the Bishop Museum.

Sharing his knowledge about the ukulele is one of Nunes' passions. In 1978, he founded Hawaii's Musical Museum, a traveling exhibit of ukuleles from his private collection that has appeared at Bloomingdale's in New York; Yamano Music Stores in Tokyo, Japan; and the Institute of Music in Funchal, Madeira. Said Nunes, "I can do an exhibit to accommodate the size of any room." To date, his most ambitious effort has been a display of twenty-six instruments and forty-nine historical photographs for Liberty House department store's two-week promotion on Portugal in September of last year. Nunes also regularly prepares lectures and mini exhibits for Hawaii's schoolchildren.

Although his life has virtually revolved around the ukulele, Nunes said, "I don't play well. People are always amazed at that. They think I'm a virtuoso because I have so many instruments and my interest is so deep."

Others, though, have perpetuated the ukulele through song. Ukulele master Ernest Kaai was an outstanding performer, composer, arranger and impresario in the early 1900s. In 1916, he authored the first instructional book on the ukulele, *The Ukulele: A Hawaiian Guitar*. With detailed descriptions of various strokes, chords and playing techniques, the informative manual was applauded in its time as the most thorough and systematic study of its kind.

Emphasizing the ukulele's impor-

164

Young musicians with their ukuleles, c. 1884.

A student from the Kohala Girls' School on the Big Island strums a chord, c. 1911.

tance as a rhythmical accompaniment, Kaai wrote, "The effect is very brilliant and fascinating, and any quintet, glee or musical club in the Islands without the ukulele is far from being perfect. It is as needful to any Hawaiian quintet club as a snare drum is to a military brass band."

Largely due to Kaai's efforts, the ukulele had, by the 1920s, become a mainstay of Hawaiian ensembles, but it was the gifted Jesse Kalima who brought it into the spotlight as a solo instrument. Kalima was fifteen years old when he appeared in a 1935 Territorial Amateur Hour Contest with his ukulele and won first place with his lively rendition of the "Stars and Stripes Forever." This "Hawaiianized" version of the march became an instant hit in the Islands, and Kalima became an instant star. It remained his "theme song" throughout his career, and was included for decades in every aspiring young ukulele player's repertoire.

Meanwhile, other notable Island musicians, including Andy Cummings, were following Kalima's lead and using the ukulele as a springboard for their creativity. In 1938, Cummings signed up to tour the Mainland and Canada for eight months as a member of the Paradise Island Revue, led by premier showman E.K. Fernandez. In mid-December, the troupe arrived in Lansing, Michigan, where, recalled Cummings, "the temperature was between five and ten degrees. For us Islanders, it was unbearably cold! We were walking back to our hotel from the theater where we were playing and I thought of Waikiki with its rolling surf, warm sunshine and palm trees..." The rest is history. Cummings went immediately to his room, picked up his ukulele and composed, "Waikiki," a song that has become a beloved classic in the annals of Hawaiian music.

Following his return to Hawaii, Cummings formed a group, Andy Cummings and the Hawaiian Sere-

Ukulele virtuoso Andy Cummings.

naders, which played "Hawaiian music in the Hawaiian way" at various Honolulu clubs. The Japanese attack on Pearl Harbor in 1941 ushered in World War II, and during the four tumultuous years that followed, Cummings said, "I hardly played a note. There wasn't any entertainment happening for awhile." After the war, the Hawaiian Serenaders slipped back into show business. For the next decade, they traveled the Waikiki circuit, taking the stage at such posh, prestigious spots as the Outrigger Canoe Club, Queen's Surf and the Royal Hawaiian Hotel's Monarch Room.

From 1956 until his retirement in 1978, Cummings was employed full-time in Hawaiian Airline's Sales and Promotion Department. For more than twenty years, he and his ukulele brought Hawaii's aloha to the world—Hong Kong, Bangkok, Rome, Athens, Norway, Peru, Australia, Saudi Arabia…"you name it, we've been there."

Today, every Sunday evening, seventy two-year-old Cummings strolls through the dining room at Buzz's Steakhouse in Moiliili with his ukulele, filling the air with nostalgia as he strums old Hawaiian favorites. "I don't get tired of it because I enjoy it," he said simply.

"When the guests enjoy it, I enjoy it even more."

Eddie Kamae understands that sentiment well. At fifty-eight, he is one of Hawaii's musical pioneers and its youngest "Living Treasure," an honor bestowed only upon the eminent few who have distinguished themselves in some aspect of Hawaiian culture.

Kamae was about fourteen years old when his brother Sam found an ukulele on a city bus and brought it home. "I loved the sound of the instrument," Kamae recalled, "so every day I would pick it up and play it, not knowing anything about chords or how to read notes." Curiosity piqued, he learned whatever he could from his brother, then scoured bookstores to find material that would teach him more. He also frequented musicians' havens, one of the most popular of which was a place called Charlie's Taxi in downtown Honolulu. It was there that he met Shoi Ikemi, and in 1948, the two teamed up as the Ukulele Rascals—Hawaii's first all-ukulele act.

The Ukulele Rascals played Latin, classical, jazz, American folk and popular tunes—everything but Hawaiian music. By expanding their repertoire, however, they stretched the ukulele to its fullest potential, coaxing from it a range of exciting new sound capabilities. An innovator, Kamae developed a method of plucking the ukulele's four strings simultaneously, so both the melody and chords could be heard at the same time.

Gradually, in the years that followed, Kamae became immersed in serious research and reflection about his Hawaiian heritage. By 1957, his focus had completely shifted, and he was devoting himself entirely to Hawaiian music. In 1960, he organized the Sons of Hawaii, a group which revolutionized Island music with its distinctive blend of ancient and contemporary rhythmic elements.

Their first job was playing at a club called the Sandbox which was located on Sand Island, in the heart of Honolulu's industrial area. It was far from the entertainment hub of Waikiki but, said Kamae, "The Sandbox became the 'in' place. We had lines outside the doors—I couldn't believe it. Buses would bring tourists there, men with tuxedos on would walk in. I knew then that people were craving for this kind of music."

Kamae's ukulele has been an inspiring companion. When he composes, Kamae often goes up to the mountains, "where there's nobody around but the birds and the beautiful scenery and the breeze. I take my ukulele, a tape recorder, and a pad and pencil, sit under a tree and write about some of the things I've experienced. Going into the mountains is an intense spiritual experience for me…it's a magical place. I've cried there many times. But it's a good cry. It's a totally good feeling when you can sit down and pour out your soul. If I'm working on a song, the only time I know I'm finished with it is when I cry. The purpose of music is to move people that way."

Kamae has had a powerful influence on many Island musicians, one of the most celebrated of whom is ukulele virtuoso Herbert Ohta, who is known professionally as Ohta-san. As a young boy, Ohta-san would spend a lot of time at Aala Park, "where all the ukulele players got together. One of them was Eddie Kamae."

Said Kamae of their first meeting, "Herbert was maybe twelve years old. He had his ukulele and we talked. I remember asking him to play a song for me. He played the 'Stars and Stripes Forever,' Jesse Kalima's song. I told him as time goes by, he should play something that would identify him. I had a feeling he was very dedicated, very serious about his music."

Kamae became Ohta-san's first mentor. He taught his talented protégé a variety of sophisticated playing techniques and urged him to apply them in all genres of music. Today, Ohta-san's vast repertoire defies classification; he can expertly deliver a soft, romantic "Tennesee Waltz," a crisp, snappy "Girl From Ipanema"—and everything in between. His lovely "Song for Anna," written for him by French composer Andre Popp, was an international hit in 1974, and has sold over two million copies.

Regarded as one of the Islands' most prolific performers, Ohta-san has recorded thirty albums on three continents (Europe, the Mainland and Asia). He is also one of the founders and charter members of Honolulu's Ukulele Club, an enthusiastic group of ukulele devotees who meet with their instruments every Monday night at Paki Park in Kaimuki for a few hours of fun and fellowship.

Ohta-san credits his mother with sparking his interest in the ukulele when he was seven. A few years later, in 1944, he played his ukulele on KGMB Radio's amateur hour and walked away with first prize—$10 and a comb and brush set. The next week, he appeared on the show again—and won first place once more. When he turned up at the station for the third time, he was denied a slot in the competition; the judges deemed him too skilled a performer to compete against the other contestants.

After World War II, while he was a student at Saint Louis High School, Ohta-san played his ukulele at the Honolulu Army/Navy YMCA on Sundays, and earned about $20 a month. From 1953 to 1963, he served in the Marine Corps and barely touched the ukulele—as an interpreter with the commanding general's staff in Japan, he "just didn't have the time." He did, however, manage to squeeze in an appearance on the "Ed Sullivan Show" in 1955.

Following his stint in the military,

Ohta-san's high school classmate, Galen Kam, who was working as a distributor for Decca Records, introduced him to Don McDiarmid, Jr., president of Hula Records. It was McDiarmid who gave Ohta-san his professional name and first recording break. In 1964, Ohta-san released "Sushi" for Hula Records. It became a smash hit, motivating hundreds of young fans, like Roy Sakuma, to take up the ukulele.

Recalled Sakuma, "'Sushi' became the number one song in Hawaii—I just *loved* that song! I started picking up the ukulele but I couldn't play it well. Then a friend of mine saw an ad in the paper that said Ohta-san was giving lessons. So I went to see him and asked if he would teach me. I studied with him for eighteen months."

From 1968 to 1972, Sakuma served as an instructor for Ohta-san's ukulele school, then he finally decided to go on his own. Today, with studios in Kaimuki, Aiea and Kaneohe, and a staff of twenty-three teachers, he operates the largest ukulele school in the state.

Sakuma's students range from four-year-olds barely bigger than their instruments to "grandmas and grandpas." His greatest satisfaction comes from "working with the children and seeing them grow. It's a great feeling to see that you've helped them and they're using what they've learned in ukulele class to better themselves in other areas."

In 1972, soon after he opened his first studio in Kaimuki, Sakuma formed the Termites, a group of four young ukulele virtuosos who entertained at birthday parties, conventions and many other special Island events for six years. In 1978, when they outgrew their name, the Termites were succeeded by a new performing group called the Super Keikis—who, in turn, have been succeeded by the Little Keikis.

Although he is justly proud of all of his youngsters, Sakuma remem-

Portrait of Ernest Kaai, c. 1915.

bers four with a special fondness. "They were students with muscular dystrophy at Jefferson Orthopedic School," Sakuma recalled. "I started off teaching three boys, then after one year, another boy saw how well the other kids were performing and he wanted to join the group. His teacher told me, 'Roy, he can't do it because he's mentally retarded.' His grade level was kindergarten and below. But he wanted to try, so I let him. The other kids were so encouraging, and what happened was, within six months, that boy advanced to third and fourth grade level work. The teachers all felt the music had opened him up."

In 1975, the four boys formed a group called ESP, Extra Strumming Power, and during the few years they were together, they made several public appearances, including televised performances for the Muscular Dystrophy and Easter Seals telethons. Said Sakuma, "Music was good therapy for them. They were very independent and they didn't give up easily. Even though they were handicapped, they were perfect kids."

Hawaii's annual Ukulele Festival is Sakuma's brainchild, the very successful realization of his "dream to

give the ukulele more recognition." The free show is usually held the last Sunday afternoon in July at Waikiki's Kapiolani Park, and for the past eight years, KCCN Radio has broadcast the entire program live. According to Sakuma, who has remained the moving force behind the event, the first festival in 1971 drew 800 spectators. Today, the crowd numbers about 6,000, with people coming as early as 5:30 in the morning to reserve seats. In fact, it has become so popular, Sakuma said, "There are visitors who plan their trips to Hawaii around the festival. They call me up and say, 'We want to know the exact date of the festival because we're planning our vacation now and want to be there.'"

Danny Kaleikini has been the festival's master of ceremonies since its inception. In addition, the show has featured such other "big name" Island entertainers as Ohta-san, Melveen Leed, Frank DeLima, Moe Keale, Mel Cabang, Bill Kaiwi and Bla Pahinui. One year, the festival spotlighted a performer from Maui who is ninety percent blind. "But," said Sakuma, "he jumps, rolls on his back on stage, strums with his toes and plays the ukulele behind his back. He's absolutely incredible."

Last year, Clarence Hirakawa, Japan's top ukulele player, participated, and even though Sakuma hopes to expand this international theme by one day signing up ukulele masters from Portugal, Panama, Brazil and Tahiti, he emphasizes the real stars of the festival are the 400 or so Island keikis who perform. "The biggest spotlight," he said, "will always be on the children."

There is another facet of ukulele artistry—craftsmanship of the instrument which, for the past seventy years, has been dominated by Kamaka Hawaii, Inc. In 1916, Samuel K. Kamaka began making ukuleles as a hobby in the basement of his Kaimuki home. Kamaka, who had learned the trade as an apprentice to Manuel

Nunes, produced about a dozen ukuleles a week and sold them for $5 apiece. In response to the demand for the beautiful koa instruments, Kamaka's hobby soon turned into a business.

Kamaka Hawaii now occupies a spacious, two-story building on South Street in downtown Honolulu, with Sam Kamaka's sons—Sam, Junior and Fred—managing operations. Over the years, Kamaka Hawaii has created instruments for comedians Laurel and Hardy, actor Theodore Bikel, singer Tiny Tim, astronaut Scott Carpenter, Prince and Princess Takamatsu of Japan, and many of the top entertainers in Hawaii.

Custom-made Kamaka instruments cost $500 and up because of the special attention that's paid to workmanship. "Production line quality" instruments, which also must meet stringent inspection criteria, range in price from $135 for a standard four-string ukulele to $400 for an eight string ukulele. The firm also manufactures lutes, dulcimers, tiples, guitars and, on occasion, *balalaikas*, a Russian stringed instrument with a triangular body.

Interestingly, two-thirds of Kamaka Hawaii's twelve craftsmen are handicapped—some have muscular dystrophy, some are mildly retarded, a few are even deaf. Sam Kamaka, Junior began hiring the handicapped in 1957 through the encouragement of his wife, Gerry, who is an occupational therapist. "You may think it's ironic that deaf people should be making musical instruments," Kamaka said, "but you don't have to hear to put a fine instrument together. The deaf have a fine sense of touch. They gauge the correct thickness of the sound boxes by drumming their fingers on the wood. When the wood has reached the proper thickness, they can tell by feeling the vibrations."

Kamaka Hawaii, which produces about 400 ukuleles a month, spe-

cializes in koa instruments but has also worked with other woods such as spruce, walnut, kou, milo, ohia and kamani. Seventy-five percent of their inventory is sold in the Islands; other major markets are the West Coast, Tahiti, Samoa, Japan, Denmark and Sweden.

Said Kamaka, "Customers sometimes buy multiple-string ukuleles and aren't sure how they're supposed to be tuned. So they call us up all the time and ask us to tune their instruments over the phone. We've gotten calls from England, Australia—and calls from the West Coast are common. We pluck out the correct notes over the phone, they tune it, and once we hear that it's pretty close, we have them play a test chord. When they hear it sound like it's supposed to, they're so happy."

Each year from November through June, more than 2,000 fourth graders, who are studying Hawaiian culture as part of their school curriculum, visit Kamaka Hawaii. They are treated to a tour of the factory as well as a lecture on the history of the ukulele by one of the staff members. Said Kamaka, "The kids love it. They're so excited to see the shop, smell the sawdust."

Kamaka sees the experience as a way of preserving the ukulele's unique place in Hawaii's history and culture. As *Paradise of the Pacific* noted in 1917, "The ukulele, that little taro-patch guitar...is a symbol of innocent merriment...We should take off our hats to the little Hawaiian ukulele."

169

An instrument made by Manuel Nunes' son, Leonardo, and a 1930s pineapple-shaped ukulele developed by Sam Kamaka, Senior.

"Ukulele: The Strings That Bind" was first published in March/April 1986.

THE IRON MEN OF KONA

A biker participates in the ultimate test of endurance.

THE TRIATHLON CRAZE

BY CAROL HOGAN

Looking back in history, it wasn't so long ago that swimmers were swimmers, bike riders were bike riders, runners were runners—and the wrangling between them was constant over which sport was most healthful, arduous and best.

But somewhere between a barroom challenge and the Waikiki Swim Club's (WSC) annual fall banquet, a singular idea emerged that changed the entire direction of sports history and set in motion a new era of sports that generated from Hawaii like ripples in a pond and is now the latest sports craze around the world.

The idea: The Hawaiian Ironman Triathlon, an ultimate endurance test featuring a 2.4-mile swim from Queen's Beach to Fort DeRussy in Waikiki, a 112-mile bike ride around Oahu and a 26.2-mile run, all done consecutively.

The challenge: To see if it could be done, and if so, who would survive best: swimmer, cyclist or runner.

Sound crazy? That's what everyone thought. But on February 18, 1978, fifteen undaunted men dove into the ocean off Waikiki and swam the WSC roughwater course, jumped on bicycles (few of which were actual racing bikes) and rode around Oahu. Once they reached Aloha Tower in downtown Honolulu, they jumped off their bikes and immediately started running (or walking), following the route of the annual Honolulu Marathon, to Hawaii Kai and back, to a finish at Kapiolani Park.

Except for coverage by Dick Fishback, then a sportswriter for the *Honolulu Advertiser,* the event went virtually unnoticed. Prior to the start, Navy Commander John Collins, a member of WSC and the originator of the race, had called Fishback to see if the paper would be interested in covering the event.

"Everyone thought he was crazy," said Fishback, who later wrote in an advance article, "The Hawaiian Ironman Triathlon seems to be an inhumane attempt to tax the body beyond all comprehension and award the survivor—if any—with a trophy." Further, Fishback joked, "Maybe an iron lung should be on hand, Preparation-H sought as a sponsor, an entire embalming firm put at the ready."

His words were funny, but the competitors were dead serious. Not only did fourteen out of fifteen finish (one athlete lost his support crew to car problems and had to pull out), but Gordon Haller, a Navy man, won it in 11:46:58. Although they were sore and tired, nobody died.

In fact, the triathlon was repeated again the following year! Nautilus Fitness Center took over race direction, and fourteen men and one woman plunged into the ocean off Queen's Surf. This was San Diegan

171

A triathlon enthusiast takes a break.

Tom Warren's year to win, and he established a time of 11:15:56. Lyn Lemaire, of Boston, crossed the line in 12:55:38, ahead of many of the twelve men who finished that year.

Sports Illustrated published an in-depth feature article on the "lunatic" competition, and still nobody paid much attention to something that appeared so patently impossible.

However, by January 10, 1980 enough people had read about the Ironman to bring the starting field to 108. Most of the competitors were good at one endurance sport; few could be called expert in all three.

Single-sport and armchair athletes alike still thought the few who competed were "crazies," which was sufficient to attract the attention of ABC-TV's "Wide World of Sports" producers, who sent a film crew to cover it.

With few exceptions, those who entered had no real knowledge of how to train for such a race. But Dave Scott, a twenty-six-year-old Masters swimmer and three-time winner of the annual WSC Roughwater Swim had designed his training around all three disciplines and came from Davies, California prepared to win. So did John Howard, a six-time national cycling champion, Pan American gold medal winner and Olympic competitor who thought his cycling would pull him through. Others looked for top positions based on one skill, but most of the other men and two women from every walk of life were entered because it seemed the ultimate challenge. They only hoped to finish.

Stormy Kona weather forced race director Hank Grundman, of Nautilus, to move the swim from its scheduled offshore Waikiki venue to a calmer area in Ala Moana Park. The adverse weather conditions provided high drama; ABC-TV was delighted.

Only after the race began did organizers see they had real problems on their hands. With fifteen competitors, logistics had been relatively simple. With 108 bike riders and their support crews circling the island most of the day—charging through Waikiki stoplights, battling with tour buses and weekend drivers for space on the two-lane highway, and runners spread out for twenty-six miles late into the night—it was horribly unsafe. Nobody knew exactly where all the competitors were.

A somewhat modest Dave Scott finished just before sunset, proving that he was made of flesh, blood—and iron. He had raced what was then a perfect Ironman in 9:24:33—one hour and fifty-one minutes faster than the previous record. Women's division winner Robin Beck turned in an excellent time of 11:21:00.

Unused to being beaten, a disgruntled John Howard said, "What we have here is an impossible event, not so much from a point of view of endurance, but you cannot run a bike race around an island with 200 stoplights. I can do it, but a less skillful rider could get killed. You have a potential disaster situation. If I had any less skill on the bike I wouldn't have done the things I did."

He hinted that he *might* be back next year, allowing that being an Olympic cyclist had enabled him to catch up and finish third. He pointed out what Scott already knew: To win an Ironman you have to train and excel in all three sports.

ABC-TV's coverage was viewed worldwide and polled the most popular "Wide World of Sports" program for 1980. It was a critical turning point in the history of the Ironman. Still, no one quite realized the impact it was to have.

Coaches and trainers doubted the human body could endure, without serious and permanent injury, the arduous training required. Few people actually knew how to train, eat properly, work a full eight-hour day,

and get enough sleep to repeat the process again the next day. Many quit jobs to train. Families separated. Athletes were struggling with new concepts in cross-training. Their friends and loved ones struggled to live with and understand the excitement of triathlon obsession.

By the spring of 1981, triathlons blossomed all over the Mainland. In some areas, winter sports such as canoeing and cross-country skiing replaced swimming and biking. Nevertheless, triple-sport contests made their mark on the nation, with the Ironman as the goal—the triathlon Olympics.

In 1981, Valerie Silk took over race directorship, and reorganized and moved the event to Kailua-Kona on the less populated island of Hawaii. A new course traversing 140.6 miles of Kona and Kohala was established. Headquarters were set up at the Kona Surf Hotel, seven miles south of town in Keauhou.

Economically, Kailua got a much-needed boost. Internationally, it put the small town on the map as triathletes and their entourages poured into town. The town buzzed with activity; banners welcomed the superstars to the superbowl of triathlons.

That year Howard returned, a slimmer, wiser, better swimmer and runner than before. He had trained to a peak few athletes could hope to duplicate. Dave Scott was injured and didn't return to defend his title.

Howard performed flawlessly, establishing a time on the new course of 9:38:29. Already an internationally recognized cyclist, he became the articulate spokesman of triathlon training, lending an air of common sense and respectability to the Ironman.

Twenty-one women competed, and twenty-two-year-old college student Linda Sweeney from Arizona won the women's division in 12:00:32.

But it wasn't just participants in

Competitors get set to dive into the first leg of the grueling triathlon.

Pedaling along the Kohala coast highway.

their prime who stole the show. It was competitors like blind athlete Harry Cordellos, fourteen-year-old Robin Tain, seventy-three-year-old Walt Stack, and other people with just a burning desire to finish who gave the Ironman the drama and color that inspired the world.

In the post-race months, Howard followed his win with clinics and consultation on triple-sport training. Scott had already begun a fitness consultation business, and Sally Edwards, second-place winner in the 1981 women's division, published the book *Triathlon, The First Complete Guide to Challenge You to New Total Fitness.*

By February 1982, 580 contestants had taken the bait. They stood in the waters of Kailua Bay waiting to begin their "day without end." ABC-TV was again on hand to film the "gruelathon," as it has come to be known. Budweiser Light was the new sponsor.

It was a hot day and Scott Tinley was "hot" too. The twenty-five-year-old aquatics instructor from California finished first overall, and set a new record of 9:19:41, toppling Dave Scott, who had been highly trained and favored to win. Jeff Tinley, the winner's younger brother, finished third. The Tinley brothers made their debut on the triathlon scene in unforgettable style.

So did twenty-three-year-old Julie Moss of California, who led the women's division throughout most of the run. Out front and pushed to the limit, Moss fell to her knees just 100 yards from the finish, while a crowd of spectators watched in silent horror. A dazed Moss stood, ran, collapsed, stood, ran, collapsed, stood, collapsed and crawled to the finish line with television cameras whirring inches from her face. Meanwhile, other finishers ran past, one of them Kathleen McCartney, of California, who, without noticing Moss on the ground, went on to become the first woman finisher by

a mere thirty-nine seconds.

Moss reached the line and stretched out her arm one more time. But instead of moving forward, she fell on her back, unconscious. Through the medium of television, Moss and the Ironman triathlon were instantly famous. Moss spent several hours in the medical tent recovering from her ordeal but was back on her feet, well and healthy the next day.

Several hundred photojournalists in Kailua saw the finish and their accounts of it went around the world. It was telecast internationally. Ironman became the standard bearer, *the* ultimate competition. Watching Moss' emotionally packed finish in Hawaii gave world viewers new parameters. If this slightly built heroine, an unknown from California, could take herself to the limits—and beyond—so could thousands of others. She not only inspired athletes but non-athletes alike. People who never before dreamed of participating in the Ironman clamored to get in the next one. Four months before the event, with 700 people on the waiting list, race directors were turning people away.

After the February race, officials changed the date from early February to October to accommodate athletes who lived in wintry climates where they couldn't train. The fifth Ironman was held eight months later on October 9, 1982.

Race director Silk had promised an even bigger and better event. ABC was on hand and Kailua-Kona played host to over 500 journalists who represented tabloids from all over the world. No single sporting event had ever drawn so much attention to Hawaii. By early September, Kailua was booming. By mid-September not a single rental car was available, hotel rooms were scarce, and the town vibrated with energy.

The central meeting place for triathletes was the Kailua pier. Every morning from daybreak to dusk,

A runner heads toward the finish line in Kailua-Kona town.

competitors would gather extemporaneously to evaluate their competition, exchange training tips and gossip, swim the course or just hang out. Traveling bike mechanics set up shop in the backs of their cars. Triathletes met each other for distance rides out into the lava fields. A nearby telephone pole became the downtown triathlon bulletin board.

After months of arduous training, 850 swimmers, bikers, and runners were peaked and ready to go.

Perhaps Silk, herself an Iron Maiden who has nurtured the complicated event from its early stages into a sophisticated, smoothly run three-act play, said it best when asked about her role as race director: "If I had known what it was gonna take before I did it, I never would have done it." Many triathletes feel the same way.

Most have dedicated three to eight hours a day, just to make it through and the training tells. On race day,

Dave Scott stole the show, finishing first in each event to set a new record, 9:08:23. He became the first person to win it twice. Julie Leach, twenty-five, of California, won the women's division in 10:54:08, becoming the first female to break the eleven-hour barrier and earning a place in the triathlon hall of fame.

The real unsung heroes and heroines are the 2,500 volunteers who work to make the Hawaiian race a success. They are the ones who act as water safety personnel on surfboards, build and assemble the bicycle racks for 900 machines, set up the showers and cover them with palm fronds, wash the sand off the pier, and write all the numbers on the clothing bags each entrant turns in before the race. They are the ones who ferry water and ice to desolate aid stations along the lava desert, who quarter thousands of oranges, make guava jam sandwiches, and provide bananas and chocolate chip cookies to keep the athletes fed on race day. They are the ones who staff the aid stations tirelessly until every competitor is finished.

For the volunteers and spectators as well as those who participate, the Ironman has become more than just an endurance event. It is a race in which everyone is emotionally involved. A free Ironman magazine lists competitors by name and number, enabling easy identification so that people can call contestants by name, personally encouraging them to keep going, telling them how wonderful they are. The admiration is boundless—the feeling is mutual.

The Ironman's impact and the resultant races it has inspired around the world have made triathlons in the eighties what marathons were to the seventies. Surveys are being conducted and questionnaires generated about endurance cross-training, food habits and injuries. Coaches are reevaluating their thinking and advocating new and more complicated training regimens. Training camps have sprung up around the country, including one at Kona. Equipment is now labeled "triathlon." What was once thought impossible is now possible. Kailua is now a major destination and training center for some of the world's best athletes.

King Kamehameha, who ruled from Kailua, would be proud of the events taking place in his hometown. If he returned today he would find the cream of the crop in male and female warriors, made of iron and with endurance and dedication beyond imagination.

"The Iron Men of Kona: The Triathlon Craze" was first published in September/October 1983.

Crowds cheer the triathlon finishers—every one of whom is a winner.

175

DEFINING OUR KEY WORD... ALOHA

BY PEGGY BENDET

Alice Holokai opens the door to her small frame house in Papakolea and says, "Come in, please," nodding her head slightly to convey that if she was going to do this properly and say what she really means, it would be "Anoai ke aloha."

Inside is a four-year-old who has twisted her silky corkscrew curls around the wheel of an automated toy truck, squealing with mixed horror and delight as she further involves her hair in the spinning trap. It appears inextricable.

Her great-grandmother sets it free for the second time that day, softly reasoning with the child, "Do you want to be gorgeous or do you want to be funny kind?"

"Gaw-jus," the little girl says, but she lacks conviction, and so this time, Holokai keeps the truck.

In that house in Papakolea the woman raised twenty-six children. Only one of them was her own.

It all began half a century ago, she explains, settling in a rocker with another great-grandchild in her lap, this one in diapers. She received a letter from a much-loved uncle of hers in Kohala on the Big Island, who described his wife's latest pregnancy, saying, "The cow is mine, but the calf is not." He told Holokai that she could have this child if she wanted it.

Young friends at Lei Day festivities, Kahala Elementary School, Oahu.

178

She raised that child, one of her own, five from a sister, another several from assorted relatives and many more from people she barely knew. It became a way of life for her. When seventy-eight-year-old Holokai was nominated for a statewide community service award several years ago, her sponsor estimated that she assists some 300 people a month with food, clothing, job counseling, medical advice and good common sense, acting as an herb therapist, surrogate mother and, possibly most important, as a dependable friend to anyone who knocks on her door. And for all of this she has never collected any fee.

If aloha is defined by genuine human warmth and acts of kindness and compassion, then Holokai's life serves as a definitive statement.

She describes an incident from her childhood, a lesson in aloha she received from her mother, a British-Hawaiian woman who was, in many ways, more Hawaiian than British.

"One payday my father came home from work with his pockets bulging with silver," Holokai says. "We didn't use much paper money in those days. 'I have something for you,' he said to my mother, and he started pouring the coins into her lap.

"She asked him if he had won the money gambling, and when he said, 'Yes,' she started throwing it at him, saying, 'Who is going to feed the children of those men?' She returned the money to the men's wives the next day, taking her own children with her in the cab so they would remember the lesson."

Six-year-old Alice didn't understand it at the time. "I thought we needed the money ourselves," Holokai recalls, "but a few years later I talked with her about it, and then I knew." What she knew, she lived,

A kupuna shares her aloha.

Piialoha Woodward and her son, Kalamaku.

and as she lived it, her understanding of aloha deepened.

Many of her children were unhealthy when she first got them—victims of malnutrition, paralysis, leprosy and worse—and they were healed by her in the time-honored Hawaiian fashion.

"I don't believe in doctors," Holokai says. "My son-in-law is a surgeon, and *still* I don't believe in doctors. The only medicine I ever give is herbs, red dirt and ha.

"Ha is the breath," she explains. "The Hawaiians knew how to use the breath. This is why Kamehameha was great. He understood the breath. You don't blow like those *aikido* people do: 'Hhhaaauuuuuuugh.' I laugh at them. I breathe lua style (as in the Hawaiian martial arts). My father taught it to us. You don't make a sound."

She explains that the power of the breath is identified by the Hawaiians as more than the air one draws in and expels from the lungs—it is the impulse to breathe, the very life force itself, the divine spirit in man. And this, as Holokai explains it, is the secret of aloha.

"Ha means both 'the breath' and 'God.' This is the old way of speaking, the way I learned from my mother. Alo means 'in the presence of.' So aloha means 'in the presence of God.'"

Pilahi Paki speaks of that little syllable "ha" in much the same way: "It isn't that ha means 'breath'—that is just a human thought, a surface understanding—ha is the life force itself."

Paki, a Hawaiian linguist who has been designated a "living treasure" by the state of Hawaii, has written a book on the history of her people, *The Legends of Hawaii: Oahu's Yesterdays*, and she is completing work on another, *Gems of Antiquity.* In 1970, Paki stunned participants in a much-publicized conference on the state's economic future by standing on the convention floor and elucidating the qualities of aloha, something she told the delegates they had overlooked.

She is a philosopher in the true sense of the word in that she lives what she knows. "I live the life of an individual," is the way she puts it, adding, "but in this day and time an individual is often looked at as a visitor from Mars."

She was born seventy-two years ago in Kaanapali, Maui. Her mother and father were both full-blooded Hawaiians. Her mother, who died when Paki was seven, was a Roman Catholic convert, but when her father died thirty years later, Paki says, "He was certain that Akua, the God he had prayed to his entire life, was the same God other people were talking about, and so he saw no reason to change his religion."

And Paki's religion?

"Aloha is my religion. I practice it every day."

According to Paki, "Aloha is not something that you do, it's not even the way you do something. It is being in touch with yourself. When you are in that state, whatever you do expresses aloha.

"Say the word aloha," Paki smiles. "Now close your eyes and feel it. Take that word inside yourself and consider what it really means, consider the love inside yourself. Get in touch with that love, really feel it, and when you do feel it then open your eyes and say that word again.

"Words are man's greatest weapons," Paki says, "and yet when people speak today most of the time they have no sense of what they are saying. We have this idea that the faster someone speaks the greater his intellect is, and so people use words frivolously, with no feeling of what they are saying.

"Aloha is being destroyed," she

Alice Holokai

179

Kumu hula Frank Hewett and a young friend share a tender moment.

says, "because people are using that word without any feeling."

Paki speaks dramatically, often beginning statements with the qualifier "in the teachings of my ancestors and in the experience of Pilahi."

"The people of Hawaii speak from the diaphragm," she says. "The ha, the life force, is in their voices. You can hear it as they speak."

According to Paki, it was the lack of ha evinced by the early visitors to Hawaii that inspired the term haole, foreigner, which is the etymological opposite of aloha: ole, "without," and ha, "life force" or "soul." The etymology was shuffled aside in the intervening years—at least one would hope so, because haole is now used to refer to any and all Caucasians in Hawaii.

The racial issue doesn't concern Paki, who explains that the names of different races and nationalities were kapu in her father's house: "He always told us, 'There is no Japanese, no Chinese—there are only human beings.'"

And this is what does concern Paki: The human issue, the problem that people have lost touch with their own essence, their aloha.

"Two and two is not four, you know," she says with a mischievous smile. "Do you know what it is? It's five. Do you know why? Because the one who considers, 'What is two and two?' has to be counted. That is the most important one. We are so interested in what is happening out there we forget that one."

She adds, "What is 500 feet away from me, I don't concern myself with. I only concern myself with what is inside me and directly around me. And when I come to know that, then I am also privileged to know the essential nature of what is out there, 500 feet away."

In old Hawaii, the children were not taught conceptually, the way today's children are. "The kupuna, the elders, never taught their chil-

Pilahi Paki

dren," says Nana Veary, a seventy-five-year-old full-blooded Hawaiian woman who is now a kupuna herself. "If you asked them how to do something, they would say, 'Watch!'

"So the children would watch and then try it themselves, and then watch some more and try again," and in this way they would actually teach themselves.

Veary is a handsome woman, formerly the private secretary to Doris Duke, one of the world's wealthiest women, and the mother of Emma Veary, known as "The Songbird of Hawaii."

"My son tells me what a terrible grandmother I am," Veary says with a smile. "I don't live the way my grandparents lived, and so his children cannot learn from me the way I learned from them. In this way the Hawaiian culture is dying."

Veary, who greets almost everyone she sees with an all-engulfing hug, says she rarely uses the word aloha. "Only when I really mean it," she says.

"When you heard the kupuna saying 'Aloha,' you could feel it, because to them it expressed a feeling. Aloha is not a greeting; it is a feeling."

And who uses the word with feeling today?

"It would be unfair for me to say that there isn't anyone now who uses the word aloha with feeling. There must be some people living in the country, on the outer islands. In the country there is nothing else to get involved in, except, perhaps, going fishing."

Veary was reared by foster parents—the father Scot and the mother Hawaiian—and some of her fondest childhood memories are of visits with her Hawaiian grandparents, who lived in the fishing village that was then at the mouth of Pearl Harbor. She says it was from her grandmother that she first learned of aloha.

"I think I was about six or seven," she recalls. "I was playing with the other children one day when we saw a stranger coming down the road. We hollered to my grandmother, and she came out and said that as soon as he got in front of the house we should call her."

This amazed the young girl, but even more amazing was what happened when the stranger arrived: her grandmother asked him inside not just to ai, eat, but to paina, dine.

"My Scot foster father was a very difficult man to grow up with—very, very strict—but I did get one thing from him," Veary recalls. "He taught me that if I didn't understand something I should ask about it.

"So when all of the other kids began to bid this stranger farewell, crowding around him in that beautiful way that children do, I walked right over to my grandmother and I asked her, 'Was he really a stranger?'

"She said, 'Yes, he was.'

"And so I said, 'Then why did you feed him?'

"My grandmother said, 'That is your Scotsman father's influence,' and she got very upset with me. She said, 'I want you to remember this one thing as long as you live: I was not feeding the man—I was entertaining the spirit of God.'"

Embracing each other, members of a halau utter words of thanksgiving.

Nana Veary

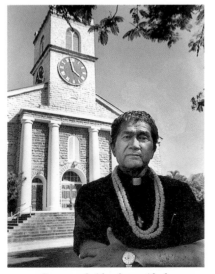

Reverend Abraham Akaka

Seeking peace and comfort through a moment of silent prayer.

"When I think of aloha," says the Reverend Abraham Akaka, "I think of God."

When many other people think of aloha, they think of the Reverend Akaka, the gracious Hawaiian man who for the past quarter century has been rector of historic Kawaiahao Church, built by Kamehameha III on the spot where Christian missionaries preached their first sermon in Hawaii. Some of the services are still sung in Hawaiian today, and, in true Hawaiian tradition, Akaka does more than just marry and bury—he launches many of the state's business enterprises with his blessings.

On March 13, 1959, the day after Hawaii was granted statehood, Akaka delivered to the legislators of the new Aloha State a moving sermon entitled "Aloha ke Akua," "God is aloha."

"As I told them that day," he says in a quiet interview in his office at the church, between two meetings in his busy day, "the first words my mother taught me were 'Aloha ke Akua.'"

Akaka defines aloha as "the feeling that God is present."

How do you know God is present?

"The same way you know love is present," he says, with a smile. "Aloha isn't an idea. It is a reality. Somehow today—and this is true of everybody, not just Hawaiians—we have to come to an experience of the reality of aloha."

He paints a vivid metaphor of people living in aloha in the same way fish live in water, and says that our lack of awareness of this force is like a fish that has closed its gills and refuses to let water in. Just as the fish would die for lack of nourishment, "we need to know our total dependence on aloha," Akaka says. "I don't think we can live without it."

He attributes his own certainty of aloha to his upbringing, which he says was filled with the love of God. He says that every day of his childhood his father would call the entire family into the living room at 6:00 A.M. and again just before bedtime for a hymn, a prayer, and, from each child, the recitation of a Bible verse in both English and Hawaiian.

"I feel I had an advantage, having the kind of parents I had," Akaka says. "I don't have any excuse."

He laughs, and then he amends his statement slightly, saying, "I feel very fortunate. I think people who miss the experience of aloha are really deprived. And the saddest thing is that many of them don't know what they missed.

"I look at the difficulty (our country's leaders) are having in trying to find a common ground for peace in the world. That common ground has to be aloha. Unfortunately, we are using force. We are trying to maintain an advantage of power, so the idea of sharing power has a hard time getting in edgewise."

Almost to himself, he muses, "It is how you were raised, I guess."

"Aloha is a two-way street," says Walter Ritte. "We Hawaiians have been giving aloha; the problem is, it hasn't been coming back. Now the door is starting to close. I don't give my aloha to just anybody anymore."

The thirty-eight-year-old Hawaiian activist props his feet up on the desk in front of him because, it seems, it is comfortable and the desk is there and, besides, he really doesn't take desks that seriously, even in the Office of Hawaiian Affairs (OHA). Ritte likes the country, living in the style of old Hawaii, and he has little regard for the trappings of business. He is a hunter, for instance, and at the time of the interview he was looking ahead to indictment on three felony counts—illegal possession of ammunition, illegal possession of a firearm, and assault—all related to an incident in March when he was, as he says, exercising his right to gather food from the land.

Ritte lives on Molokai with his wife, a former Miss Hawaii, and their four children, flying to Honolulu only for his work as an OHA trustee, a position jeopardized by the felony charges, a position he does take seriously. Very seriously. Ritte speaks with concern about the future of his people and their land.

"My greatest touch with aloha is through the land," he says. "There is a term that was coined by George Helm, aloha aina, love of the land. I get my strongest feeling of aloha when I am on the land. It's a great feeling. It's a feeling I wish I could have all the time."

Helm, who died in 1977, is thought to have drowned trying to rescue Ritte and another young Hawaiian man, Richard Sawyer, who were themselves trying to rescue Kahoolawe, the island just off Maui's windward coast, from U.S. Navy bombardment.

Kahoolawe became an issue for Ritte a year before, almost by accident, he says, admitting that he went only because some friends of his were going. On that trip, he and Molokai physician Emmett Aluli spent three days on Kahoolawe, ending their stay with an experience Ritte now says was a turning point in his life.

"The Navy picked us up in a helicopter," he says, "and as the helicopter took off from the island, I was focusing on a rock. As the helicopter lifted from the land, it went straight up, and the point that was the rock seemed to grow until it encompassed the entire island.

"I thought, 'God, they're going to kill this island, and nobody is going to do anything about it.' And I knew what I had to do."

He says for the next four hours, during the time he was being questioned by reporters, policemen and Navy officials, he could not stop crying.

And a year later, he returned to the island, this time with provisions for twenty days, with more support and, finally, with the attention of the

Walter Ritte

Hawaii legislature, which passed a resolution asking the Navy to stop the bombing.

His departure from Kahoolawe was again momentous for him, but in a different way. "The second time the Navy picked me up, instead of flying me right to jail, they flew me really low over all of Pearl Harbor, over all their aircraft carriers and destroyers, over all of that might.

"I knew then that I was going to have to find another way. I can't fight this guy with my anger, because if I do I'm going to lose."

In the last seven years, Ritte has translated aloha aina into a set of blueprints for a community that would be formed along the lines of an ahupuaa, a land unit where people could live as the ancient Hawaiians did by hunting, farming and fishing—gathering the resources of the mountains, the plains and the sea.

"What we are looking for at this point is not to replace what has happened here in Hawaii," Ritte says. "What we want to do is set up an alternative, a place to be Hawaiian."

Describing himself as "half-Hawaiian, half-haole," Ritte says, "From my youngest days I was aware that the kupuna on my Hawaiian side gave out this good feeling—you can call it aloha, you can call it whatever you want—and I loved to be around them. The relatives on my haole side were always so strict and so pompous and so controlled. With them nothing was free-flowing, everything was regimented.

"So I went with the natural flow. I became supportive of the Hawaiian side of my nature because, at the very essence of it, I wanted to be like the Hawaiian kupuna.

"I haven't accomplished that yet," he says. "I have too much anger in me yet. I have to return that anger to positive things."

He adds that his own problem is a lack of aloha, a statement not supported by his eyes or his voice or the easy affection he shows people who interrupt to talk with him.

"If I wanted to be a haole," he says, "all of the doors would open. I have the resources and the capability to be a very successful haole. What I'm looking for is a place to be Hawaiian."

He adds, "We're pretty close to losing aloha. Our kupuna are fast dying, and not many of us opio, youth, are picking it up. There is a lot of hatred in us, a lot of anger.

"Aloha is the Hawaiians' contribution to the world. Entire religions are based on it. People all over the world search for it. And we have it. If we lose aloha, we have lost it all."

183

"Defining Our Key Word...Aloha" was first published in November/December 1983.

OAHU

The power and grace of winter waves at Waimea Bay.

Windsurfers hit the water, Lanikai.

Rainbow of mailboxes brightens a North Shore street.

Polynesian beauty.

Tropical blossoms, Kaimuki yard.

184

The hands tell the story.

One family's place in the sun.

Full moon over Koko Head.

The majestic Koolau Mountains.

Natatorium at sunset, Waikiki.

Colorful sails, Lanikai.

185

MAUI

Waterfalls grace the West Maui Mountains.

Field of vanda orchids, Kahului.

Imposing Buddha, Lahaina Jodo Mission.

186

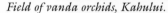

Hawaiian hut, Kepaniwai.

Paddlers from the Kihei Canoe Club, silhouetted at dusk.

Windsurfers scattered on the beach, Wailea.

Waterfall on the road to Hana.

Pastoral Kula scene.

Winsome hula dancer.

Up-country farmer.

THE BIG ISLAND

A hula kahiko dancer stretches his muscles, Merrie Monarch Hula Festival, Hilo.

A North Kohala rainbow.

A blazing field of lava.

Tikis at sunset.

Amaumau ferns.

Lush Waimea ranchland.

A glimmer of molten lava in a sea of mist, Kalapana.

Waterfalls, North Kohala coast.

The summit of Mauna Kea at dawn.

Sugarcane worker on his way home.

The fury of Kilauea Volcano.

Horses graze on a verdant hillside.

KAUAI

Sunset, Kalalau.

View of Niihau from Kauai.

Flowers through a Kokee cabin window.

Islander and his kayak, Kalalau Beach.

Kukuilono Park, Kaloa.

Taro farm, Hanalei.

Kalalau, near Na Pali, at twilight.

Intriguing leaf pattern, north shore.

MOLOKAI

Ranch, east Molokai.

School buses even run to the isolated eastern areas.

Many waterfalls line the north shore.

Tropical palms.

LANAI

Keomuku Church.

Dancer at Puu Pehe.

Pineapple workers.

Rainbow over pineapple fields.

Rita Moon and her daughter, Janelle,
Lanai City.

PHOTOGRAPHY CREDITS

Pages 2, 3: JOE CARINI, *Hawaiian Legends*®.

Page 4: JOE CARINI, *Hawaiian Legends*®.

Page 5: JOE CARINI.

Page 6: BILL YOUNG, *Stock Photos Hawaii*.

Page 7: JOE CARINI.

Page 8: MARC SCHECHTER, *Photo Resource*.

Page 9: VERONICA CARMONA.

Page 10: DOUGLAS PEEBLES.

Page 11: Clockwise from left— DAVID DAVIS, DAVID DAVIS, BOB CHINN.

Page 12: Top, RITA ARIYOSHI. Bottom, GREG VAUGHN.

Page 13: Top, WILLIAM WATER-FALL. Bottom, DAVID DAVIS.

Pages 14, 15: JOE SOLEM, *Photo Resource*.

Page 15: BOB CHINN.

Page 16: RON DAHLQUIST.

Page 17: CHUCK PLACE.

Page 18: R.J. SHALLENBERGER.

Page 19: Left, SUNSTAR. Right, VERONICA CARMONA.

Page 20: RITA ARIYOSHI.

Page 21: Top, RITA ARIYOSHI. Bottom, VERONICA CARMONA.

Page 22: ALLAN SEIDEN.

Pages 22, 23: VERONICA CARMO-NA.

Pages 24, 25: JOE CARINI, *Hawaiian Legends*®.

Page 26: Top, ALLAN SEIDEN. Bottom, DOUGLAS PEEBLES.

Page 27: Top, GREG VAUGHN. Bottom, RITA ARIYOSHI.

Page 28: ALLAN SEIDEN.

Page 29: Left, DOUGLAS PEE-BLES. Right, GREG VAUGHN.

Page 30: JOHN BOWEN.

Page 31: CAMERA HAWAII.

Page 32: ALLAN SEIDEN.

Page 33: Clockwise from left: PAT DUEFRENE, GREG VAUGHN, ALLAN SEIDEN.

Page 34: KYLE ROTHENBORG.

Page 35: DOUGLAS PEEBLES.

Page 36: JIM ARIYOSHI.

Page 37: PETER FRENCH.

Page 38: DOUGLAS PEEBLES.

Page 40: DOUGLAS PEEBLES.

Page 41: FRANCO SALMOIRAGHI, *Photo Resource*.

Page 42: BILL WALTERS.

Page 43: CLIFF HOLLENBECK.

Page 44: AARON CHANG.

Page 45: MONTE COSTA.

Page 46: WILLIAM WATERFALL.

Page 47: FRANCO SALMOIRAGHI, *Photo Resource*.

Pages 48, 49: JOE CARINI.

Page 49: JOE CARINI.

Page 50: JOE CARINI, *Hawaiian Legends*®.

Page 51: FRANCO SALMOIRAGHI, *Photo Resource*.

Page 52: JOE CARINI, *Hawaiian Legends*®.

Pages 52, 53: ALLAN SEIDEN.

Page 54: WILLIAM WATERFALL.

Page 55: ALLAN SEIDEN.

Page 56: FRANCO SALMOIRAGHI, *Photo Resource*.

Page 57: JOE CARINI.

Pages 62, 63: MONTE COSTA.

Page 64: ALLAN SEIDEN.

Page 65: *Hawaii State Archives*.

Pages 70, 71: DOUGLAS PEEBLES.

Page 72: *Hawaii State Archives*.

Page 73: JOE CARINI.

Page 74: Left, VERONICA CARMO-NA. Right, RITA ARIYOSHI.

Page 77: *Hawaii State Archives*.

Page 78, 79: KYLE ROTHENBORG.

Page 80: *Hawaii State Archives*.

Page 81: KYLE ROTHENBORG.

Pages 82, 83: WILLIAM WATER-FALL.

Pages 84, 85: RITA ARIYOSHI.

Page 86: *Whalers Village Museum, Kaanapali, Maui*.

Page 87: NICKI CLANCEY, *Sea Life Park*.

Page 88: JOE CARINI.

Page 90: Top, JIM ARIYOSHI. Bottom, *Sea Life Park*.

Page 91: JOE CARINI. *Scrimshaw from Whalers Village Museum*.

Page 92: JOE CARINI.

Pages 100, 101: ARNA TODD.

Pages 102-105: *Photos courtesy of Sam "Steamboat" Mokuahi*.

Pages 106, 107: JOE CARINI, *Hawaiian Legends*®.

Page 107: ALLAN SEIDEN.

Page 108: JOYCE TORREY.

Page 109: JOE CARINI.

Page 110: VERONICA CARMONA.

Page 111: JOE CARINI.

Page 112: RIC NOYLE.

Page 113: Clockwise from left—JOE CARINI, JOE CARINI, GREG VAUGHN.

Pages 144, 145: JOE CARINI, *Hawaiian Legends*®.

Page 146: SHUZO UEMOTO.

Page 147: JOE CARINI, *Hawaiian Legends*®.

Page 148: JOE CARINI, *Hawaiian Legends*®.

Page 149: Top (left to right), RITA ARIYOSHI, RITA ARIYOSHI, JOE CARINI, *Hawaiian Legends*®. Bottom, JOE CARINI, *Hawaiian Legends*®.

Page 150: Left, *JOE CARINI, Hawaiian Legends*®. Right, SHUZO UEMOTO.

Pages 151-153: SHUZO UEMOTO.

Pages 154, 155: RAE HUO.

Pages 156, 157: DANA EDMUNDS.

Page 160: KYLE ROTHENBORG. Inset, DESOTO BROWN.

Pages 162, 163: DANA EDMUNDS.

Pages 164, 165: JAMES WILLIAMS, *courtesy of Robert Van Dyke*.

Page166: RAY JEROME BAKER, *courtesy of Robert Van Dyke*.

Page 167: JOE CARINI.

Page 168: *Hawaii State Archives*.

Page 169: DANA EDMUNDS.

Page 170, 171: PETER FRENCH.

Page 172: WILLIAM WATERFALL.

Page 173: Top, WILLIAM WATER-FALL. Bottom, PETER FRENCH.

Page 174: PETER FRENCH.

Page 175: CAROL HOGAN.

Page 176, 177: RITA ARIYOSHI.

Page 178: ALLAN SEIDEN.

Page 179: Left, JOE CARINI, *Hawaiian Legends*®. Right, WILLI-AM ING.

Page 180: Left, JOE CARINI. Right, WILLIAM ING.

Page 181: Top, JOE CARINI. Bottom, WILLIAM ING.

Page 182: JOE CARINI.

Page 183: WILLIAM ING.

Page 184: Clockwise from top— DAVE BJORN, *Photo Resource;* GREG VAUGHN; TAMI DAWSON, *Photo Resource;* AARON CHANG; SUNSTAR.

Page 185: Clockwise from top left— WILLIAM WATERFALL, VERONI-CA CARMONA, WILLIAM WA-TERFALL, JOE CARINI, SUN-STAR, JOE CARINI.

Page 186: Clockwise from top left— TAMI DAWSON, *Photo Resource;* SUNSTAR; RON DAHLQUIST; KYLE ROTHENBORG, Stock *Photos Hawaii;* RITA ARIYOSHI.

Page 187: Clockwise from top— DARRELL WONG; DOUGLAS PEEBLES; RON DAHLQUIST *(CATTLE);* VERONICA CARMO-NA; VAL KIM, *Photo Resource*.

Page 188: Clockwise from top left— WILLIAM WATERFALL; DAVE BJORN, *Photo Resource;* PETER FRENCH; GREG VAUGHN; RITA ARIYOSHI; DOUGLAS PEEBLES.

Page 189: Clockwise from top left— RON DAHLQUIST; VAL KIM, *Photo Resource;* JOE CARINI; PETER FRENCH; FRANCO SALMOIRAGHI, *Photo Resource;* PETER FRENCH.

Page 190: Clockwise from top— STEVEN KASTNER; FRANCO SALMOIRAGHI, *Photo Resource;* FRANCO SALMOIRAGHI, *Photo Resource*.

Page 191: Clockwise from left— WILLIAM WATERFALL, WILLIAM WATERFALL, DOUGLAS PEEBLES, BEN RODRIGO, PETER FRENCH.

Page 192: Clockwise from top— ALLAN SEIDEN, MONTE COSTA, GREG VAUGHN, ALLAN SEIDEN.

Page 193: Clockwise from top left— ALLAN SEIDEN, WILLIAM WATERFALL, WILLIAM WATER-FALL, RITA ARIYOSHI, ALLAN SEIDEN.

ALOHA ALOHA ALOHA ALOHA